Praise for *Forward!*
The Leadership Principles of Ulysses S. Grant

In his new book, *Forward! The Leadership Principles of Ulysses S. Grant*, Craig von Buseck gives us a timeless and fascinating look at what made Grant not only a great general but also one of the greatest leaders in American history.

~Wendy Griffith
Co-host, *The 700 Club*

Craig von Buseck provides insight into Grant's leadership principles and supports his conclusions about Grant's principles through the use of contemporary leadership theories and concepts. *Forward! The Leadership Principles of Ulysses S. Grant* is an excellent resource for leaders and students of leadership who wish to understand leadership through the life and accomplishments of an exemplary military leader of the mid-1800s. Also, von Buseck's book is an excellent tool for contemporary leaders to conduct a 360-evaluation through subordinate/self/peer/superiors' evaluations and follow-up discussion about how one measures up to Grant's leadership principles. I recommend Dr. von Buseck's book to anyone interested in understanding leadership.

~Dr. Bruce Winston, PhD
Director in Organizational Leadership Program, Regent University

Craig has captured the leadership skills of Ulysses S. Grant and unearthed principles we can all benefit from. Grant's rise from a humble store clerk to commander of the Union armies to president of the United States is the American dream fulfilled. Observing Grant's willingness to trust and to listen to those who worked with him, we should all seek to better understand his visionary leadership. I promise you can do no better than this excellent book.

~Andy Freeman, Television Producer
The Huckabee Show, The 700 Club

Every serious student of leadership needs to read this book. Most casual history fans are familiar with the "Cliff Notes" version of Ulysses S. Grant—that he was the dogged, persistent general who was willing to sacrifice thousands of his troops to wear down and defeat Gen. Robert E. Lee. However, Craig von Buseck delves into the nuts and bolts of what made Grant the most successful general of the Civil War. He examines Grant's qualities of boldness, tenacity, and doing the right thing, along with his knack for choosing the right people. I was fascinated to learn how Grant became a master logistician and excelled at keeping his supply lines open and his troops superbly fed and equipped. This book offers excellent lessons for those who strive to become better leaders.

~Lieutenant Colonel Baxter Ennis, US Army, Ret.
author of *When Leadership Mattered*

This book is the perfect union of leadership principles and history. In *Forward! The Leadership Principles of Ulysses S. Grant*, Dr. Craig von Buseck has provided a guidebook for leaders, drawing on wisdom from a well-loved historical figure coupled with applications relevant for today. The book's practical progression will equip leaders in all fields and, I predict, become a mainstay for everyone in a leadership role.

~Edie Melson
Director, Blue Ridge Mountains Christian Writers Conference

Dr. Craig von Buseck does it again with his new book on the leadership principles of Ulysses S. Grant. This book gives more insights into one of the greatest American military and political leaders in United States history. However, most people are not aware of all the work Grant did as a general, a businessman, and as president. Dr. von Buseck draw out insights and historical facts that few scholars are able to do. If you love learning about leadership principles and great historical figures, you must read *Forward! The Leadership Principles of Ulysses S. Grant*.

~Daniel B. Gilbert, PhD
Assistant Professor, Regent University School of Divinity
President, Empowered Living Int'l Ministries & Bible Schools

Dr. Craig von Buseck's extensive research into the civilian, military, and family life of Ulysses S. Grant enabled the author to masterfully connect leadership qualities in a nineteenth-century general to much-needed leadership principles for the twenty-first century trailblazer. Our favorite principle? Have faith in God and family. As von Buseck points out, "A study of the life of Ulysses S. Grant shows that his devotion to God and to his family served as an anchor in every season of his life—rich or poor, in sickness and in health, during times of fame and times of obscurity." That's a quality that would richly serve us all!

~Lieutenant Commander David R. Lavender, US Navy, Ret.
and **Julie Lavender**
Author of *365 Ways to Love Your Child*

Leaders are expected to set goals and achieve them. Through this book, you will discover the skills to apply to be a great leader in difficult times. The insights you will realize from *Forward! The Leadership Principle of Ulysses S. Grant* will help you rise above the challenges that attempt to hinder or defeat you, especially when called to do the right thing—even if doing right is unpopular and confronted with powerful opposition. Great leaders choose to stand firm, hold fast, and honor their word. I highly recommend the tested leadership principles you will discover in this book.

~Peter M. Kairuz
President and CEO, CBN Asia

Craig von Buseck gives readers a closer look at Ulysses S. Grant to see what outstanding leadership looks like from his actions, words, and the testimonies of those who knew him well, including President Abraham Lincoln. The author presents ten principles of leadership, each one supported with thoroughly researched evidence from Grant's life and work.

~Dr. Mitch Land
Dean of Media and Worship Arts, The King's University

I recommend *Forward! The Leadership Principles of Ulysses S. Grant* to you all. Dr. Craig von Buseck has accurately mined the historical records of another worthy American figure, this time to portray a wealth of leadership concepts for us to savor. This enjoyable read is a well-reasoned narrative of strategic decisions and real-world illustrations of altruistic behavior often rare in the public arena. Far beyond Grant's battlefield choices, *Forward!* skillfully portrays his personal dedication throughout an enduring life of service. As I read the book, it awakened my hopes for our great nation and those who would serve well. Dr. von Buseck's rediscovery and commanding presentation of Ulysses S. Grant at this troubled time is a treasure of inspiration. We are given here a demonstration and paradigm for the moral leadership we so deeply desire.

~Rev. Joel Palser, PhD, Retired Chaplain
Vice President Ministry Relations, The Christian Broadcasting Network

A timeless, timely book! Never have I read a book that so brilliantly weaves together eye-opening biography, crucial-to-know history, and essential life application principles for modern readers in one page-turning read. Bravo, Dr. von Buseck! Not only have I gotten to know Ulysses S. Grant, but I have also surprisingly fallen in love with this misunderstood man, general, president, and civil rights pioneer that I once brushed aside. America owes him a tremendous debt, and hopefully we can apply Grant's leadership principles to "Let us have peace" in an era that has not been this tumultuous and divided since the Civil War. *Forward! The Leadership Principles of Ulysses S. Grant* should be required reading for every high school and college student in America.

~Jenny L. Cote
Award-winning Author of *The Amazing Tales of Max and Liz*
and *Epic Order of the Seven* series

Craig von Buseck is well versed, not only in Civil War history but also in modern leadership theory. These principles come to life through the narrative—specific accounts of Ulysses S. Grant which prove him a military hero, a moral example, and a leadership champion.

~**Rob Dickson**
Doctor of Strategic Leadership
and Vice President of Partner Relations, Inspiration Ministries

Forward! The Leadership Principles of Ulysses S. Grant is a brilliant collection of practical advice, leadership principles, and examples of life experiences that further support leaders from all walks of life. The numerous examples provided by von Buseck on Grant's life offer up opportunities to support both informal and formal leadership roles. This book weaves both life experiences and leadership principles that can be wonderful resources for any reader.

~**Dr. Almarie E. Donaldson**
Associate Professor of Leadership, Indiana Wesleyan University

In chapter after chapter, Dr. Craig von Buseck weaves historical references, leadership insights, and trusted confirmation from other well noted authors to compound the depth of Grant's leadership principles. Every chapter has a great synopsis along with a summarized takeaway to create conversation and fuel for any business looking for a new approach to teach leadership. What makes this even more unique is the level of historical research invested in these lessons.

~**April Ballestero**
Leadership Coach
Founder, One Light Ahead

Forward! The Leadership Principles of Ulysses S. Grant is a beautifully written, well documented, and timely book. In story after story, Craig von Buseck eloquently unfolds the genius leadership of one of our most humble generals and presidents. A must-read for anybody fascinated by history and for all who wonder what authentic servant leadership resembles.

~Muriel Gregory
Writer for Planting Roots Military Outreach
Author of *Rise Up: Awaken the Leader in You*

FORWARD!

THE LEADERSHIP PRINCIPLES OF ULYSSES S. GRANT

DR. CRAIG VON BUSECK

LPC Books

Imprint of Iron Stream Media

Birmingham, Alabama

Straight Street Books is an imprint of LPCBooks
a division of Iron Stream Media
100 Missionary Ridge, Birmingham, AL 35242
ShopLPC.com

Cover design by Elaina Lee

Quotation of Proverbs 22:29 taken from The Holy Bible, Modern English Version. Copyright © 2014 by Military Bible Association. Published and distributed by Charisma House. All rights reserved.
Quotation of Psalm 19:9 taken from the King James Version of the Bible. Public domain.

Library of Congress Control Number: 2021937411

ISBN-13: 9781645263173
E-book ISBN: 9781645263180

To my daughter, Margo
This book began as your idea, and so I dedicate it to you.
Through your remarkable creativity, compassion, and wisdom,
you are already an amazing leader.
I look forward to the ways you will make a difference
through your God-given talents.
Remember, what Sam said to Frodo:
"Folk in those stories ... kept going,
because they were holding on to something. ...
That there's some good in this world, Mr. Frodo,
and it's worth fighting for."

ALSO BY DR. CRAIG VON BUSECK

Victor! The Final Battle of Ulysses S. Grant

I Am Cyrus: Harry S. Truman and the Rebirth of Israel

Nobody Knows: The Harry T. Burleigh Story

Praying the News

Netcasters

Jesus at the Well

Seven Keys to Hearing God's Voice

Living the Christian Life

TABLE OF CONTENTS

FOREWORD

Dr. Craig von Buseck is an intriguing man, fascinated by history as well as understanding and knowing God. His most recent books drew my attention as a retired Army Colonel. *Victor! The Final Battle of Ulysses S. Grant* and *Forward! The Leadership Principles of Ulysses S. Grant* are both exceptional works, the first a riveting biography of the last two years of Grant's life after his second term as US president and the latter a superb compilation of the leadership principles Grant exemplified and implemented.

I first met the author at a Carolina Christian Writer's Conference a few years ago. The conference's staff congregated at Linda and John Gilden's home, who directed the conference. While we ate, reviewed attendee comments, and gained an understanding of the participants' takeaways, I conversed with Dr. von Buseck, who introduced himself as Craig. His lighthearted banter drew me in, and his description of his work caught my attention. Never a man to waste a moment, he welcomed me into his circle, and together we worked, ate, and shared stories. He thoroughly impressed me.

Later, when I found Craig had written two Civil War books, I immediately gravitated toward them. After reading *Victor!*, I leaped at the opportunity to read *Forward!* Having taught leadership principles as part of the curriculum for US Army students in the Adjutant General Officers Advance Course, I'm constantly pursuing new perspectives on understanding and implementing the critical elements of leadership in battle and in life.

Leadership is a highly valued characteristic of a fine military officer. Refined by years of planning, preparation, and tested by the fire of battle, leadership is best exhibited by those with a fully integrated character. Comprised not only of major concepts applied in the crucible of combat, leadership forms the decisions in day-to-day operations in the military and in home life. The true leader is a fully integrated individual, caring and concerned for the large and small actions they take and their impact on those around them.

When I served on active duty in the US Army, the expressed core concept of leadership was an acronym, LDRSHIP, which stood for Loyalty, Duty, Respect, Selfless Service, Honor, Integrity, and Personal Courage. Dr. von Buseck easily captures Grant's embodiment of these overarching principles, but more importantly, he includes Grant's development of a variety of underpinning concepts that support the whole.

In colorful fashion, the author uncovers Grant's thorough understanding of leading others, a sterling example of leadership in numerous situations. *Forward!* shows how Grant not only lived the simple values of leadership but also reveals the details of those principles in actions. Starting the book with one of the most critical elements of a leader, serving others, the examples from Grant's life illustrate how that principle, along with accompanying supporting actions, provided the best result not only for Grant but also for his unit and his country. Dr. von Buseck clearly lays out Grant's underlying premise in the ultimate leader's mind—the people you work with have value above and beyond their contributions to the overall goal. In combination with this factor, each of the other principles in the first chapter meld together to create unassailable leadership traits that will motivate others to follow that leader wholeheartedly to complete the mission, regardless of peril.

As a friend, I watched Craig produce a Facebook Live show in which he discussed his book, *Victor! The Final Battle of Ulysses S. Grant*. His original plan was to include another person in the broadcast, but when that failed, he pressed on, providing a detailed account of many of Grant's battles fought in the Civil War. After the broadcast, I asked how he managed to leaf through his notes without glancing away from the screen. He smiled and told me the lessons and stories came from memory, without the need for notes. I sat back in my chair, amazed at his ability to fully integrate years of research into cohesive understanding for his listeners.

Examples and stories help us understand how to apply what we've learned in our lives. *Forward! The Leadership Principles of Ulysses S. Grant* takes the reader into the formative background and understanding of how and why Grant became a great leader. The author illuminates Grant's principles for all leaders, especially those in the military. Each reader will benefit from concepts such as don't give up, press forward, think strategically, find advantages in every setback, take calculated risks, and do what's right even if it's unpopular. The stories lodge these lessons and their background into the reader's mind, providing a crucial resource when under extreme pressure, on a battlefield or in an office.

Dive into this book with your mind open, ready to soak up every valuable bit of data and detail possible. Study this work. Memorize the principles. Each one will make your leadership better. More comprehensive. More complete. Once you've digested, internalized, and applied each principle and the supporting tenets, you'll be ready for your next battle.

Aaron M. Zook, Jr.
Colonel, US Army, Ret.

INTRODUCTION

GRANT IN THE AMERICAN PANTHEON

In 1900, Vice President Theodore Roosevelt made a remarkable statement regarding the place of Ulysses S. Grant in the American political pantheon:

> As the generations slip away, as the dust of conflict settles, and as through the clearing air we look back with keener wisdom into the nation's past, mightiest among the mighty dead loom the three great figures of Washington, Lincoln, and Grant. There are great men also in the second rank; for in any gallery of merely national heroes Franklin and Hamilton, Jefferson and Jackson, would surely have their place. But these three greatest men have taken their place among the great men of all nations, the great men of all time.[1]

This statement by one of the great leaders of the early twentieth century may seem shocking to some in the early twenty-first century. But it was likely accepted at face value by those who heard him speak.

Many people forget that, in his era, Grant was nearly as popular as Abraham Lincoln. His 1885 funeral in Manhattan saw 1.5 million mourners—still the largest funeral in American history. After filling the streets, front porches, and storefronts, people crowded dangerously onto rooftops and even dangled from tree branches and telephone poles to view the funeral procession.

Grant's tomb quickly became New York's number one tourist destination.[2] The mausoleum became a sacred pilgrimage spot for Union veterans and their families from all over the country. Until 1916, it attracted five hundred thousand to six hundred thousand people annually, more visitors than even the Statue of Liberty. It maintained extremely high levels of visitation through the 1920s.[3]

By that time, however, Grant's reputation faced a dual challenge. First, the Civil War generation was dying, and the struggle was drifting into distant memory. Second, and more ominously, since the 1870s, when he led the fight to silence the Ku Klux Klan and to protect the former slaves throughout the South, Ulysses S. Grant had become the target of the "Lost Cause" school of historians and writers—a group of Southern sympathizers embarrassed to admit that the Civil War was about slavery. Of the true cause embraced by the Confederate States of America, Grant declared it was "one of the worst for which a people ever fought, and one for which there was the least excuse." Lost Cause writers were determined to change the narrative. Instead of slavery, the war was about "states' rights" and "tariffs."

Rather than recognizing that Ulysses S. Grant was the strategic genius who orchestrated the surrender of three rebel armies and ultimately the defeat of the Confederacy through a concerted national effort, conceived and directed by him, the Lost Cause writers tagged Grant a "butcher," who mindlessly wore down the South with overwhelming Northern resources and men. The same negative campaign was used against Grant's presidency—prompting historians to consider him one of the worst chief executives.

Quite a tumble from Roosevelt's vaunted triumvirate. So what precipitated this fall?

LAMENTING THE LOST CAUSE

Before and during the Civil War, Confederate leaders themselves made it clear that the conflict was about race-based slavery. This sentiment was stated by Confederate Vice President Alexander Stephens in a March 1861 address that has become known as "The Cornerstone Speech."

In his book, *Freedom on Trial*, Scott Farris writes that General James "Old Pete" Longstreet, Robert E. Lee's top lieutenant, scoffed at the Lost Cause notion that the war was about anything other than slavery. "I never heard of any other cause of the quarrel than slavery." Like Grant, Longstreet supported civil rights for the freed slaves—"even leading African-American militia and others in trying to rebuff an 1874 attack on the Louisiana state Capitol by eight thousand armed members of the White League, an offshoot of the Ku Klux Klan, who were unhappy with election results. ... In retaliation," Farris writes, "Lost Cause advocates have engaged in a century-and-a-half-long campaign to besmirch Longstreet's military reputation."[4]

The Lost Cause writers inflated Robert E. Lee and the Confederacy, in what they called the War of Northern Aggression, while they worked to disparage Grant's reputation. In their retelling, Grant directed the merciless slaughter of his soldiers to overwhelm by sheer numbers the courageous Southern army.

Historian Joan Waugh writes, "For the 'unreconstructed,' it was not enough to idolize Robert E. Lee; Ulysses S. Grant's reputation had to be destroyed. ... The elements that define the Lost Cause are familiar," she explains. "The war was caused not by slavery but by states' rights; southern armies were never defeated, but instead were overwhelmed by numbers; the southern soldier was brave and true, echoing the perfection of the patron saint of the Lost Cause, the courtly Virginia gentleman of impeccable lineage, Gen. Robert E. Lee. ... Lee and Grant's historical reputations assumed distinctly different trajectories at this time, Lee's ever upward, Grant's downward."[5]

"When Grant is remembered," historian Ronald White explains, "he is too often described as a simple man of action, not of ideas. Pulitzer Prize winning Grant biographer William McFeely declared, 'I am convinced that Ulysses S. Grant had no organic, artistic, or intellectual specialness.' Describing Grant's midlife crisis, he wrote, 'The only problem is that until he was nearly 40 no job he liked had come his way, and so he became a general and a president because he could find nothing better to do.'

"No!" White emphatically counters. "I believe Grant was an exceptional person and leader. A popular 1870s medallion depicted George Washington, Abraham Lincoln, and Ulysses S. Grant as the three great leaders of the nation. Lionized as the general who saved the Union, he was celebrated in his lifetime as the hero of Appomattox, and the warrior who offered magnanimous peace terms to General Robert E. Lee. Elected president twice, he would be the only leader of the United States to serve two consecutive terms between Abraham Lincoln and Woodrow Wilson. Even with the scandals that tainted his second term, he retained enormous popularity with the American people and probably would have been elected to a third term in 1876 if he had chosen to run."[6]

So who is right? An examination of the historical record reveals that Grant is the victim of one of the greatest smear campaigns in American history. Then a change started to take place soon after the Civil Rights Movement of the 1950s and 1960s. Beginning in the latter part of the twentieth century, writers and historians like Bruce Catton, Ronald White, Jean Edward Smith, and Ron Chernow conducted a reexamination of Grant's life and arrived at very different conclusions from the Lost Cause writers.

What emerged was an American leader who was remarkably ahead of his time—someone worthy of praise from leaders such as Teddy Roosevelt, Walt Whitman, Frederick Douglas, and many others.

THE CLASH OF THE TITANS

During the first half of the Civil War, Grant had built an impressive list of successes in the western theater. The ultimate test of his leadership, however, came when President Lincoln appointed him as commanding general of all the Union armies.

For the first three years of the Civil War, Abraham Lincoln was plagued with a string of generals who failed to lead. "Grant was the antithesis of everything Lincoln had deplored in his predecessors," biographer Ron Chernow explains, "as eager to fight as they were reluctant; as self-reliant as they were dependent; as uncomplaining as they were petulant. Grant did not badger or connive for more troops or scapegoat others. There would be no more grumbling from Lincoln about dilatory generals as Grant converted the Union army into a scene of ceaseless activity. With his zest for combat, Grant was itching for a fight."

Soon after Grant's elevation to head all the Union armies, one of Lincoln's personal secretaries, William O. Stoddard, entered the president's office and found him resting on the sofa. Curious about the new commander, Stoddard asked Lincoln what he thought of Grant. "Well ... I hardly know what to think of him, altogether," Lincoln answered. "He's the quietest little fellow you ever saw. Why, he makes the least fuss of any man you ever knew. ... The only evidence you have that he's in any place is that he makes things git! Where he is, things move!"[7]

"Grant is the first general I've had!" Lincoln exclaimed. "He's a general! ... You know how it has been with all the rest. They wanted me to be the general. I am glad to find a man who can go ahead without me."

"May I ask, sir," Stoddard inquired, "what exactly do you mean by that?"

"As soon as I put a man in command of the army he'd come to me with a plan of campaign and say, 'I don't believe I can do it, but if you say so I'll try.' They tried to put the responsibility of success or failure on me.[8] It isn't so with Grant. He hasn't told me what his plans are. I don't know, and I don't want to know. I'm glad to find a man who can go ahead without me."[9]

Grant's elevation set up the inevitable clash of the titans—the South's best general, Robert E. Lee, would be confronted by the North's most successful commander, Ulysses S. Grant. Both leaders had enjoyed a string of successes in the previous two years of the conflict—Grant in the West and Lee in the politically charged East.

Grant was the seventh Union commander who tried to defeat the Confederacy in Virginia and bring the rebellion to an end. In 1861, Irvin McDowell was defeated at First Manassas and his troops "skedaddled" back to Washington in a panicked retreat. In 1862, George B. McClellan was within sight of the spires of Richmond when Robert E. Lee took command of the Army of Northern Virginia. McClellan was immediately out-generaled and pushed back down the Virginia Peninsula to the James River in another embarrassing retreat. John Pope was routed by Lee at Second Manassas. Ambrose Burnside led the disaster at Fredericksburg. In 1863, Joe Hooker's pride preceded his fall at Chancellorsville.

While George Gordon Meade defeated Lee at Gettysburg in Pennsylvania, he failed to follow up on the victory, raising the ire of Abraham Lincoln and allowing Lee to take his army back over the Potomac into the safety of Virginia. Later that year, Meade called off a hopeless attack on Lee's fortified position at Mine Run, pulling his troops back across the Rapidan River into winter camp.

Many in the South believed Grant would simply be the seventh name added to the list of Yankee generals humiliated by Robert E. Lee. And so far, the Southerners weren't impressed.

Confederate General Evander M. Law declared the "universal verdict" among rebel soldiers asserted that Grant "was no strategist and that he relied almost entirely upon the brute force of numbers for success."[10] On the evening when the news was received that Grant intended to give personal direction to the Army of the Potomac, one officer present spoke confidently of being able to easily whip the western general.

Confederate General James Longstreet, Robert E. Lee's right-hand man, knew better.

"Do you know Grant?" Longstreet asked. The braggadocious officer did not. "Well, I do," Old Pete replied. "I was in the corps of cadets with him at West Point for three years. I was present at his wedding. I served in the same army with him in Mexico. I have observed his methods of warfare in the West, and I believe I know him through and through. And I tell you we cannot afford to underrate him and the army he now commands. We must make up our minds to get into line of battle and stay there, for that man will fight us every day and every hour till the end of this war. In order to whip him we must outmaneuver him, and husband our strength as best we can."[11]

Just as Grant was underrated in the Confederate army, Lee was greatly overrated by the Union forces.

After hearing multiple officers repeat the mantra, "Grant hasn't faced Bobby Lee," Chief of Staff John Rawlins wrote in frustration to his wife: "There is a habit contracted among officers of this army anything but praiseworthy, namely, of saying of western successes: 'Well, you never met Bobby Lee and his boys; it would be quite different if you had.' And in speaking of the probabilities of our success in the coming campaign: 'Well, that may be, but, mind you, Bobby Lee is just over the Rapidan.'"[12]

To defeat the rebellion, Grant knew he had to exorcise the specter of General Lee from the psyche of the Army of the Potomac. From his experience in Mexico, Grant had observed the vaunted Southern commander in person and believed he could be beaten. Grant later wrote, "I knew Lee was mortal."[13]

The Battle of the Wilderness was fought in a thick tangle of second-growth forest in central Virginia. After two days of some of the most gruesome fighting in the entire war, Grant's patience regarding Lee's invincibility finally ran out. Grant and Meade stood together discussing the day's events when suddenly staff officers and couriers came galloping into headquarters with word that Lee had attacked the extreme right and that a part of General John Sedgwick's line had been driven back in confusion.

Grant immediately took the matter in hand. "In the darkness of the night," staff officer Colonel Horace Porter recalled, "in the gloom of a tangled forest, and after men's nerves had been racked by the strain of a two days' desperate battle, the most immovable commander might have been shaken. But it was in just such sudden emergencies that General Grant was always at his best. Without a change of a muscle of his face, or the slightest alteration in the tones of his voice, he quietly interrogated the officers who brought the reports; then, sifting out the truth from the mass of exaggerations, he gave directions for relieving the situation with the marvelous rapidity which was always characteristic of him when directing movements in the face of an enemy."

His orders given, General Grant seated himself on a stool in front of his tent and lit a fresh cigar. Couriers continued to bring messages and reports from the right. Grant acknowledged these dispatches, calmly puffing on his tobacco and staring into the campfire.

Suddenly an officer came thundering into the firelight. Leaping from his horse, he spoke rapidly with considerable excitement. "General Grant, this is a crisis that cannot be looked upon too seriously. I know Lee's methods well by past experience; he will throw his whole army between us and the Rapidan, and cut us off completely from our communications."

In a most uncharacteristic manner, the general rose to his feet, took the cigar out of his mouth, and for the first time since taking command of the Army of the Potomac, raised his voice in reply. "Oh, I am heartily tired of hearing about what Lee is going to do. Some of you always seem to think he is suddenly going to turn a double somersault, and land in our rear and on both of our flanks at the same time. Go back to your command, and try to think what we are going to do ourselves, instead of what Lee is going to do."

It was the beginning of the Army of the Potomac becoming Grant's army.

Grant returned to his camp chair, picked up a stick, and commenced whittling, while the startled officers and staff quietly resumed their business. Grant had confronted and corrected the popular thinking, putting it to rest forever. No one ever looked on Grant—or Lee—in the same way again.

The Wilderness had been a horrific battle with thousands of Union troops killed and wounded—many were burned alive or asphyxiated in the fires that raged in the tangled forest. After similar battles, all previous Union commanders had retreated across the Rapidan toward Washington to refit and plan an attack for a later date.

But Grant was not that kind of commander.

The day after the Battle of the Wilderness, Grant ordered the Army of the Potomac to move out. When he came to the crossroads that led either north or south, the Union troops watched with anticipation. When Grant turned right on the road leading south toward Richmond, the Federal troops erupted in loud celebration.

Grant was moving forward!

This was the general Lincoln had been seeking all along. In the heat of the next fight, the Battle of Spotsylvania, Grant wrote to President Lincoln: "I propose to fight it out on this line if it takes all summer."[14]

It not only took all summer but also the fall, winter, and the following spring. Then, on a chilly April day, Robert E. Lee surrendered the Army of Northern Virginia at Appomattox Court House. The aristocratic Lee surrendered to the common man Grant, and America was changed forever.

TRUTH WINS

As the English poet, writer, and politician John Milton famously declared, "Let [Truth] and Falsehood grapple; who ever knew Truth put to the worse in a free and open encounter?"[15]

In other words, truth wins in the end. In the serious reexamination of Ulysses S. Grant by historians over the last quarter of a century, the truth of Grant's accomplishments—along with his important role in American history—is finally being revealed and restored.

As General David Petraeus declared in a discussion of the Civil War commander, the truth is that "Grant had that quiet determination in spades. It just oozes out of him. I found it incredibly inspirational."[16]

"In a story of transformation," Ronald White observes, "Grant moved in ... seven years from clerk at his father's leather goods store in Galena, Illinois, to commander of all the Union armies, and finally to being president of the United States. His remarkable rise constitutes one of the greatest stories of American leadership."[17]

In light of these facts, two compelling questions emerge: (1) What latent character traits in Grant during his early years emerged during the Civil War, enabling him to rise so high so fast? (2) What can we learn from this titan of the Civil War that could possibly be relevant to twenty-first-century leaders?

This nineteenth-century general embodied so many of the leadership principles now being taught by twenty-first-century experts. In writing this book, I have endeavored to match Grant's leadership principles with some of the key research emerging from contemporary leadership scholars. In so doing, I believe the reader will see that many of the leadership practices that led to Grant's success in the mid-nineteenth century have become "best practices" identified by modern leadership scholars.

Throughout his life—and for a century after his death—Ulysses S. Grant was underestimated. But the truth is that he was a strategic genius, a man of character, and a leader who refused to turn back when facing an enemy. I invite you to join me in an examination of the life and leadership principles of this extraordinary American hero.

Forward!

Chapter One

LEADING IS SERVING

The ultimate measure of a man is not where he stands in moments of comfort and convenience, but where he stands at times of challenge and controversy. — Martin Luther King Jr., from the speech "Strength to Love."[18]

Before Abraham Lincoln finally found his general in the person of Ulysses S. Grant, he endured several officers who failed their troops, their president, and ultimately their country because of their self-centered leadership style. To fully appreciate Grant's approach to leadership and the reasons President Lincoln eventually chose him to lead, it is helpful to compare him to the commanders who preceded him.

General Irvin McDowell: As the result of pressure from his mentor, Secretary of the Treasury Salmon Chase, General Irvin McDowell was pushed into command of the Army of Northeastern Virginia despite a lack of experience commanding troops in the field. This led to the disastrous defeat of Union troops at First Bull Run.

Later, McDowell became a corps commander under General John Pope. In 1879, a board of review commissioned by President Rutherford B. Hayes attributed much of the loss in the Second Battle of Bull Run to McDowell's indecision, lack of communication, and inept behavior. The commission found he failed to deliver vital communication to one of his key commanders, Fitz John Porter, he failed to forward intelligence of Southern General James Longstreet's position to General Pope, and he neglected to take command of the left wing of the Union army at a critical moment in the battle.

General George B. "Little Mac" McClellan: Other than Douglas MacArthur, there may have never been a more insubordinate commanding general than George McClellan. While he was unsurpassed in the preparation of troops, when it came time to take them into battle, he was inexplicably slow and cautious. In utter frustration, President Lincoln declared, "If General McClellan isn't going to use his army, I'd like to borrow it for a time."[19]

At another time, the president reportedly declared, "I would be willing to hold McClellan's horse if he would only give us victories."[20]

On one occasion, President Lincoln, Secretary of War Edwin M. Stanton, and presidential secretary John Hay paid a visit to McClellan at his home. They were told that the general was out at the moment and were invited to wait in the parlor for his return. After an hour, McClellan entered through the front door and was told by a porter that the president was waiting. McClellan ascended the stairs to his room without saying a word to his guests. Amazingly, after Lincoln waited another half hour, he was finally informed that McClellan had retired to bed.

Hay felt that the president should have been greatly offended, but Lincoln replied it was "better at this time not to be making points of etiquette and personal dignity." Lincoln, however, made no more visits to the general's home after the discourteous snub.[21]

McClellan, on the other hand, was exceedingly disrespectful to the president, at various times calling him a "coward," "an idiot," and "the original gorilla." He privately referred to Lincoln, whom he had known before the war as a lawyer for the Illinois Central Railroad, as "nothing more than a well-meaning baboon" and "ever unworthy of … his high position."[22]

On September 17, 1862, McClellan's Army of the Potomac fought Robert E. Lee's Army of Northern Virginia to a standstill at the Battle of Antietam near Sharpsburg, Maryland—the bloodiest day of the war. While the Yankees suffered approximately 12,400 casualties, McClellan still had plenty of fresh troops that were never used in the fight. The Confederates, on the other hand, were greatly damaged—losing 10,320 casualties—which was a larger percentage of their total troop strength.[23] That forced Lee and the crippled Army of Northern Virginia to retreat into Virginia.

For six weeks after Antietam, McClellan ignored Lincoln's urging to pursue Lee. In late October, McClellan finally began moving, but he took nine days to cross the Potomac. By that time, Lee's forces were safely guarded behind well-constructed entrenchments. Lincoln had enough. He was convinced that "Little Mac" could never defeat Lee, and on November 5, 1862, Lincoln fired George McClellan.

After his removal, McClellan battled with Lincoln yet again—for the presidency in 1864. In a moment of poignant irony, Lincoln defeated McClellan with the support of the majority of the soldiers in McClellan's old command, the Army of the Potomac.

General John Pope: In Ken Burns's documentary, *The Civil War*, Shelby Foote explained that many people saw General John Pope as a liar and a braggart. "Yes," said Abraham Lincoln of the accusation, "I knew his family back in Illinois. All the Popes were liars and braggarts. I see no particular reason why a liar and a braggart shouldn't make a good general."[24]

Sadly, General Pope was not the strong leader Lincoln was seeking. After the disastrous defeat at Second Bull Run, Pope was sent to Minnesota to fight in the Indian wars.

General Ambrose Burnside: Unlike Pope and McClellan, some Union officers understood their limitations—and Ambrose Burnside was one of them. In contrast to many of the other leading generals of the time, Burnside did not want to be in command. But Lincoln chose Burnside to lead the Army of the Potomac despite the general turning down the appointment two previous times.[25] Yet once he was in command, Burnside determined to aggressively lead the army against the rebels and show the fighting spirit McClellan lacked.

On a frigid day in December 1862, Burnside directed the Army of the Potomac to cross a pontoon bridge across the Rappahannock River to attack the Confederates in Fredericksburg, Virginia—walking into Robert E. Lee's well-laid trap. When the battle was over, the Union had endured 12,653 casualties, including 1,284 killed. In the aftermath of that bloodbath, Lincoln wrote, "If there is a worse place than hell, I am in it."

Burnside was reassigned a month later.

General Joseph Hooker: "My plans are perfect," General Hooker said before going into battle against the Army of Northern Virginia. "May God have mercy on General Lee, for I will have none."[26] Unfortunately, this was yet another historic example of pride coming before a fall. Hooker's attack at Chancellorsville ended in a Union debacle—and Lee's most brilliant victory in the war.

Abraham Lincoln soon lost confidence in Hooker, and he was eventually replaced.

General George Gordon Meade: The final commander of the Army of the Potomac was George Meade, a competent administrator who took charge only three days before the critical Battle of Gettysburg.[27] While he was often short-tempered, Meade was a loyal, industrious, and subservient commander. He ably led Union forces to victory at Gettysburg, but he did not aggressively pursue the badly damaged Confederate army—much to Abraham Lincoln's consternation. Meade later initiated a feeble attack against Lee in northern Virginia in the winter of 1863, but he turned back when he saw the seemingly impenetrable rebel fortifications at Mine Run.

Lincoln respected Meade, but he was looking for a general who would aggressively pursue Lee and not turn back. Unlikely as it seemed to officers who knew him at West Point and in remote West Coast garrisons, Lincoln found that leader in General Ulysses S. Grant.

FAILING FORWARD

With ten years of failure and disgrace behind him, Ulysses S. Grant could have been just a tragic and forgotten figure of history, but he rose from near obscurity to become one of America's greatest leaders. How did Grant achieve so much in his remarkable life?

First, let's establish a working definition of leadership. In his aptly titled book, *Leadership*, James MacGregor Burns offers this description:

> Leadership is leaders inducing followers to act for certain goals that represent *the values* and the motivations—the wants and needs, the aspirations and expectations—of both leaders and followers. And the genius of leadership lies in the manner in which leaders see and act on their own and their *followers' values* and motivations.[28]

One reason Grant caught Lincoln's attention is that they both appeared to have the same values and motivation. Unlike the seemingly timid McClellan, Grant was an aggressive fighter.[29] But Lincoln also observed in Grant a man who truly cared for his officers and his men and a commander who put the cause ahead of his own personal ambition. Today, leadership scholars would identify this as the behavior of a servant leader.

ULYSSES S. GRANT: SERVANT LEADER

Just as God placed natural laws in the universe, like the laws of gravity and thermodynamics, he also provided principles of wisdom and leadership that are equally unchanging. While these leadership principles have existed from creation, they have recently been discovered and defined by scholars, much as the natural laws were discovered by scientists.

By pairing the principles now accepted by leadership scholars as "best practices" with the actions and behaviors of great leaders of the past—like Ulysses S. Grant—we can learn much about why such a person overcame adversity and rose to a position of prominence in a time of crisis. Through this study, we can then apply these universal principles to our lives and experiences to hopefully gain success as well.

Robert K. Greenleaf was a pioneer in the leadership philosophy that has come to be known as servant leadership. One of his students, Larry Spears, extracted from Greenleaf's writings a set of ten characteristics of the servant leader. It is fascinating to see that more than one hundred years earlier, Ulysses S. Grant displayed all ten of these characteristics in his military leadership during the Civil War.

1. Listening. According to Greenleaf, the servant leader seeks to identify the will of the group and helps to clarify that will. "He or she listens receptively to what is being said and not said. Listening also encompasses hearing one's own inner voice. Listening, coupled with periods of reflection, is essential to the growth and well-being of the servant leader."[30]

Grant was a listener. It was one of his greatest attributes. He would talk too—eventually. Once he became comfortable with you as a friend, he became a veritable raconteur.

General Lew Wallace recorded his impression of Grant's calm demeanor just prior to the assault on Fort Donelson: "From the first his silence was remarkable. He knew how to keep his temper. In battle, as in camp, he went about quietly, speaking in a conversational tone; yet he appeared to see everything that went on, and was always intent on business. He had a faithful assistant adjutant-general [John Rawlins] and appreciated him; he preferred, however, his own eyes, word, and hand. ... At the council—calling it such by grace—he smoked, but never said a word."[31]

In 1864, after several months of fighting and travel with the Army of the Potomac, Grant had grown quite comfortable in the presence of his staff officers and corps commanders. Horace Porter described Grant's behavior at headquarters during those challenging days: "While the general's manners were simple and unconstrained, and his conversation with his staff was of the most sociable nature, yet he always maintained a dignity of demeanor which set bounds to any undue familiarity on the part of those who held intercourse with him. ... He was scrupulously careful under all circumstances not to neglect the little courtesies which are the stamp of genuine politeness."[32]

2. Empathy. "One assumes the good intentions of coworkers and colleagues and does not reject them as people," wrote Greenleaf, "even when one may be forced to refuse to accept certain behaviors or performance. The most successful servant leaders are those who have become skilled empathetic listeners."[33]

Although Grant tried for three years to run a farm, he failed to make it productive. Then, in October 1857, the American economy went into a free fall. In one of the worst depressions in American history, thousands of banks closed along with tens of thousands of businesses and farms. Millions of Americans lost their jobs. Even the small amount of money Grant made selling firewood dried up.

To purchase Christmas presents for his wife, Julia, and their three children that year, Grant pawned his gold watch. A fourth child, Jesse, arrived two months after Christmas, increasing the financial burdens. Grant continued to make a go of the farm until his health gave out in the summer of 1858. He lacked the strength to work the land and the money to hire laborers. He eventually rented out the farm and went to work for a local real estate company as a rent collector.

During these years, Grant experienced grueling poverty, so he had empathy for those suffering the same plight, especially during an economic depression. This characteristic made Grant a tender-hearted person, but it also made him a poor rent collector. Soon he packed his family and moved to Galena, Illinois, to work in his father's leather goods store.

Yet even in those dark days, Grant looked out for his fellow man. For example, a laborer who had worked for Grant at the farm had his mule seized to satisfy a court judgment. When the mule went up for auction, Grant purchased it for fifty dollars and returned it to the original owner. Unfortunately, the writ called for a "change of possession," so the mule was seized again. Once word of Grant's generosity spread in the community, no one bid against him at the auction, and he bought the mule again—this time for just five dollars. Since no change of possession had occurred, the mule was seized for the third time. Grant bought it again, paying only one dollar. He advised the owner to take it to another county and trade it for another mule. Even if that didn't work, Grant declared, "I am going to have that old mule even if I have to buy it once a week all summer!"[34]

3. Healing. Although extending healing to others is a part of being human, servant leaders recognize that they have an opportunity to help make others whole. "There is something subtle communicated," wrote Greenleaf, "to one who is being served and led if, implicit in the compact between servant leader and led, is the understanding that the search for wholeness is something they share."[35]

In the spring of 1865, Abraham Lincoln was beset with illness and exhaustion after four years of war. "I'm a tired man," he told a friend. "Sometimes I think I'm the tiredest man on earth."[36]

Unable to rise from bed, he was forced to hold his cabinet meeting in his bedroom. Photographs from the time show the care-worn look on his face, making him look far older than his years. "It looked care-ploughed, tempest tossed and weather beaten," observed Horace Greeley.[37]

Reading similar comments in the newspapers, Julia Grant suggested that her husband issue an invitation for the president to visit them at City Point. By that time, Grant and Lincoln had grown to be more than just partners in the war—they had truly become friends. Ulysses agreed that a vacation from Washington would be a refreshing break for the careworn leader. "Can you not visit City Point for a day or two?" Grant telegraphed Lincoln on March 20. "I would like very much to see you, and I think the rest would do you good."[38]

With his wife, Mary, and their son Tad, he took a steamboat to Grant's headquarters at City Point. There they met their eldest son, Robert, then serving on the commanding general's staff, at the wharf with General Grant. Surrounded by the Army of the Potomac and the Army of the James, Lincoln enjoyed one of his best vacations during his time in the White House.

Sadly, it would be his last.

4. Awareness. "Awareness is not a giver of solace," wrote Greenleaf, "it is just the opposite. It is a disturber and an awakener.

Able leaders are usually sharply awake and reasonably disturbed. They are not seekers after solace. They have their own inner serenity."[39]

Serving as quartermaster for his regiment early in his career, Grant traveled on the journey from New York to California with the 650 soldiers of the Fourth Infantry, along with sixty army wives and twenty children. Unfortunately for Grant and his unit, a cholera epidemic had broken out in Panama shortly before they left New York. The unit surgeon had warned the War Department that it would be "murder" to send the regiment into a cholera zone, but he was overruled.

As they made their way across the Isthmus of Panama, the cholera epidemic was in full strength, with dead and dying railroad workers clustered in huts all along the track. The regimental commander left Grant in charge of the women, children, and the sick—along with all the regimental baggage—while he forged ahead with the healthy soldiers. As Grant's group trudged along the muddy trail, cholera took its toll.

"Almost every mile between the Atlantic and the Pacific, Grant had to bury someone in the mud," writes biographer Geoffrey Perrett. "Grant himself avoided cholera by never touching water and drinking only wine. He urged others to do the same and the soldiers tended to heed his advice, but the women and children were likely to ignore it—the sign of what looked like attractive springs gushing pure, cool water was too tempting. But the springs were polluted by cholera sufferers who had tried to wash away the traces of diarrhea from their clothes and their bodies. And it was not only the water that spread the disease. So did the flies, which transported it from the feces of the dead to the food of the living."

On July 26, Grant and the survivors arrived at the Pacific Ocean. Of those who had set off from the Atlantic port of Cruces two weeks earlier, one in three had perished. According to one officer, Grant "took a personal interest in each sick man. [He was] a man of iron, so far as endurance went, seldom sleeping, and then only two or three hours at a time. ... He was like a ministering angel to us all."

The ordeal haunted Grant for the rest of his life, and he became convinced that no one should ever be forced to go on such a dangerous, primitive journey. In his first message to Congress as president, Grant called for a canal to be built across Panama to carve "a path between the seas."[40]

5. Persuasion. "The servant leader seeks to convince others, rather than coerce compliance. This particular element offers one of the clearest distinctions between the traditional authoritarian model and that of servant leadership. The servant leader is effective at building consensus within groups."[41]

If there was ever a time that required the skill of persuasion, it was during the preparations for the assault on Vicksburg. As a centerpiece to his plan of attack, Grant asked the navy to run the dangerous rebel batteries perched high on the bluff above the Mississippi River. Whatever ships survived would then ferry the army in an amphibious crossing downstream. When Grant announced his strategy to his generals on March 30, William Tecumseh Sherman, his most trusted subordinate and friend, shook his head in unbelief. Grant's plan broke many of the rules they had learned at West Point. Ulysses understood this, but he was a pragmatist—one of the reasons he had been somewhat half-hearted in his study of strategy at West Point. Grant knew then, as he understood during the war, that not all circumstances fit neatly into textbook theory.

Sherman preferred returning north to Memphis and moving south on the overland route through central Mississippi. But this would be a tactical retreat, and Grant didn't like to retreat (more on this key trait in another chapter). Though daring, Grant believed his plan would work.

"Grant is brave, honest, & true," Sherman had concluded earlier that month, "but not a Genius."[42]

"To anyone who would listen," writes biographer Brooks Simpson, "he [Sherman] recited his doubts about running the batteries and coming at Vicksburg from the south, ending with the almost fatalistic rejoinder that he would obey orders. Believing that Grant was down to his last chance, he distanced himself from his friend's proposal even as he professed his loyalty."

Sherman handed Grant a written protest of the operation, making sure his concerns were placed in the official record. And Grant was okay with that.

In the end, Sherman went along with Grant's bold strategy. "Whatever plan of action he may adopt will receive from me the same zealous cooperation and energetic support as though conceived by myself."[43]

"It was a daring plan," writes Simpson, "made no less daring by the failure of alternatives. It was also a plan shaped by concerns not purely military. Grant knew that even the appearance of a setback might cost him his job. He was confident his plan would work. It had to work."[44]

It did work—and military colleges still teach Grant's strategy to their students. True to form, Sherman gave Grant all the credit for the victory.

6. Conceptualization. "Servant leaders seek to nurture their abilities to dream great dreams," Greenleaf observes. "Servant leaders are called to seek a delicate balance between conceptual thinking and a day-to-day operational approach."[45]

Colonel Horace Porter, one of Grant's most trusted staff officers, gives a fascinating description of Grant's methods for conceiving a plan of action during the Overland Campaign in Virginia:

> He would sit for hours in front of his tent, or just inside of it looking out, smoking a cigar very slowly, seldom with a paper or a map in his hands, and looking like the laziest man in camp. But at such periods his mind was working more actively than that of any one in the army. He talked less and thought more than any one in the service.
>
> He was one of the few men holding high position who did not waste valuable hours by giving his personal attention to petty details. ... He held subordinates to a strict accountability in the performance of such duties, and kept his own time for thought. It was this quiet but intense thinking, and the well-matured ideas

which resulted from it, that led to the prompt and vigorous action which was constantly witnessed during this year [1864], so pregnant with events.[46]

That is how Grant conceived his plans for both the brilliant Vicksburg and Overland Campaigns.

7. Foresight. "This enables the servant leader to understand the lessons from the past, the realities of the present, and the likely consequence of a decision for the future. It is deeply rooted within the intuitive mind. Closely related to conceptualization, the ability to foresee the likely outcome of a situation is hard to define but easier to identify."[47]

In May 1864, Grant ordered all the armies of the United States—more than a million men—to move out of winter camp and to advance upon the enemy. The general maintained his headquarters in the field, traveling with the Army of the Potomac and their commander, General George Meade. "This advance by General Grant inaugurated the seventh act in the 'on to Richmond' drama played by the armies of the Union," said General John B. Gordon of the Army of Virginia.[48]

Since the beginning of the war, the Army of the Potomac had positioned itself primarily on the eastern side of Richmond so that while fighting the battles against the rebels, they could still defend Washington, DC. This position also allowed them to transport supplies, troops, and the wounded by the various rivers flowing southeastward toward the Chesapeake Bay and then on to Washington or Fortress Monroe.

Grant understood the importance of defending the capital, but he was also completely focused on defeating Lee's army. He comprehended, as previous commanders had not, that to defeat Lee and the Army of Northern Virginia was to defeat the Confederacy. The only way to weaken Lee's army to the point where it could be driven to its knees was to do what he did in Vicksburg—cut off all supplies to the enemy. Those goods flowed into Richmond nearly unhindered from the south and the west—the opposite side of where the Army of the Potomac had focused its efforts up to that time.

Grant believed Lee would defend Richmond first and foremost, rather than pulling away to attack Washington in full force. So if he could engage the Army of Northern Virginia—and the other Union forces could keep the smaller rebel armies in check—Lee would have no forces available to attack Washington, and Grant could move around to the southern and western side of Richmond to begin the siege that would eventually choke off the supplies and defeat the rebel army.

"We can defend Washington best by keeping Lee so occupied that he cannot detach enough troops to capture it," Grant declared.[49]

Grant could hold enough troops around Washington to keep it safe from any small rebel force Lee might send against it. In a crisis, he could rush more troops from south of Richmond by water down the James River, around Old Point Comfort on the Chesapeake Bay, and then up the Potomac River to Washington. In the meantime, he would lay siege to the Army of Northern Virginia—and as General Lee warned Jubal Early—"then it would only be a mere question of time."[50]

This played out exactly as Grant foresaw it. There was a siege. One by one, Grant cut off the supply lines that fed Lee's army. The blockade brought the Southern economy to its knees. Responding to desperate letters from home, soldiers left the Army of Northern Virginia in droves in late 1864 and early 1865 until Lee's lines were too weak to hold back the Union forces. As Lee foresaw, it was a mere question of time.

8. Stewardship. Greenleaf's view of institutions was one in which CEOs, staffs, and trustees all played significant roles in holding their organizations in trust for the greater good of society.[51]

"I want to push on as rapidly as possible to save hard fighting," Grant wrote to Julia. "These terrible battles are very good things to read about for persons who lose no friends, but I am decidedly in favor of having as little of it as possible. The way to avoid it is to push forward as vigorously as possible."[52]

Grant was keenly aware of his stewardship responsibilities as the general in chief—and they weighed heavily on him. To end the war, Grant understood, the Union needed to fight hard against the rebellious South to bring it to its knees. President Lincoln promised to support Grant in any way possible.

> To Lieutenant General Ulysses S. Grant
> April 30, 1864
>
> I wish to express, in this way, my entire satisfaction with what you have done up to this time, so far as I understand it. The particulars of your plans I neither know, or seek to know. You are vigilant and self-reliant; and, pleased with this, I wish not to obtrude any constraints or restraints upon you. ... If there is anything wanting which is within my power to give, do not fail to let me know it.[53]

Grant responded to Lincoln's kind letter of support with his gratitude. "I have been astonished at the readiness with which everything asked for has been yielded without even an explanation being asked." Fully equipped, Grant knew the responsibility was on him to bring victory to the Union. "It will be my earnest endeavor that you, and the country, shall not be disappointed."[54]

In his groundbreaking documentary, *The Civil War*, Ken Burns describes the way Lincoln fulfilled his promise to sustain Grant in his fight with the rebels:

> Near Petersburg, the Union camp at City Point on the James River suddenly found itself one of the world's busiest seaports, with bakeries, barracks, warehouses, 200-acre tent hospital, more than a mile of wharves, and a new 70-mile railroad built by Herman Haupt in record time to bring supplies and fresh troops right up to the Union trenches.
>
> "Not merely profusion, but extravagance," a visitor wrote. "Soldiers provided with everything." An industrial machine of unparalleled power now kept the war supplies streaming to the front.[55]

9. Commitment to the Growth of People. "Servant leaders believe that people have an intrinsic value beyond their tangible contributions as workers. The servant leader recognizes the tremendous responsibility to do everything in his or her power to nurture the personal and professional growth of employees and colleagues."[56]

By the time of the Battle of Shiloh, General Sherman understood that his old friend Ulysses S. Grant was a man of both vision and detail. He knew Grant would go into battle prepared with a strategy for victory and fully equipped with the means to achieve it. "When you have completed your best preparations, you go into battle without hesitation ... no doubts, no reserve," Sherman wrote to Grant. "I tell you that it was this that made us act with confidence. I knew wherever I was that you thought of me, and if I got in a tight place you would come—if alive."[57]

Grant also played a key role in the personal and professional growth of numerous other commanders, including James B. McPherson, Horace Porter, Phil Sheridan, Rufus Ingalls, and George Meade.

10. Community Building. "All that is needed to rebuild community as a viable life form for large numbers of people," Greenleaf explained, "is for enough servant leaders to show the way, not by mass movements, but by each servant leader demonstrating his or her unlimited liability for a quite specific community-related group."[58]

Porter wrote of the atmosphere of community, democracy, and respect among officers at Grant's headquarters:

"Whether receiving the report of an army commander or of a private soldier serving as a courier or a scout, he listened with equal deference and gave it the same strict attention. ... He never criticized an officer harshly in the presence of others. If fault had to be found with him, it was never made an occasion to humiliate him or wound his feelings.

"The fact that he never 'nagged' his officers, but treated them all with consideration, led them to communicate with him freely and intimately; and he thus gained much information which otherwise he might not have received. To have a well-disciplined command he did not deem it necessary to have an unhappy army."

As the siege of Petersburg dragged on, Grant changed his habits about going to bed early and began to sit up and chat with his men late into the night. "Many a night now became a sort of 'watch-night' with us," Porter explained. "But the conversations held upon these occasions were of such intense interest that they amply compensated for the loss of sleep they caused."[59]

This is the servant leader Lincoln chose to bring the war to a close. Modern-day leaders can learn much from his example. Grant was able to accomplish what he did in large measure because of the character trait we will examine in the next chapter.

GRANT'S LEADERSHIP PRINCIPLES

- Serve others, both individually and collectively, understanding that the achievements of the group will bring success to the individual.
- Manifest these traits in everyday behavior:
    1. Listening
    2. Empathy
    3. Healing
    4. Awareness
    5. Persuasion
    6. Conceptualization
    7. Foresight
    8. Stewardship
    9. Commitment to the growth of people
    10. Community building

Chapter Two

NO BACKWARD STEPS

There are risks and costs to a program of action. But they are far less than the long-range risks and costs of comfortable inaction. —John F. Kennedy[60]

A young reporter, Henry Wing from the *New-York Daily Tribune*, approached General Grant at the end of the second day of the Battle of the Wilderness. Wing was leaving in the morning to take dispatches from the battle to Washington for his newspaper. Did Grant have a message for the president?

Grant walked with him beyond the hearing of the officers, then reached up and placed his hand on Wing's shoulder. "If you see the president," Grant said quietly, "tell him from me that whatever happens, there will be no turning back."[61]

Wing made it through the gauntlet of marauding armies and arrived in Washington. Meeting with Lincoln, the intrepid reporter relayed Grant's message. Overjoyed, Lincoln leaned over and kissed the reporter on the brow.[62] Lincoln then turned to his aide, John Hay, and said, "I believe if any other general had been at the head of that army it would have now been on this side of the Rapidan. It is the dogged pertinacity of Grant that wins."[63]

By choosing Grant to lead the Armies of the United States, Lincoln had tapped into a tremendous force—and it almost always moved forward.

"One of my superstitions," Grant wrote in his memoirs, "has always been when I started to go anywhere or to do anything, not to turn back or stop until the thing intended was accomplished. I have frequently started to go to places where I had never been and to which I did not know the way, depending upon making inquiries on the road, and if I got past the place without knowing it, instead of turning back, I would go on until a road was found turning in the right direction, take that, and come in by the other side."[64]

In the midst of the most intense fighting in American history, during the Battle of Spotsylvania, Grant wrote to General Henry Halleck, the army's chief administrator in Washington, DC:

> The enemy hold our front in very strong force, and evince a strong determination to interpose between us and Richmond to the last. *I shall take no backward steps.*[65]

VISIONARY LEADERSHIP

Earlier in the war, Grant was frustrated by the lack of support from General Halleck, his superior at the time, in his desire to move south into enemy territory with his troops. "I am very sorry that I have not got a force to go south with, at least to Columbus," he wrote to Julia. "But the fates seem to be against any such thing. My forces are scattered and occupy posts that must be held." This defensive stand was undoubtedly the work of Halleck and not Grant, as the first was overly cautious and the second was highly aggressive.

"What I want is to advance," Grant exclaimed.[66]

"Leadership is about going somewhere," writes Ken Blanchard. "All good leadership starts with a visionary role—the leadership aspect of servant leadership."

Blanchard explains that servant leadership includes "setting goals and establishing a compelling vision, which gives people a sense of direction. Once people are clear on where they're going, the leader's role shifts to a service mindset for the task of implementation—the servant aspect of servant leadership. This is where leaders turn the hierarchical pyramid upside down to serve their people and help them live according to the vision and accomplish the established goals."[67]

In *Servant Leadership*, Blanchard and co-author Renee Broadwell say, "Some people say that leadership is really the visionary/direction role—doing the right thing—and management is the implementation role —doing things right … let's think of these both as leadership roles."[68]

Grant had the dual gifts of being a visionary on the one hand—providing direction to the Union army and striving to do the right thing—and a spirit of excellence to do the job right and permanently. According to General David Petraeus, this was equally true in each position Grant held up the chain of command:

> I think that Grant is unique in American military history, and quite unique in global history. There are very few people who have demonstrated true excellence at the tactical level—and that would be division level and below, in those days 15,000 or less; the operational level—this is now a corps in modern days, it would be multiple divisions … the operational masterpiece was Vicksburg, one of the greatest campaigns in world history; and then as a strategist. …To do all three is really quite extraordinary.[69]

Both concepts of "doing the right thing" and "doing things right" were served by Grant's insistence on constantly moving forward. This character trait almost caused a disaster early in the Overland Campaign as General Grant and General Meade rode their horses late at night on a thickly wooded road from the Wilderness to Spotsylvania. Grant's trusted aide, Colonel Horace Porter, shares the harrowing tale in his classic book, *Campaigning with Grant*:

> At eleven o'clock word came to Grant and Meade that their headquarters escorts and wagons were delaying the advance of Warren's corps, and they decided to move on to Todd's tavern in order to clear the way. The woods were still on fire along parts of the main road, which made it almost impassable, so that the party turned out to the right into a side road.
>
> The intention was to take the same route by which the cavalry had advanced, but it was difficult to tell one road from another. The night was dark, the dust was thick, the guide who was directing the party became confused, and it was uncertain whether we were going in the right direction or riding into the lines of the enemy. The guide was for a time suspected of treachery, but he was innocent of such a charge, and had only lost his bearings.

Colonel Comstock rode on in advance, and hearing the sound of marching columns not far off on our right, came back with this news, and it was decided to return to the Brock road. General Grant at first demurred when it was proposed to turn back, and urged the guide to try to find some cross-road leading to the Brock road, to avoid retracing our steps. This was an instance of his marked aversion to turning back, which amounted almost to a superstition. He often put himself to the greatest personal inconvenience to avoid it. When he found he was not traveling in the direction he intended to take, he would try all sorts of cross-cuts, ford streams, and jump any number of fences to reach another road rather than go back and take a fresh start.

The enemy who encountered him never failed to feel the effect of this inborn prejudice against turning back. However, a slight retrograde movement became absolutely necessary in the present instance, and the general yielded to the force of circumstances.[70]

Porter reported that after they arrived at Todd's Tavern later that night, they learned that Anderson's corps had been marching parallel to Grant and Meade at a distance of less than a mile. Imagine the outcome if the generals had not turned back and both had been taken prisoner that night!

IF IT TAKES ALL SUMMER

The fighting between Northern and Southern forces at Spotsylvania reached a new level of barbarity as both sides sensed that this campaign would likely decide the war. At the infamous "bloody angle" during the Battle of Spotsylvania, a brigadier in General Horatio Wright's corps said that in a space measuring no more than fifteen by twelve feet, he counted 150 bodies.

According to one Pennsylvania officer, there were places along the line where dead men were sprawled eight or ten bodies deep. Some rifle pits were filled with dead bodies as though they were mass graves.

A member of the Fifth Maine found one of his officers whose body had been so mangled by rifle fire that "there were not four inches of space about his person that had not been struck by bullets."

A rebel soldier from Louisiana observed, "We have met a man this time who either does not know when he is whipped, or who cares not if he loses his whole Army, so that he may accomplish an end."[71]

During the worst part of the battle, Grant's friend and local congressman Elihu B. Washburne, who had been observing the fight, announced that he was leaving for Washington. He asked General Grant if he could relay a message to the president and secretary of war. Grant stepped to the field table inside his tent and wrote words which have echoed down through time:

> Hon. E. M. Stanton,
> Sec. of War. Washington D. C.
>
> We have now ended the sixth day of very heavy fighting. The result to this time is much in our favor. But our losses have been heavy as well as those of the enemy. ... *I propose to fight it out on this line if it takes all summer*" (emphasis added). [72]

LEVEL 5 LEADERSHIP

In his landmark book, *Good to Great*, author Jim Collins and his research team identified a set of companies that made the leap from adequate to great results and then sustained those achievements for fifteen years. In examining these corporations, the researchers asked, "Why did one set of companies become truly great performers while the other set remained only good?" They discovered certain attributes common to every company they identified as having gone from "good" to "great." The first was what Collins called "Level 5 Leadership."

"We were surprised, shocked really, to discover the type of leadership required for turning a good company into a great one. Compared to high-profile leaders with big personalities who make headlines and become celebrities, the good-to-great leaders seem to have come from Mars."

Collins's team identified some of the common traits of Level 5 Leadership and described them in their best-selling book. Astonishingly, they describe many of the key leadership qualities Ulysses S. Grant manifested. "Self-effacing, quiet, reserved, even shy—these leaders are a paradoxical blend of personal humility and professional will," Collins writes.[73]

"In contrast to the very I-centric style of the comparison leaders, we were struck by how the good-to-great leaders didn't talk about themselves. ... Those who worked with or wrote about the good-to-great leaders continually used words like *quiet, humble, modest, reserved, shy, gracious, mild-mannered, self-effacing, understated, did not believe his own clippings*; and so forth."[74]

That statement describes Grant, Grant, and Grant.

Ironically, Collins identifies Level 5 Leadership as being "more like Lincoln and Socrates than Patton or Caesar."[75] The one person Grant respected more than any other was Abraham Lincoln. He adopted Lincoln's views and policies as the Civil War unfolded; he guarded them through the turbulent years of the Andrew Johnson administration; he implemented and enforced them in his own presidency; and then he defended them to his dying day—most notably in his groundbreaking final achievement, *Personal Memoirs of Ulysses S. Grant*.

Collins describes what he calls the "flywheel" of good-to-great transformation. These principles can be clearly seen in the leadership style of Ulysses S. Grant.

1. First Who ... Then What. Collins explains that good-to-great leaders "first got the right people on the bus, the wrong people off the bus, and the right people in the right seats—and then they figured out where to drive it. The old adage 'People are your most important asset' turns out to be wrong. People are not your most important asset. The *right* people are."[76]

When Grant was promoted in 1864 to lieutenant general and given command over all the Union forces, he went right to work on getting the right people into the right seats. His first choices raised some eyebrows but proved to be prescient.

To replace himself in command of the western armies, Grant chose the energetic, brilliant, yet sometimes volatile William Tecumseh Sherman—a controversial move as he was outranked by the calm and steady General George Thomas. But Grant and Sherman had forged a trust over the years that could not be broken. Grant knew Sherman would fight with the same dogged determination as he did until victory was won.

Sherman famously said of their comradeship, "Grant stood by me when I was crazy and I stood by him when he was drunk, and now, sir, we stand by each other always."[77] The truth is that Sherman was not crazy and Grant was not drunk, at least not when it mattered (more on Grant's struggle with alcohol in chapter 12). Both men saw how their talents complemented each other. Their friendship was one of the most important and strategic relationships in the war.

While General Thomas was a competent commander, he was sometimes afflicted with the same disease as George McClellan—a severe case of what Lincoln called "the slows."[78] Thomas was meticulous in his planning, but he too often waited to attack until he knew he had everything in place—as he did late in the war before the Battle of Nashville. Grant knew he needed someone who agreed with his views on the necessity of what he called celerity, or speed of action, in battle.

Nearly eighty years later, the Germans in World War II called this military tactic *blitzkrieg*.

Grant gained success by his belief in celerity—timely execution and then pressing forward with the momentum gained along the way. He was critical of officers who took too long to prepare under the excuse of being what he labeled "thorough." If a commander lacked celerity, Grant noted, "the enemy organizes and improves as rapidly as yourself, and all the advantages of prompt movement are lost."[79]

Grant and Sherman shared this fondness for rapid movement. Like Grant, Sherman was also an expert at strategy and logistics— vital characteristics for a successful army commander.

History has shown that Grant's choice of Sherman for this role helped bring the war to a more rapid close. Sherman's timely victory in Atlanta later in 1864 turned the tide of national opinion and helped reelect Abraham Lincoln to the presidency.

Another key personnel move was placing Phil Sheridan in charge of the cavalry for the Army of the Potomac. Within weeks of taking command, Sheridan's charismatic, disciplined leadership brought the Yankee cavalry on par with the Southerners' for the first time in the war. Soon Northern horsemen surpassed the haggard Confederate cavalry. The Confederate cavalry's fate was forever sealed with the death of their commander, Jeb Stuart, at Yellow Tavern outside Richmond—killed by Sheridan's cavalry.

Later, when neither Generals Fran Siegel nor David Hunter could dislodge the Confederates from the strategic Shenandoah Valley, Grant appointed Sheridan to lead the attack in that strategic breadbasket of the Confederacy. Within weeks of ascending to this command, Sheridan defeated the rebels under Jubal Early and closed the valley to Confederate use forever. That decisive victory further secured Lincoln's election victory in November 1864.

KEEPING HIS SEAT ON THE BUS

One person who remained in his position until the end of the war was General George Meade, commander of the Army of the Potomac. When Grant first met with Meade after being appointed general in chief, Meade immediately suggested that Grant might want to replace him with an officer who had served with him in the west, mentioning Sherman, to take his place. "If so, he begged me not to hesitate about making the change," Grant wrote in his memoirs. "He urged that the work before us was of such vast importance to the whole nation that the feeling or wishes of no one person should stand in the way of selecting the right men for all positions. For himself, he would serve to the best of his ability wherever placed.

"I assured him that I had no thought of substituting any one for him. This incident gave me even a more favorable opinion of Meade than did his great victory at Gettysburg the July before. It is men who wait to be selected, and not those who seek, from whom we may always expect the most efficient service."[80]

After this surprising encounter, Grant was most impressed with Meade's response. "He spoke so patriotically and unselfishly that even if I had had any intention of relieving him, I should have been inclined to change my mind after the manly attitude he assumed in this frank interview," Grant later explained.[81] Meade served ably and with the same admirable humility and submission to Grant's leadership for the remainder of the war. Meade's able administration of the massive Army of the Potomac freed Grant to concentrate on the oversight of all the armies across the continent. Grant was grateful for such a talented and valuable subordinate. Meade was right where he needed to be on the bus, and he remained there for the remainder of the war.

2. Confront the Brutal Facts (Yet Never Lose Faith). "Every good-to-great company embraced what we came to call the Stockdale Paradox [named for former POW Admiral James Stockdale who survived torture and imprisonment in Vietnam]: You must maintain unwavering faith that you can and will prevail in the end, regardless of the difficulties *AND at the same time* have the discipline to confront the most brutal facts of your current reality, whatever they may be."[82]

If anyone confronted the cold, brutal facts at the opening of the Civil War, it was William Tecumseh Sherman.

"Sherman was maybe the first truly modern general," said historical writer Shelby Foote. "He was the first one to understand that civilians were the backers-up of things and that if you went against civilians, you'd deprive the army of what kept it going. So he quite purposely made war against civilians. ... He saw from the very beginning how hard a war it was going to be. And when he said how hard a war it was going to be, he was temporarily retired under suspicion of insanity—and then brought back when they decided that maybe he wasn't so crazy after all."[83]

Like Sherman, Grant took stock of the realities of the war, but he never lost his optimistic belief that the Federal forces would prevail.

3.The Hedgehog Concept. "In his famous essay 'The Hedgehog and the Fox,' Isaiah Berlin divided the world into hedgehogs and foxes, based upon an ancient Greek parable: 'The fox knows many things, but the hedgehog knows one big thing.'"[84] Collins and his team observed this about the good-to-great companies: "They stick with what they understand and let their abilities, not their egos, determine what they attempt."[85]

Collins shared a fascinating discovery from their research: "In over two thirds of the comparison cases, we noted the presence of a gargantuan personal ego that contributed to the demise or continued mediocrity of the company."

During the Civil War, President Lincoln had encountered several gargantuan egos. But he quickly recognized the servant leadership trait in Grant's character—one of the positive characteristics that distinguished Grant from the other generals Lincoln encountered. The president observed that Grant "doesn't worry and bother me. He isn't shrieking for reinforcements all the time. He takes what troops we can safely give him … and does the best he can with what he has got."[86]

Once Grant made up his mind to do something, he took no backward steps. "One of his greatest traits was his perfect willingness to accept responsibility," remembered M. Harrison Strong, who worked on the general's staff. "He was perfectly sure of himself. There was no such thing as failure for him."

Mortimer D. Leggett, who commanded a brigade under Grant during his time in the west, commented that Grant's "confidence in his own judgment seemed unbounded." Leggett believed he was "remarkably quick in his comprehension and perception. He was a very accurate observer and a careful listener, and when he had the facts before him he was the quickest man to arrive at a conclusion that I have ever met."

Phil Sheridan agreed. "He inspired me with confidence. He was so self-contained, and made you feel that there was a heap more in him than you had found out."[87]

Abraham Lincoln concurred. "The great thing about Grant, I take it, is his perfect coolness and persistency of purpose. I judge he is not easily excited,—which is a great element in an officer,—and he has the grit of a bull-dog! Once let him get his 'teeth' in, and nothing can shake him off."[88]

4. A Culture of Discipline. Collins observed that few companies have a culture of discipline. "When you have disciplined people, you don't need hierarchy. When you have disciplined thought, you don't need bureaucracy. When you have disciplined action, you don't need excessive controls. When you combine a culture of discipline with an ethic of entrepreneurship, you get the magical alchemy of great performance."[89]

When Grant was named colonel of the rowdy, undisciplined Twenty-First Illinois Regiment, he employed some of the techniques he learned from General Zachary Taylor in Mexico. For several days, Grant meandered through Camp Yates in rumpled civilian clothes, observing what was going on. If a veteran of the Mexican War had been present, he would have recognized Old Zack's mannerisms immediately. Once Grant understood what was happening in the camp, he was ready to act.

"In accepting this command," he informed his new subordinates, "your commander will require the cooperation of all the commissioned and non-commissioned officers in instructing the command and in maintaining discipline. ..." Instruction on discipline began immediately. "Hereafter no passes to soldiers to be out of camp after sun down will be valid unless approved by the commanding officer of the regiment."

Of course, the men immediately tested Grant. He responded with more instruction and a warning. "It is with regret that the commanding officer learns that a number of the men composing guard of last night deserted their posts, and their guard. This is an offense against all military rule and law. ... It cannot, in time of peace, be accompanied with a punishment less than the forfeiture of $10 from the pay of the soldier, together with corporal punishment such as confinement for thirty days with ball and chain at hard labor."

Then he added the kicker. "In time of war the punishment of this is death."

As this was the first offense under his command, he gave the soldiers grace, interpreting their actions as ignorance of the rules rather than deliberate disobedience. But he warned the entire regiment: "It will not be excused again."

In the end, the soldiers appreciated the firm leadership of their new colonel. "It was in a terribly disorganized state when I took it," Ulysses wrote to Julia, "but a very great change has taken place. ... I don't believe there is a more orderly set of troops now in the volunteer service. I have been very strict with them and the men seem to like it. They appreciate that it is all for their own benefit."[90]

"We called him 'the quiet man,'" one soldier remembered, "and in a few days he reduced matters in camp to perfect order."[91] Whipping the Twenty-First Illinois into shape led to victory in battle, which led to promotion. More discipline, more victory, more promotion.

5. Technology Accelerators. "Good-to-great companies *think* differently about the role of technology. They never use technology as the primary means of igniting a transformation. Yet, paradoxically, they are pioneers in the application of carefully selected technologies."[92]

The US Army under Ulysses S. Grant was the best equipped in history up to that point. Manufacturers throughout the North refocused their productive capacity and technological ingenuity to building weapons—and it made a major difference to the outcome of the war.

Technology we take for granted today was in its infancy during the Civil War, but it modernized and changed the tactics and strategies of modern warfare. The railroads played a major role in warfare for the first time, not only for rapid transportation, which was vital but also through the introduction of the first railroad artillery. The war witnessed the first military telegraph, the first landmines, and the first telescopic sites.

The telegraph allowed Grant to oversee his national strategy in 1864 and 1865. From his headquarters—the saddle, a tent, or his small wooden hut at City Point, Virginia—Grant dispatched orders via telegraph to every army commander across the continent. This amazing electrical innovation changed warfare forever.

In 1862 alone, 240 patents were issued for military weapons. Lincoln was fascinated by new military inventions, approving and ordering ten Union repeating guns, forerunners of the machine gun. But he was no pushover, so he passed on a scheme to manufacture canoe-shaped footwear for walking on water, among many other crazy contraptions.

Another of the most significant innovations to influence the war was the rifled musket, along with Captain Claude Minie's new bullet: an inch-long lead slug that expanded into the barrel's rifled grooves and spun as it left the muzzle. The Minie ball could kill at half a mile and was accurate at 250 yards, five times as far as any previous one-man weapon. This new rifle alone raised the casualty rate in the Civil War dramatically.

The age of massing your men and charging with the bayonet had ended, yet most officers did not know that when the Civil War began.[93] After the war, Grant admitted that most officers did not start entrenching until after the massacre at Shiloh.

> "General, you know of course that you have been criticized for not having intrenched [sic] against Albert Sidney Johnston at Shiloh; is this true?" *Century Magazine* associate editor Robert Underwood Johnson inquired.
>
> "Yes, at that stage of the war we had not yet learned to intrench," Grant admitted.[94]

After the massive casualties at Shiloh—23,800 wounded, killed, or missing in two days of fighting—Grant, along with most of the country, changed his mind about the war and how to fight it. From then on, Grant's troops "made use of the spade for protection," as he later said at Petersburg.

Another key invention that further tipped the scales to the Union's favor later in the war was the Spencer repeating rifle. After the battle of Spotsylvania, Northern and Southern troops raced to the next strategic crossroads. Once again, the Southerners, with knowledge of the country and shorter interior lines, arrived ahead of the Yankees. But when General Sheridan swooped in on May 31 with two cavalry divisions, he moved forward to take the crossing. Rebel cavalry held the position with a handful of infantry, but Sheridan's men carried the newly issued Spencer repeating rifles, capable of shooting up to twenty rounds per minute.

Southern forces facing this new technology referred to the sixteen shooter as "that damned Yankee rifle that you load on Sunday and shoot all week."[95]

"Level 5 leadership is not just about humility and modesty," Collins concluded. "It is equally about ferocious resolve, and almost stoic determination to do whatever needs to be done to make the company great."[96] Grant had all of these qualities and brought them to bear in the American Civil War to secure victory over the Confederacy.

GRANT'S LEADERSHIP PRINCIPLES

- Whatever happens, be determined to finish the job.
- Be a visionary—provide direction and strive to do the right thing.
- Manifest a spirit of excellence to do the job right and permanently.
- Continually embody words such as *quiet, humble, modest, reserved, shy, gracious, mild-mannered, self-effacing, understated, did not believe his own clippings*.

- Utilize what Collins calls the "flywheel" of good-to-great transformation:
    1. First Who ... Then What
    2. Confront the Brutal Facts (Yet Never Lose Faith)
    3. The Hedgehog Concept
    4. A Culture of Discipline
    5. Technology Accelerators

Chapter Three

FIND THE ADVANTAGE IN EVERY SETBACK

You could not be quiet at home for a week when armies were moving. —William Tecumseh Sherman to Ulysses S. Grant when he contemplated resigning from the army at a low point after the Battle of Shiloh.

My father's favorite saying was "every burden becomes a blessing, and every blessing has its burdens." This was surely true in the life of Ulysses S. Grant, who traded blessings for burdens and burdens for blessings on an ongoing basis. The first of many such incidences occurred at the time of his appointment to West Point.

Ulysses's father, Jesse Grant, was a tanner, and the stench from the dead animals and the tanning solution that wafted across the street from his shop to their home sickened Ulysses as a lad, much to his father's annoyance and disappointment. Knowing his eldest son was repulsed by his profession—a seeming setback—Jesse looked for other educational options for the lad.

A staunch abolitionist, Jesse always had a hand in Whig politics. When he received word that a local boy had washed out of West Point by failing the rigorous exams, Jesse saw his chance. It wasn't that the elder Grant envisioned a military career for his boy. At that time, West Point was one of the leading engineering schools in the country, and Jesse gravitated to the idea of his son receiving a free education that would prepare him for a prestigious career. In this, Ulysses had a definite advantage—he was excellent at mathematics, a necessary component of engineering. With this in mind, Jesse set out to secure the appointment for his son.

A problem arose, however, that could have derailed Jesse's plans. The local congressman, Thomas Hamer, had been Jesse's close friend until their views on slavery drove them apart. To finalize the appointment, Jesse had to request Hamer's endorsement for the West Point opening, something the headstrong elder Grant dreaded. Seeking to avoid this encounter, Jesse tried to circumvent the process by appealing directly to the War Department for a nomination. His attempted end run was immediately rejected, so Jesse had no choice but to swallow his pride and send a letter to his political rival, asking Hamer to nominate Ulysses to West Point.

A rumor circulated that Ulysses's mother, Hannah Grant, visited Hamer's wife to extend an olive branch. As it turned out, Jesse's letter reached Hamer on his final day in Congress. Tending to last-minute details, Hamer rushed to forward his endorsement for the appointment. In an oversight that echoed through history, Jesse neglected to include his son's full name in the letter—a requirement for the West Point application. Without time to verify, Hamer took a guess at the name and got it wrong.

When word arrived of the appointment, Jesse informed his son that he would be attending the United States Military Academy at West Point—the first time Ulysses had heard of the plan. "But I won't go," Ulysses protested. His father replied, "I think you will." Grant pondered the reply for a moment and then meekly answered, "Well, if you think I will, then I guess I will."[97]

No one knew about Hamer's mistake until a young man by the name of Hiram Ulysses Grant arrived at West Point to register months later. The congressman knew the lad was called Ulysses by his family and friends and had assumed his middle name was his mother's maiden name, Simpson—a common custom of the time. So when Ulysses arrived at West Point, he was informed that he was registered under the name Ulysses S. Grant. When the lad protested the bureaucratic blunder, he was told in no uncertain terms that the name on the form was the name that would be used—and if he didn't agree, he would not attend.

The adjutant informed him that there was no appointment waiting for Hiram Ulysses Grant, and his name had to match the roll. He would either be Elihu Grant from New York or Ulysses S.

Grant from Ohio.[98] Without further protest, the young man agreed and became Ulysses S. Grant. The error was actually a godsend for the Ohioan, as it changed his initials from the embarrassing H.U.G. to the almost patriotic U.S.G.

"I remember Grant's first appearance among us," said Sherman. "I was three years ahead of him. I remember seeing his name on the bulletin board, where all the names of the newcomers were posted. I ran my eye down the columns, and there saw 'U.S. Grant.' A lot of us began to make up names to fit the initials. One said, 'United States Grant.' Another, 'Uncle Sam Grant.' A third said, 'Sam Grant.' That name stuck to him."[99]

Other than excelling in mathematics, Grant was an average student. He didn't lack intelligence; he just wasn't involved in the choice to attend West Point, so his heart wasn't in it. He tolerated classes in strategy, drill, and French—doing just enough to get by.

He was also one of the best horsemen at West Point. Today Grant would be considered a horse whisperer.

The army passed along awards based on grades and demerits, and while they admired Grant's skill with horses, his graduation in the middle of his class earned him an infantry appointment. Ironically, the best horseman at West Point eventually served as a quartermaster in the infantry.

But that appointment was yet another instance where providence intervened. Had Grant joined the cavalry, he never would have received the training in supply, logistics, and organization required of a quartermaster. Those skills—which were absolutely vital for a successful general—were so highly honed in Grant that, years later, quartermasters and supply officers serving under him in the Civil War were amazed at the completeness of his supply request orders.

DESIGNED FOR SUCCESS

One of Grant's greatest strengths was his ability to quickly discern the results of an action, then learn both from the successes and the failures. "Grant was not just twice as successful or three times as successful as a military leader compared to a business leader, he was a thousand times more successful," writes Sean Murray. "Finding the profession most suitable to your talents and most aligned with your purpose might be the biggest factor impacting your success as a leader. It was for Grant."[100]

THE DILIGENCE OF U. S. GRANT

King Solomon of the Bible wrote, "Do you see a man diligent in his business? He shall stand before kings" (Proverbs 22:29).[101] In *The Richest Man Who Ever Lived*, Steven K. Scott writes of Solomon, "Diligence is a learnable skill that combines: creative persistence, a smart-working effort rightly planned and rightly performed in a timely, efficient, and effective manner to attain a result that is pure and of the highest quality of excellence."[102]

Scott lists the rewards of true diligence, which were all evident in the life of Ulysses S. Grant.

1. You will gain sure advantage. Diligence gives a unique advantage that results in greater productivity, achievement, wealth, and fulfillment.[103]

Grant's diligence at Donelson, Shiloh, Vicksburg, and Chattanooga led to his promotion to head all the Union armies. His continued tenacity during the Overland Campaign shocked the Confederacy. Despite tremendous casualties in the Overland Campaign—including nearly 7,000 men, dead and wounded, in less than thirty minutes at the Battle of Cold Harbor—Grant refused to stop his forward momentum.[104]

"He had proven that he was not about to give up," biographer Brooks Simpson writes of the disappointment at Cold Harbor. "Setbacks such as that suffered at Cold Harbor simply redoubled his determination to try again."[105]

"Grant will take Richmond, if only he is left alone," declared headquarters staffer Captain Charles Francis Adams. "Of that I feel more and more sure. His tenacity and strength, combined with his skill, must, on every general principle, prove too much for them in the end."[106]

In one of the most important strategic moves in the Civil War, Grant put the Cold Harbor defeat behind him and led the Army of the Potomac south to the James River, where they crossed the eighty-foot-deep tidal river on a quickly assembled pontoon bridge. In this move, Grant completely out-generaled Robert E. Lee, who remained in the dark concerning the Army of the Potomac's location for several days (more on this in chapter 6). He also initiated the siege of Petersburg that eventually led to the surrender at Appomattox.

2. You will be in control of the situation, rather than have the situation control you. "Those who are truly diligent not only control their own destiny, but enhance the achievements of those around them as well."[107]

After the humiliating defeat of Union forces at the Battle of Chickamauga, Federal troops had been surrounded and were under siege in Chattanooga, facing complete destruction. In this emergency, Lincoln called on his top general, U. S. Grant, to fix the mess. As soon as he arrived on the scene, Grant relieved the current commanding general, William Rosecrans, and then collected information from the top officers on the scene. Taking the recommendation of Chief Engineer General William F. "Baldy" Smith, Grant approved the plan to open up what he called the "Cracker Line" at Kelley's Ferry on the Tennessee River. This allowed food, supplies, and ammunition to flow into Chattanooga. Reinforced by troops under William Tecumseh Sherman and Joseph Hooker, Grant attacked the Confederates and broke the siege (more on the Battle of Chattanooga in chapter 10).

3. You will experience true fulfillment. "Imagine being so contented and fulfilled that you crave nothing. That's the kind of fulfillment that is promised to the diligent."[108]

After eight long years of service as president of the United States and fifteen years of diligently serving his country, Ulysses S. Grant finally had time to rest and enjoy life. "We had peace, and order, and observance of law, and the world had a new illustration of the dignity and efficiency of the Republic," Grant declared upon finishing his second term. Grant told reporter John Russell Young that he was never happier than the day he left the White House. "I felt like a boy getting out of school."[109]

After leading the Union forces to victory in the Civil War and then serving two terms as president, Grant was known around the world. Bidding the Grants farewell, incoming president James Garfield noted: "No American has carried greater fame out of the White House than this silent man who leaves it today."[110]

Diligence brought Grant this fame.

Ulysses and Julia had always wanted to travel, so they set off on a two-year world tour. "People throughout the world opened their hearts and their doors to 'General Grant,'" biographer Jean Edward Smith observed. "He was received not as an ex-president but as the Hero of Appomattox, the victor of the world's greatest war since the fall of Napoleon. To heads of state and the public alike he was the most famous soldier of the era, personifying the marvel of a modern industrial power."[111] His *Personal Memoirs* went on sale only months after his death, becoming the second-biggest seller of the nineteenth century.

Grant's diligence paid off—for himself, for his family, for America, and for the world.

4. You will attain the respect and admiration of those in authority. "While others fight to be noticed, the diligent are sought out by people in positions of authority or prominence."[112]

In the first months of the Vicksburg campaign, Grant's various military experiments looked like multiple missteps to the general public and most politicians in Washington. Despite several creative attempts to crack the Vicksburg defenses, no progress was made. At the same time, scores of Northern soldiers were contracting numerous diseases, and many were dying. "All Grant's schemes have failed," Cadwallader Washburn, a cavalry commander involved in the Vicksburg campaign, wrote to his brother, Congressman Elihu Washburne. "He is frittering away time and strength to no purpose."[113]

During this time, the editor of *The Cincinnati Commercial* sent a letter to Treasury Secretary Salmon P. Chase, who passed it along to President Lincoln. The editor called Grant "a jackass in the original package. He is a poor drunken imbecile. He is a poor stick sober, and he is most of the time more than half drunk, and much of the time idiotically drunk." Chase counseled Lincoln that "reports concerning Grant similar to the statements made by Mr. Halstead are too common to be safely or even prudently disregarded."

Lincoln concluded that the time had come to investigate the accusations against Grant and find out if they were based on truth or mere jealousy. The president sent Assistant Secretary of War Charles Dana, a former journalist, to check on Grant's drinking. Dana arrived at Grant's headquarters at Milliken's Bend, Louisiana, northwest of Vicksburg, on April 6. Secretary of War Stanton had given Dana the cover story of heading a special commission to investigate the pay service of the western armies, "but your real duty will be to report to me every day what you see."[114]

Everyone on Grant's staff knew Dana was there to spy on Grant and the western army. "Dana was about as popular in camp as a case of measles," said Captain Samuel H. Beckwith.[115]

Instead of being defensive and trying to conceal a problem, Grant told his officers to be transparent. Instead of snubbing Dana, Grant received him with respect and openness. In their first interview, Grant revealed his plan for taking Vicksburg. Dana was impressed by Grant's civility and his military prowess.

It didn't take long for the Northern commander to win Dana's admiration.

Grant was, Dana wrote to Washington, "the most modest, the most disinterested, and the most honest man I ever knew, with a temper that nothing could disturb, and a judgment that was judicial in its comprehensiveness and wisdom."[116]

Regarding the drinking, Dana wiped the slate clean for the general. "I have been able, from my own knowledge to give a decided negative."[117] Dana later observed a few slips in that area but never a fall. Grant never drank when vital military movements were taking place.

By being genuine and transparent, Grant won a strong ally in Charles Dana.

5. Your needs will be satisfied. Scott quotes Solomon when he writes, "'He that tills his land shall be satisfied with bread, but he that follows vain persons is void of understanding' (Proverbs 28:19). Here he warns that if you stray from your field of endeavors to follow vain people or their advice, you will lose the path of understanding."[118]

Due to the lies and deceit of Grant's business partner, Ferdinand Ward, the firm of Grant & Ward crashed in a spectacular implosion in 1884. For years, Ward had been secretly running a colossal Ponzi scheme—the Bernie Madoff of the nineteenth century.

While Grant was nearly spot-on in judging character in the military, he had difficulty doing so in civilian life. The problem was that Grant had a hard time believing that other people did not hold to the same high standards of conduct he did. As a result, he suffered because of his support of friends who were involved in terrible scandals during his presidency. He then endured the humiliation and financial purgatory from the crash of Grant & Ward.

Grant had let down his guard and followed a "vain" person, as Solomon would say. He trusted that Ward was running the firm in a legal, ethical manner. Grant testified during the deposition for James D. Fish of the Marine Bank, co-conspirator then on trial for embezzlement in the failure of Grant & Ward. The defendant's counsel asked whether the general had "any mistrust on your part in respect to Mr. Ferdinand Ward?" Grant replied, "I am sorry to say that I did not. I had no mistrust of Mr. Ward the night before the failure, not the slightest. It took me a day or two to believe it was possible that Ward had committed the act he had."

"There is nothing wrong in being engaged in government contracts more than in anything else," Grant testified, "unless made wrong by the acts of the individual, but I had been President of the United States, and I did not think it was suitable for me to have my name connected with government contracts. I did not think it was any place for me."

Ulysses and his son Buck were exonerated of any involvement in the Ponzi scheme, but that didn't change the tragic fact that the finances of every member of the Grant family were wiped out by Ward's deception. "We were literally without means," Julia wrote, "when a gentleman from Lansingburgh, N.Y., sent the general five hundred dollars, saying, 'General, I owe you this for Appomattox.'"[119]

Once again, the general needed to find another source of income. He did that first by writing articles that gave his perspective on several battles during the Civil War for *The Century Magazine*. When the articles were enthusiastically received by the public, the Century Company offered Grant a contract to write his memoirs. At that time, Grant learned he was dying of incurable throat cancer, so he wanted to ensure that his wife was cared for financially after his death.

Fortunately for Grant, his good friend Mark Twain owned his own publishing company and had heard a rumor about the Century offer. Twain had urged Grant to write his memoirs two years earlier, so he paid a visit to the general to see where matters stood. This was a fortunate development, as Grant was about to accept a deal that offered far less than the memoirs were worth.

Grant ended up signing a contract with Twain and spending the rest of his life writing his memoirs in terrible pain. In this act of diligence and love, Grant not only restored his family's fortune and secured his wife's future, but he also redeemed himself in the eyes of the public, further cementing his place as one of the greatest leaders in American history (more on this moving story in my book *Victor! The Final Battle of Ulysses S. Grant*).

LEARNING AT SHILOH

One of Grant's most serious setbacks during the war was the bloodbath at the Battle of Shiloh. Historians agree that the Northern commander was surprised by General Albert Sydney Johnston at Pittsburg Landing on the Tennessee River in the spring of 1862. Grant was caught flatfooted several miles upriver from his troops at Savannah, Tennessee, when Johnston attacked. After hearing the muffled sound of artillery, Grant and his staff hurriedly boarded his flagship, the *Tigress*, and ordered the captain to steam forward to the sound of the battle.

As the *Tigress* approached Pittsburg Landing, the crackling of muskets and the booming of cannon became deafening. Grant and his staff arrived at 9:00 a.m. to a mixture of military gallantry, bedlam, and cowardice. On certain parts of the field, his troops bravely held the line against the Confederates. At the same time, hundreds of skulkers, who had run from the battlefield in terror, lined the bluffs of the river for half a mile.

Grant immediately went to work, coordinating the ammunition train to properly supply the troops at the front—the quartermaster training serving him well once again. After that was accomplished, his chief of staff, Colonel Joseph Webster, hoisted the hobbling Grant onto his horse. The general had recently been injured when he was pinned under his horse, so Webster lashed the commander's crutches to the saddle, and Grant rode forward into the battle.[120]

Arriving at the front, he found the divisions of Generals Mc-Clernand, Prentiss, and Sherman all fighting a pitched battle. The Southerners caught the Union troops off guard as they prepared breakfast, throwing their six divisions at the drowsy Federal soldiers.

Despite his injury, Grant rode rapidly back and forth across the battlefield, heedless of danger even in the midst of a shower of cannon fire and musket balls. When Grant's friend John Rawlins arrived on the Shiloh battlefield, he told a fellow officer looking for Grant: "We'll find him where the firing is heaviest."[121] Sure enough, that's where he was. As the general moved from one section of the fight to another, a bullet made a direct hit, bending the scabbard of his sword. Grant acknowledged the shot for only a second, then returned his focus to the fight.[122]

The general raced from unit to unit, talking to regimental and brigade commanders, sometimes positioning troops himself as needed. At times he rounded up stragglers and led them back to the fight, telling them, "Now boys pitch in."

Confederate infantry flanked the left end of the Union line, causing General Stephen A. Hurlbut's division to retreat toward Pittsburg Landing. This exposed the troops of General Benjamin Prentiss, who fought in the center of the battlefield—a place that earned the name "the Hornet's Nest" for the ferocity of the fight. A final Confederate assault on the Hornet's Nest included ten thousand Confederate troops, who incurred approximately 2,400 casualties.[123] Grant's line north of the Hornet's Nest finally caved as the Confederates outflanked Prentiss on both the left and right, and he surrendered.

When the news of the surrender arrived, one of Grant's officers asked the Northern commander if this was a sign of a rebel victory. "Oh, no," Grant answered confidently. "They can't break our lines tonight. It is too late. Tomorrow we shall attack them with fresh troops and drive them, of course."

"Do you think they are pressing us, General?" Rawlins asked nervously.

"They have been pressing us all day, John," replied Grant coolly, "but I think we will stop them here."[124]

In midafternoon, the general had directed Colonel Joseph D. Webster to create a line of defense in front of Pittsburg Landing on the shore of the Tennessee River. Gathering every gun he could find from the reserve artillery and from any retreating units, Webster created a seventy-cannon line, which checked the advance of the enemy.

An Illinois surgeon standing by fearfully exclaimed, "General, things are going decidedly against us."

"Not at all, sir," Grant responded confidently, "We're whipping them now." The doctor told friends later that no other man in the army would have responded as Grant did.[125]

By nightfall, the Union army had backed up more than a mile from where it had been at dawn, but Grant remained optimistic. Lieutenant Colonel James B. McPherson asked whether the army should retreat across the Tennessee River. "Retreat?" Grant responded. "No, I propose to attack at daylight and whip them."[126]

Grant brought this positive attitude to each of his division commanders that evening as they discussed plans for the counterattack in the morning. "So confident was I that the next day would bring victory if we could only take the initiative that I directed them to throw out heavy lines of skirmishers in the morning as soon as they could see, and push them forward until they found the enemy, following with their entire division, and to engage the enemy as soon as found."[127]

That evening the Federal forces of General Juan Carlos Buell and General Lew Wallace arrived on the battlefield to reinforce Grant.

After midnight, Grant was still awake, seeking shelter from the pouring rain under a giant oak tree. Just then General Sherman approached, seeking a final consultation with his commander. Sherman had worked five hours to prepare his division to attack, but it seemed like a hopeless endeavor. His troops had been thoroughly beaten that day, and Sherman thought the wise move would be "to put the river between us and the enemy." He sought out Grant to see when and how the retreat could be arranged.[128]

Sherman caught sight of Grant from a distance, huddled under the tree with a lantern and a lit cigar. He started to approach to discuss a withdrawal but was "moved by some wise and sudden instinct not to mention retreat."[129]

"Well, Grant," Sherman said as he drew near, "we've had the devil's own day, haven't we?"

"Yes," answered Grant, taking a long drag on his cigar. "Lick 'em tomorrow though."[130]

The next day the reinforced Union army did exactly what Grant had foreseen. Except for a few costly counterattacks, the Confederates were pushed back all day. Pressed by the overwhelming force from four of Grant's divisions and three of Buell's, the haggard Confederates fell back in a fighting retreat. By 2:30 in the afternoon, Confederate General Pierre Beauregard feared his army would disintegrate and ordered an immediate withdrawal. As the Southern troops fled into the deep woods, Union soldiers fell to the ground, exhausted, cold, and soaked by the persistent rain.

Of more than one hundred thousand soldiers who fought in the Battle of Shiloh, nearly twenty-four thousand had been killed or wounded. The casualties from these two days of ferocious fighting eclipsed the total of the Revolutionary War, the War of 1812, and the Mexican War combined. Grant's losses came to thirteen thousand killed, wounded, and missing; the Confederates had lost close to twelve thousand.[131]

"Shiloh was the severest battle fought at the West during the war, and but few in the East equaled it for hard, determined fighting," Grant wrote in his memoirs. "I saw an open field, in our possession on the second day, over which the Confederates had made repeated charges the day before, so covered with dead that it would have been possible to walk across the clearing, in any direction, stepping on dead bodies, without a foot touching the ground."[132]

"The second day at Shiloh was a reflection of Grant's determination," writes biographer Jean Edward Smith. "As Sherman's comment suggests, a general imparts attitude to an army. It is not simply a matter of issuing orders, but infusing spirit and initiative. An inchoate bond develops between a successful commander and the army. His will becomes theirs. Grant's relationship with the Army of the Tennessee at Shiloh exemplified that bond. ... The men fought because they knew Grant expected them to, and they trusted his judgment that they could do so."[133]

Shiloh was also a wake-up call for Grant and the country.

"Up to the battle of Shiloh I, as well as thousands of other citizens, believed that the rebellion against the Government would collapse suddenly and soon, if a decisive victory could be gained over any of its armies," Grant wrote in his memoirs. "But when Confederate armies were collected which not only attempted to hold a line farther south, from Memphis to Chattanooga, Knoxville and on to the Atlantic, but assumed the offensive and made such a gallant effort to regain what had been lost, then, indeed, I gave up all idea of saving the Union except by complete conquest."[134]

Rightly or wrongly, Grant received the blame for the carnage. The mistakes of Shiloh led to people calling Grant a drunk and demanding his removal. An influential Pennsylvania Republican who had supported Lincoln early for the presidency, Alexander McClure, visited the White House to voice what people across the country were saying after Shiloh. "I shared the almost universal conviction of the President's friends that he could not sustain himself if he attempted to sustain Grant by continuing him in command. ... I simply voiced the admittedly overwhelming protest from the loyal people against Grant's continuance in command."

Lincoln listened intently and then pondered what McClure had to say for some time. "He gathered himself up in his chair," McClure remembered, "and said in a tone of earnestness that I shall never forget: 'I can't spare this man; he fights.'"[135]

GRANT'S LEADERSHIP PRINCIPLES

- Find the profession most suitable to your talents and most aligned with your purpose.
- After setbacks, redouble your determination to try again.
- Diligence leads to fulfillment.
- The fruit of your diligence will be rewarded because people in positions of authority or prominence will eventually seek you out.
- Avoid following vain people or their advice.
- Communicate confidence in victory while at the same time working diligently to achieve that victory.

Chapter Four

SURROUND YOURSELF WITH TRUSTWORTHY PEOPLE

The friend in my adversity I shall always cherish most. I can better trust those who helped to relieve the gloom of my dark hours than those who are so ready to enjoy with me the sunshine of my prosperity. — Ulysses S. Grant[136]

No one achieves success by himself. True success can only be accomplished by a team of people working together in pursuit of the same vision. Wherever Grant went, he built a strong team around him that worked to fulfill his vision. Despite this, he limited the friends he allowed into his inner circle.

"General Grant was a man who made friends very slowly," observed his friend and pastor John H. Vincent. "While he had a great many acquaintances, I think he had a very limited circle of friends—I mean men who he trusted or whose advice he accepted."[137]

Those in Grant's inner circle had earned his trust—and most of them remained lifelong friends.

GRANT AND RAWLINS

An exception was his chief of staff and former Galena neighbor, John Rawlins, who was also the lawyer for Jesse Grant's leather goods store. Rawlins and Ulysses Grant recognized each other's strengths and formed a partnership that drew on those strengths. In time, the two men grew to trust one another. Rawlins became one of the few officers close enough, as biographer Ron Chernow asserts, to confront Grant with uncomfortable truths and fiercely contest his judgment.[138]

However, when Grant moved east, Rawlins's influence on the commanding general waned—partly because he was no longer the bigger fish in the smaller pond. Rawlins remained in Grant's inner circle, but he no longer held sway over the general as he once had. Despite this cooling, Rawlins worked with Grant throughout the war and later served as Secretary of War until his early death from tuberculosis.

"A small cult sprang up dedicated to the proposition that Rawlins had been the unacknowledged genius of the Civil War," Ron Chernow observed, "that it was Rawlins's military insights that had been decisive and that Grant cheated Rawlins of his just deserts. ... This belief ... flamed into a full-blown crusade when Grant later published his *Memoirs* and only made brief, fleeting references to his dead comrade."[139]

William Tecumseh Sherman believed Grant's omission of Rawlins was deliberate. "Some of Rawlins' flatterers gave out the impression that he, Rawlins, had made Grant, and had written most of his orders and dispatches at Donelson, Shiloh, and Vicksburg—Grant disliked to be patronized—and although he always was most grateful for all friendly service he hated to be considered an 'accident.'"[140]

Despite Grant's omission of Rawlins in the memoirs, Rawlins was an important aide and friend to his Galena neighbor throughout the war. This was especially true regarding Rawlins's campaign to keep Grant sober.

"Through four years of fighting, Rawlins kept Grant's drinking problem within manageable bounds," Chernow explains. "He was an inspired choice as chief of staff and extremely valuable as a vocal devil's advocate, sometimes questioning Grant's tactical moves where others feared to tread. ... Nevertheless, in the last analysis, Rawlins could never have substituted his judgment for Grant's superior military acumen."[141]

GRANT AND INGALLS

When Grant inspected his new command in the spring of 1864, he was impressed by how well-equipped and well-fed the Army of the Potomac was. He gave much of the credit for this to his old friend from West Point, Quartermaster General Rufus Ingalls, who "could move and feed a hundred thousand men without ruffling his temper."[142]

Ingalls had been Grant's roommate for two years at West Point and had lured him into a dangerous excursion to a nearby tavern, Benny Havens. Being caught at Benny's was risking dismissal from the Academy. With the offer of tobacco, alcohol, flapjacks, and a roaring fire, Benny's provided an oasis of normalcy in the desert of disciplined drill and study at West Point. After one visit to Benny's, Grant's curiosity was satisfied, and he had proved to his fellow cadets that he could be daring when he wanted to be.[143]

Later, Ingalls stood with him when Grant faced being drummed out of the army for drinking in California. Ingalls and other fellow officers tried without success to convince Grant to fight the charges and remain in the army.

After Grant became general in chief, he came east to take command of all the Union armies. He was greatly pleased when he arrived at army headquarters at Brandy Station, Virginia, on March 10 in the pouring rain and saw among the strangers Ingalls's familiar face. Together, and with the enthusiastic support of Abraham Lincoln, Grant and Ingalls went to work equipping the Army of the Potomac for the campaign that was to come—where the South's best general would be pitted against the North's best general in a fight to the death.

When the army advanced toward Richmond on May 4, 1864, at the start of the Overland Campaign, Ingalls observed with confidence that "probably no army on earth ever before was in better condition in every respect than was the Army of the Potomac."[144]

Grant agreed. His old western army friend, Grenville Dodge, remembered Grant saying that the Army of the Potomac was "the finest army he had ever seen, far superior to any of ours in equipment, supplies and transportation."[145]

After Grant and the Union army crossed the James River in mid-June of 1864, they settled in for a siege of Petersburg. Working with his old friend Ulysses, Rufus Ingalls oversaw the building of a remarkable military base at City Point, Virginia, to support the efforts of the army. This small, rural village was transformed into one of the largest ports in the world. In what amounted to a small city, Ingalls built not only the Depot Field Hospital, serving more than twenty-nine thousand patients, but also a bakery that distributed as many as one hundred thousand loaves of bread every day.[146]

Managing soldiers, civilians, and former slaves recently recruited into service for the Union, Ingalls oversaw the construction of twenty-one miles of military railroad linking City Point to the Union front lines. Ingalls was also the mastermind behind supplying the massive siege around Petersburg, acting as one of Grant's most trusted leaders.

Grant gave his close friend high praise in *Personal Memoirs* declaring, "There never was a corps better organized than was the Quartermaster Corps with the Army of the Potomac in 1864."[147]

THE POWER OF PARTNERSHIP

In their best-selling book, *The Leadership Challenge*, James M. Kouzes and Barry Z. Posner describe what they call "The Five Practices of Exemplary Leadership." All five of these best practices involve interaction with trustworthy people—something Grant understood and modeled through most of his life, although there were some notable failures, especially during his presidency.

"Through our studies of personal-best leadership experiences," write Kouzes and Posner, "we've discovered that ordinary people who guide others along pioneering journeys follow rather similar paths. ... Leadership is not at all about personality; it's about practice." Through years of research, the authors discovered a model of leadership that became the basis for their book. "When getting extraordinary things done in organizations, leaders engage in these Five Practices of Exemplary Leadership. Those five practices are 'Inspire a Shared Vision'; 'Model the Way'; 'Challenge the Process'; 'Enable Others to Act'; and 'Encourage the Heart.'"[148] At key moments, Grant engaged in each of these five best practices, leading to his overwhelming success as a general during the Civil War.

INSPIRE A SHARED VISION

"Every organization, every social movement, begins with a dream," Kouzes and Posner explain. "The dream or vision is the force that invents the future. ... Leaders have a desire to make something happen, to change the way things are, to create something that no one else has ever created before. In some ways, leaders live their lives backward. They see pictures in their mind's eye of what the results will look like even before they've started their project, much as an architect draws a blueprint or an engineer builds a model."[149]

Ulysses S. Grant shared the dream of a united nation without slavery with Abraham Lincoln and hundreds of thousands, if not millions, throughout the country. On the night of May 3, 1864, General Grant shared his vision for the coming attack that he hoped would lead to the dream becoming a reality.

He assembled his eight senior staff members in the little front room of his headquarters at Culpeper, Virginia, to receive final instructions before beginning the Overland Campaign. The general sat at his desk, preparing some final notes. When he finished, he turned to his men, crossed one leg over the other, lit a fresh cigar, and shared his thoughts on the movement of the Army of the Potomac, which would begin in the early hours of the next morning.

"I weighed very carefully the advantages and disadvantages of moving against Lee's left and moving against his right," Grant said. "The former promised more decisive results if immediately successful. It would best prevent Lee from moving north to make raids. But it would also deprive our army of the advantages of easy communication with a water base of supplies and compel us to carry such a large amount of ammunition and rations in wagon-trains, and detach so many troops as train guards, that I found it presented too many serious difficulties."

He paused and took a long drag on his new cigar. "When I considered the suffering of the wounded in being transported long distances overland, instead of being carried by short routes to water, where they could be comfortably moved by boats, I had no longer any hesitation in deciding to cross the Rapidan below the position occupied by Lee's army, and move by our left. This plan will also enable us to cooperate better with Butler's forces, and not become separated too far from them."

Then he repeated what he had shared with them individually and with each of the separate army commanders. "I shall not give my attention so much to Richmond as to Lee's army, and I want all commanders to feel that hostile armies, and not cities, are to be their objective points."

General Grant considered it likely that Lee would fall back upon Richmond in case of defeat and place himself behind its fortifications. In his instructions to Meade, Grant declared, "Should a siege of Richmond become necessary, ammunition and equipment can be got from the arsenals at Washington and Fort Monroe."

The general in chief then rose from his seat, stepped up to an impressive military map hanging on the wall, and with a sweep of his forefinger, created an arching semicircle around Richmond, stopping at Petersburg. "When my troops are there, Richmond is mine. Lee must retreat or surrender."[150]

Before the Army of the Potomac ever crossed the Rapidan, Grant cast the vision, which would be fulfilled eleven months later when Lee surrendered at Appomattox.

MODEL THE WAY

"Titles are granted, but it's your behavior that wins you respect," Kouzes and Posner explain.

"The personal-best projects we heard about in our research were all distinguished by a relentless effort, steadfastness, competence, and attention to detail. We were also struck by how the actions leaders took to set an example were often simple things. ... The examples they gave were not about elaborate designs. They were about the power of spending time with someone, of working side by side with colleagues, of telling stories that made values come alive, of being highly visible during times of uncertainty, and of asking questions to get people to think about values and priorities. ... People first follow the person, then the plan."[151]

The Army of the Potomac had been through so many commanders that they were reticent to give their loyalty to the new general in chief too quickly. But something about Grant gave this often-maligned army a glimmer of hope.

"Yesterday the 6th Corps was reviewed by Lieutenant General U. S. Grant," wrote Elijah Hunt Rhodes in his diary. "He is a short, thick-set man, and rode his horse like a bag of meal. I was a little disappointed in his appearance. But I liked the look of his eye."[152]

The soldiers saw the difference clearly in the first battle and immediately after it.

Although Grant would have preferred to avoid an engagement with the rebels until they were beyond the Wilderness, he instructed his commanders that if they should encounter the Confederates, they should engage. Grant knew he would lose the advantages of more men and superior artillery in such a thick forest. But he also knew Lee would lose men and supplies that he couldn't replace every time he fought the Union forces. If the Confederates wanted a battle, then so be it.

Lee chose to attack the Federal army and fight in the woods. This gruesome battle—where men died not only from bullets but also by being burned alive in raging forest fires—did not seem much different to the veterans than the Battle of Chancellorsville, a loss on the same ground the previous year. The difference between the two engagements came the evening after the battle.

Soon after sunset, dispirited Northern troops were surprised as General Grant and General Meade galloped along the Brock Road. Staff officers rode ahead shouting, "Give way to the right. Move to the left. Clear a path."

The weary troops soon realized it was Grant on his massive bay, Cincinnati, and Meade on the familiar Baldy.[153] Every soldier watched to see the movement at the fork in the road up ahead beyond the ruins of the Chancellor mansion. After three years of retreats, most of the soldiers anticipated yet another backward march. If Grant turned left, they were following the same pattern and retreating across the Rapidan toward the capital.

Then, to the soldiers' astonishment, Grant turned to the right![154]

General Grant was clearly heading south. The Army of the Potomac was advancing, not retreating! The troops broke into spontaneous cheers. "On to Richmond! Huzzah for Grant! We will whip the rebs now!"

Despite the dismal battle in the Wilderness, Grant pushed forward to fight another day. Word passed rapidly along the column that the new chief was moving forward toward Richmond. As their officers confirmed the command to move by the left flank, which would take them south, the soldiers realized this wasn't like any of their previous offensives. They immediately understood this campaign had just begun.[155]

The cheers grew to a crescendo.

General Winfield Scott Hancock's soldiers, who were still in the woods guarding the movement of the rest of the army, sprang to their feet, forgetful of their weariness and the pain of wounds, and rushed to the roadside. Wild cheers echoed through the forest. Pinecones and branches were set on fire and waved, lighting the scene with a hypnotic, flickering glare.[156] Grant had won the respect and admiration of the Army of the Potomac.

The march became a key turning point in the war—so important that a generation later, sculptor Henry Merwin Shrady captured the moment and enshrined it forever in the Ulysses S. Grant Memorial on the western front of the United States Capitol in Washington, DC.

William Tecumseh Sherman further immortalized this important moment. "When Grant cried 'Forward!' after the battle of the Wilderness, I said: 'This is the grandest act of his life; now I feel that the rebellion will be crushed.'"[157]

CHALLENGE THE PROCESS

"Leaders venture out. None of the individuals in our study sat idly by waiting for fate to smile upon them," Kouzes and Posner observed. "Leaders are pioneers—people who are willing to step out into the unknown. They search for opportunities to innovate, grow and improve. … Leaders know well that innovation and change all involve experimentation, risk, and failure. They proceed anyway."[158]

Immediately upon taking command in the spring of 1864, Grant made it clear that it would not be business as usual—he would certainly challenge the process. His strategy would be to keep the Confederate armies separated so they couldn't reinforce each other. He also stopped the practice of prisoner exchange. He saw no need to return healthy soldiers to the Confederate army, even if it meant allowing Northern soldiers to remain in Southern prisons.

What Grant saw more clearly than almost anyone in Washington was that, from the military point of view, the war was actually going well. Since the Virginia and Georgia campaigns opened in May, the Confederacy had been placed under unceasing strain, like it had never endured. In the past, Confederate leadership could move troops to a hot spot to reinforce the various armies, but Grant's policy of unrelenting pressure kept the armies separated. His strategy of divide and conquer was working.

Something was bound to give. Under Sherman's leadership, the first cracks appeared in Georgia.[159]

Because General Joe Johnston had been unable to keep Sherman from crossing the Chattahoochee River and advancing to the outskirts of Atlanta, Confederate President Jefferson Davis relieved him of duty in mid-July. He was replaced with the aggressive General John B. Hood. Grant had known Hood in the Mexican War. "I know very well," said Grant, "the chief characteristics of Hood. He is a bold, dashing soldier, and has many qualities of successful leadership, but he is an indiscreet commander, and lacks cool judgment. We may look out now for rash and ill-advised attacks."[160]

Hood did just what Grant expected, coming out from behind his entrenchments, fighting both valiantly and foolishly. The results were so disastrous that on August 5, Davis provided his new commander with some ironic tactical advice: "The loss consequent upon attacking the enemy in his entrenchments requires you to avoid that if practicable."[161]

According to biographer Edward Bonekemper, during the preceding two months of the Atlanta campaign, Johnston had lost nine thousand men to Sherman's eleven thousand. In a little more than a week, Hood lost fourteen thousand casualties compared to Sherman's four thousand. The hundred-day campaign had cost the Union thirty-two thousand casualties and the Confederates thirty-five thousand, almost three-fourths of these rebel casualties occurring after Hood succeeded Johnston. With Sherman's two-to-one troop advantage, the Southerners could not afford to trade casualties on that scale.[162]

While the Democrats in Chicago were nominating General George McClellan for the presidency and composing a platform based on the assumption that the war was a failure, General Hood was forced to evacuate Atlanta to get his army out alive. On August 31, Hood lost more than four thousand men at Jonesboro, which gave Union forces control of all the railroads into Atlanta, cutting off Confederate supplies and compelling Hood to evacuate on September 1.[163]

After occupying the fallen stronghold, Sherman sent a dispatch to Washington:

SO ATLANTA IS OURS, AND FAIRLY WON.[164]

The Democratic convention had adjourned on August 31 in a mood of campaign euphoria. Only two days later, the bubble had burst. Secretary of State William H. Seward declared, "Sherman and Farragut have knocked the bottom out of the [Democrats'] Chicago platform"[165]—referring to the army's victory under General Sherman in Atlanta and the navy's triumph under Admiral Farragut in Mobile Bay. All this was possible, in large part, because Grant changed the rules of the game to the Union's advantage.

ENABLE OTHERS TO ACT

"Grand dreams don't become significant realities through the actions of a single person," write Kouzes and Posner. "Leadership is a team effort. . . . Exemplary leaders enable others to act. They foster collaboration and build trust. ... Leaders make it possible for others to do good work. They know that those who are expected to produce the results must feel a sense of personal power and ownership. ... Leaders enable others to act not by hoarding the power they have but by giving it away."[166]

Grant had seen brilliance in Philip H. Sheridan, a young, fiery Irishman, during the Battle of Chattanooga. The commanding general was so impressed that he brought Sheridan east to lead the previously ineffective cavalry of the Army of the Potomac. Sheridan quickly whipped the unit into shape, leading it so valiantly that Grant once again promoted him to lead the Yankee forces fighting in the strategically important Shenandoah Valley.

The two previous Union commanders had been ineffective in the Shenandoah, allowing Lee to use it as a breadbasket to feed his troops. The valley was also a gateway for attacks on Washington, DC—a pathway that nearly led to disaster in July 1864 when rebel General Jubal Early took advantage of this Union weakness.

Grant believed Sheridan could check the Confederates in the Shenandoah—and he enabled him to act. On September 15, the two met to discuss Sheridan's plan of attack. "My purpose was to have him attack Early, or drive him out of the valley and destroy that source of supplies for Lee's army," Grant wrote in his memoirs. "When Sheridan arrived I asked him if he had a map showing the positions of his army and that of the enemy. He at once drew one out of his side pocket, showing all roads and streams, and the camps of the two armies. He said that if he had permission he would move so and so (pointing out how) against the Confederates, and that he could 'whip them.' Before starting I had drawn up a plan of campaign for Sheridan, which I had brought with me; but, seeing that he was so clear and so positive in his views and so confident of success, I said nothing about this and did not take it out of my pocket."[167]

Grant could have forced his plan on Sheridan, but he trusted the young commander so much, he never even told him about his own plan. The result was that, within only a few weeks, Sheridan had led his army in triumph over the Confederates, driving them out of the decimated Shenandoah Valley for the remainder of the war.

To celebrate Sheridan's victory, Grant ordered the armies at Petersburg to fire a hundred-gun salute, just as he had done when he received news of the fall of Atlanta. He immediately wrote to the War Department and urged them to promote Sheridan to the rank of brigadier general in the regular army.[168]

Another Grant protégé was a young, intelligent officer by the name of James B. McPherson, who had risen almost as quickly as Grant from captain to major general in only three years. Grant and Sherman had grown fond of McPherson while working together in the Army of the Tennessee. McPherson was handsome and charming but also incredibly gifted. Having graduated first in his class at West Point, he had become an engineer before the war. But once hostilities broke out, McPherson became a warrior.

At the beginning of the Atlanta campaign, Sherman promoted McPherson to commander of the Army of the Tennessee—the same position both Grant and Sherman had held earlier in the war. McPherson was a gallant, effective leader who proved most valuable to Sherman in the campaign. On July 22, 1864, McPherson and some of his men trotted down a road that was reported to be free of Confederates. Without warning, rebel soldiers confronted them and ordered the general to surrender. Charmingly, McPherson raised his hat, then turned his horse and raced away. The Confederates shot him in the back.

Geoffrey Perret writes, "Grant almost reeled as he read the slip of paper in his hand. McPherson ... *dead*? He closed his eyes, wishing the news, the fact of death itself, away. His lips began to twitch spasmodically as he forced himself not to shout out in his anger and pain, then the tears began to flow, streaming down his sunburned cheeks and into his beard."

When newspaper reporters received word of Grant's reaction, the story was shared across the country. General McPherson's mother was touched by the commanding general's sadness and wrote to thank him. "A nation grieves. ... It is a selfish grief,"

Grant responded, "because the nation had more to expect from him than from almost any man living. I join in this selfish grief, and add the grief of personal love. ... I knew him well; to know him was to love. ... Your bereavement is great, but can not exceed mine."[169]

ENCOURAGE THE HEART

"Encouragement is curiously serious business," Kouzes and Posner assert. "It's how leaders visibly and behaviorally link rewards with performance. ... Leaders also know that celebrations and rituals, when done with authenticity and from the heart, build a strong sense of collective identity and community spirit that can carry a group through extraordinarily tough times."[170]

When Grant was named general in chief, the military press wrote that he planned to discourage diversions like horse racing and military balls when he arrived at the Army of the Potomac headquarters. This puritanical approach greatly concerned General George Meade, who led the Amy of the Potomac. Grant immediately set Meade's mind to rest when he refuted the allegation. He especially liked horse racing and looked forward to some of these camp pastimes, which encouraged the heart and helped men endure the tedium and terror that accompanied the life of a soldier.

"He laughed off reports that he had put an end to reviews, military balls, and various spectator sports, including horse races," biographer Brooks Simpson observes. "Doubtless Grant's sentiments were sincere ones—he well knew the fickleness of newspapers, having been a victim of their criticism."[171]

LOVE WORKS

Before Joel Manby won the respect of America with his appearance on the CBS reality TV series *Undercover Boss*, he was a highly successful corporate executive. After the show aired, many viewers wrote to him about the profound impact of his servant leadership philosophy. How does a person achieve that level of success without arrogance or pride? In his book *Love Works* Manby explained the power of Christlike love in the workplace. In years of leading thousands of men and women, Manby demonstrated that leading with love is effective, even in a business environment.

"When asked what was behind our caring culture displayed on 'Undercover Boss,' I said, 'Well we actually use love to define our leadership culture at Herschend Family Entertainment [HFE]. Not love the emotion, but love the verb.'"[172]

It may be difficult to imagine a military commander leading in love during a civil war, but that was likely the case with Ulysses S. Grant. As pointed out in various parts of this book, the atmosphere around Grant's headquarters was remarkably democratic—a clear sign of a caring, selfless commander who included "love the verb" in his leadership approach. Grant was truly concerned for the welfare of his staff and soldiers—and rank didn't matter to him when it came to respect for the individual.

"The simple truth is this," Manby explains, "there is a crisis of confidence in leadership. The level of dissatisfaction and even resentment present in the thousands of letters and email messages shocked me. People felt as if they couldn't trust their leaders and bosses. That's why our episode of 'Undercover Boss' provoked such an overwhelming response—people were hungry for something new, something better.

"Leading with love is counterintuitive in today's business environment because it turns many so-called leadership principles upside-down. Yet the outpouring of support from people who had never even heard of HFE convinced me that while we might be doing something slightly crazy by leading with love, we were also doing something that people were hungry to be a part of."[173]

There are many equally moving examples of Grant's compassion toward not only the Northern forces but also the Southern troops. Although he disapproved of their cause, Grant always saw the Southerners as his fellow countrymen.

"Leading with love is too important to be left to chance," Manby concludes. "It takes effort to lead with the principles of love—to be patient, kind, trustful, unselfish, truthful, forgiving, and dedicated . . . leading with love is worth it. On every level it is more difficult, and on every level it is more rewarding, more fulfilling, more right than you can imagine."[174]

A Friend to Abraham Lincoln

Part of being an effective leader is being a good follower of those God has placed in authority over us. Part of being a good follower is being a true friend.

Twenty years after the war, Grant shared his thoughts on President Lincoln with his physician, Doctor John Hancock Douglas. "I have been writing up my views of some of our Generals and of the character of Lincoln and Stanton [Lincoln's Secretary of War]. I do not place Stanton as high as some people do. Mr. Lincoln cannot be extolled too highly."[175]

Years earlier, as Grant completed his plans for the assault on Petersburg in the spring of 1865, he invited President Lincoln to visit City Point and get some rest.

On March 24, word arrived at headquarters that the president was steaming his way up the James River aboard the luxurious steamboat, the *River Queen*. About nine o'clock that evening the steamer approached the wharf, and General Grant, with some of his staff and Robert Lincoln, went down to the landing and met the President, Mrs. Lincoln, their youngest son, Tad, and several ladies who had come from Washington with the presidential party.

"It was after dark on the 24th when we reached City Point," recalled presidential guard William Crook. "It was a beautiful sight at this time, with the many-colored lights of the boats in the harbor and the lights of the town straggling up the bluffs of the shore, crowned by the lights from Grant's headquarters at the top.

"As soon as the River Queen was made fast to the wharf, General Grant with some members of his staff came aboard. They had a long consultation with the President, at the end of which Mr. Lincoln appeared particularly happy. General Grant had evidently made him feel that the end of the conflict was at hand, nearer than he had expected." [176]

The meeting was cordial, but it only lasted a short time as Lincoln and his family were fatigued by the trip and decided to retire.

The next day, Grant offered the president the choice of his two favorite horses, Cincinnati and Jeff Davis. Lincoln selected the magnificent Cincinnati, being the larger of the two and better suited to his tall frame. "He was a good rider and greatly enjoyed this recreation," wrote War Department employee David Homer Bates. "It was a busy camp, and everything was in motion. Just west of our troops was the long, curved line of Lee's intrenchments, stretching from Petersburg, south of the James and fifteen miles from City Point, to Richmond, northwest of City Point and nearly double that distance."[177]

"General Grant invited the president to take a ride to the front to visit with General Meade," Crook later recalled. "The president watched some lively skirmishing between the picket-lines of the two forces while we were at General Meade's headquarters. They were on a hill just east of where the troops were engaged, not more than a quarter of a mile away from the wood where the fighting was in progress. The President asked whether the position was not too close for the comfort of his party. When he was assured that there was no danger, he remained two hours watching the struggle, and turned away only when the firing ceased."[178]

Lincoln's working vacation was exactly what he needed to regain his strength—something he desperately needed in the coming weeks as the war was fought to its conclusion. He was extremely grateful to the Grants for their hospitality.

In the midst of the horrors of the Civil War, Grant and Lincoln moved beyond their official positions as president and commanding general to establish a true, enduring friendship. After Lincoln's assassination, Grant placed himself at the head of the fallen leader's coffin. During the private funeral in the White House, Grant stood erect, tears streaming down his face as he grieved not only a president but also a friend.

"My personal relations with him were as close and intimate as the nature of our respective duties would permit," Grant wrote.

"To know him personally was to love and respect him for his great qualities of heart and head, and for his patience and patriotism."[179]

A Lifelong Friend

One of the tragedies of the American Civil War was the way it pitted brother against brother and friend against friend. Members of both President Lincoln's and General Grant's extended family fought for the Confederacy, bringing sorrow and pain to both families. Grant had many friends on the rebel side from his years at West Point, the Mexican War, and his service in the army. But one lifelong friendship that brought him particular sadness was that of James "Old Pete" Longstreet.

Grant and Longstreet were good friends at West Point and during their time at Jefferson Barracks in St. Louis. Pete also had been one of the groomsmen at Grant's wedding. The two men spent many hours together, both as professional soldiers and as friends who gathered to play cards and smoke cigars.

While the war strained their friendship nearly to the breaking point, Grant purposefully sought out his old friend at Appomattox, soon after Lee's surrender. The former Confederate general recalled the moment he saw Grant at Appomattox: "The first thing that General Grant said to me when we stepped inside, placing his hand in mine was, 'Pete, let us have another game of brag ...'—a card game they had played together as fellow soldiers during the Mexican War—... 'to recall the days that were so pleasant.'

"Great God! I thought to myself, how my heart swells out to such magnanimous touch of humanity. Why do men fight who were born to be brothers?"[180] Longstreet later said that Ulysses S. Grant "was the truest as well as the bravest man that ever lived."[181]

When asked by a reporter who was the greatest Northern general, Longstreet did not hesitate: "Grant—incomparably the greatest."[182]

GRANT'S LEADERSHIP PRINCIPLES

- Appreciate faithful friendship in the midst of adversity.
- Demonstrate the "Five Practices of Exemplary Leadership": inspiring a shared vision, modeling the way, challenging the process, enabling others to act, and encouraging the heart.
- Lead with "love—the verb."
- Communicate compassion and empathy at appropriate moments.
- Build lifelong friendships with key associates.

Chapter Five

REMEMBER: YOUR OPPONENTS FEAR YOU

Never take counsel of your fears. —Thomas "Stonewall'" Jackson

Grant's first command in the Civil War was as colonel of the Twenty-First Illinois. One of his first assignments was to hunt down and destroy a Missouri Confederate regiment under the command of Colonel Tom Harris. As this was the first time he took troops into battle, Grant experienced increasing anxiety as the regiment drew near the enemy.

"My sensations as we approached what I supposed might be a field of battle were anything but agreeable," Grant wrote later. "I had been in all the engagements in Mexico that it was possible for one person to be, but not in command. If some one else had been colonel and I had been lieutenant-colonel I do not think I would have felt any trepidation.

"As we approached the brow of the hill from which it was expected we could see Harris' camp, and possibly find his men ready formed to meet us, my heart kept getting higher and higher until it felt to me as though it was in my throat. I would have given anything then to have been back in Illinois, but I had not the moral courage to halt and consider what to do; I kept right on."

When they reached the crest of the hill and looked down into the valley, Grant saw signs of a recent large encampment, but neither Harris nor his troops were present. The camp had been abandoned. "My heart resumed its place," Grant explained.

At that moment, he had an epiphany. "It occurred to me at once that Harris had been as much afraid of me as I had been of him. This was a view of the question I had never taken before; but it was one I never forgot afterwards.

"From that event to the close of the war, I never experienced trepidation upon confronting an enemy, though I always felt more or less anxiety. I never forgot that he had as much reason to fear my forces as I had his."[183]

Grant showed wisdom and diligence in preparing his troops for battle and, as a result, was named brigadier general by Major General John C. Fremont, commander of the western theater of operations. "I believe him to be a man of great activity and promptness in obeying orders without question or hesitation," Fremont later said of Grant. "For that reason I gave General Grant this important command at this critical period. ... I selected him for qualities I could not then find combined in any other officer, for General Grant was a man of unassuming character, not given to self-elation, of dogged persistence, and of iron will."[184]

Thus began the rapid rise up the military ladder for the calm and collected Ulysses S. Grant.

COOLNESS UNDER FIRE

Merriam-Webster defines *courage* as "mental or moral strength to venture, persevere, and withstand danger, fear, or difficulty."[185] Although he experienced trepidation in his first command, Grant's courage continued to grow. Later in the war, soldiers and officers marveled at how Grant would not even flinch as artillery shells exploded all around him.

In *The Millionaire Mind*, author Thomas J. Stanley writes about Erich Hartmann, the World War II fighter pilot who holds the world record for 352 air victories. Though it was a different kind of combat from Grant's experience in the Civil War, Hartmann still had to overcome his fear on his way to his many victories. "I was afraid ... of the big unknown factors. Clouds and sun were hate and love."

"Yes, even the Ace of Aces was afraid," writes Stanley, "but he acted courageously nevertheless. Fear and courage are related. Courage does not exist in the absence of fear of some danger."[186]

An example of Grant's coolness under fire occurred during the first day of the horrific Battle of the Wilderness. Headquarters for both General Grant and General Meade were established on a knoll on the edge of the thick woods where the battle raged. As soon as Grant learned that his troops had confronted Lee's forces, "he followed his habitual custom in warfare, and instead of waiting to be attacked, took the initiative and pushed out against the enemy," wrote Colonel Horace Porter.

After all the orders were given, General Grant lit a cigar, sat down on the stump of a tree, took out his penknife, and began to whittle a stick, making nothing. When one stick was consumed, he picked up another. Soon he was surrounded by small wood chips that had once been sticks, yet he continued the ritual throughout the day. Grant wore a pair of golden thread gloves—likely a gift from Julia—and did not remove them once during the entire day.

The general remained cool while the most critical movements were taking place, his rapid whittling the only indication of his nervousness. This occupation brought a sad ending to the thread gloves. Before nightfall several holes had been worn in them, from which his fingernails protruded. After that, the gloves disappeared, and the general wore the usual buckskin gauntlets when on horseback.[187]

Grant positioned himself near Wilderness Tavern at the center of the line where his commands—and his air of confidence—could be communicated to the greatest number of his troops. As he believed he could be located more readily and issue orders more promptly, he remained there almost the entire day. At times he walked up and down the knoll, gazing toward the invisible battlefield hidden behind the trees. He heard telltale sounds from the direction of the fight, but he could see only the tangled thicket before him and the smoke rising from the forest. Most of the day, he sat on the stump or on the ground with his back leaning against a tree, smoking his cigars—lighting a new one as soon as the last had been consumed.

Grant gave orders to staff officers and messengers who dashed off to different hot points along the line. "His speech was never hurried," Porter recalled, "and his manner betrayed no trace of excitability or even impatience. He never exhibited to better advantage his peculiar ability in moving troops with unparalleled speed to the critical points on the line of battle where they were most needed, or, as it was sometimes called, 'feeding a fight.' ...There was a spur on the heel of every order he sent and his subordinates were made to realize that in battle it is the minutes which control events."[188]

When Grant felt he was needed somewhere on the battlefield, he swung himself into the saddle without a word, then rode off at top speed with his staff following as best they could. Roads were not important to this master horseman. He had a sense for finding shortcuts, splashing through streams, or squeezing through hedges.[189]

The battle raged directly in front of general headquarters as General Warren's corps was driven back by the enemy. Stragglers emerged from the woods as they made their way to the rear. Suddenly enemy shells began falling on the knoll where General Grant was seated on the stump. He rose slowly to his feet to monitor the situation, making no comment.

An officer approached with a look of great anxiety. "General, wouldn't it be prudent to move headquarters to the other side of the Germanna Road till the result of the present attack is known?" The general took a few puffs on his cigar and then replied quietly, "It strikes me it would be better to order up some artillery and defend the present location."

The officer saluted and turned to tend to the order. Soon a battery was brought up to defend the knoll. The enemy was checked, and the Federal forces pushed them away from the general's position.[190]

Grant went back to his whittling.

He had learned well the lesson that the enemy is as afraid of you as you are of him. He also learned the importance of fighting to win. "In every battle there comes a time when both sides consider themselves beaten. Then he who continues the attack wins."[191]

FEARING YOUR IDEAS

Author Victor Hugo famously said, "An invasion of armies can be resisted, but not an invasion of ideas."[192] In addition to fearing the size and equipment of his army, Confederate leaders eventually began to respect Grant's strategic skill—and soon they feared his ideas—though many refused to openly admit it.

In the late nineteenth and early twentieth centuries, the Lost Cause school of historians, writers, and academics worked to convince Americans that Grant only won the war due to brute force. The seeds of this thinking were planted during the war itself. After several days of some of the bloodiest fighting ever seen on American soil, several Confederate officers accused Grant of butchery. General Robert E. Lee quieted them with his surprising reply. "Gentlemen, I think General Grant has managed his affairs remarkably well up to the present time."[193]

In *Thinking for a Change*, John C. Maxwell lists eleven life skills that highly successful people employ in their life and work. Not surprisingly, Grant utilized every one of them as general in chief of the Union armies in the Civil War—and his enemies feared him for it.

SKILL 1: ACQUIRE THE WISDOM OF BIG-PICTURE THINKING

One week after the bombardment of Fort Sumter by Southern forces—the moment that marked the outbreak of the war—President Lincoln ordered a blockade of the rebel ports. To establish a strategy for the war, Lincoln met with his first general in chief, Winfield Scott, who had gained fame in the War of 1812 and the Mexican War. Scott heartily agreed with Lincoln's blockade and proposed a strategy to cut off trade to the Confederacy and squeeze the life out of the rebellion.

Scott's proposal became known as the Anaconda Plan.

Scott's plan called for a force of eighty thousand men to travel up the Mississippi River, taking cities along the way and dividing the

Confederacy in two. They would begin the campaign with an attack on the forts below New Orleans from the south and then a thrust at the cities along the river from the north. When these strongholds fell, the river would be in Federal hands from its source to its mouth, and the Confederacy would be weakened.

The first great success in the plan came on April 24, 1862, when Admiral David Farragut ran his fleet past the forts that defended New Orleans and forced the city to surrender.[194] After repairing his ships, he sent them upriver, where they took Baton Rouge and Natchez. After these conquests, the fleet ran into a wall when they attacked Vicksburg, where Confederate batteries sat on high bluffs, rendering the city impregnable to the navy's gunboats.

Called "the Gibraltar of the West," the Vicksburg garrison valiantly resisted Union control of the Mississippi River. Other than Port Hudson, Louisiana—one hundred miles to the south—Vicksburg was the only remaining Confederate stronghold on the mighty river. Surrounded by nine major forts, Vicksburg was reinforced with 172 guns, commanding all approaches by water and land. A thirty-thousand-troop garrison protected the city.[195]

Having traveled the Mississippi by flatboat in his youth, President Lincoln knew its topography. Early in the war, Lincoln stressed Vicksburg's importance when he pointed to a national map and said, "See what a lot of land these fellows hold, of which Vicksburg is the key. The war can never be brought to a close until that key is in our pocket."[196]

Grant embraced this national strategy, supporting the blockade and working to cut off the supplies to the Confederate army. This eventually led to his signature victory at Vicksburg (more on the Battle of Vicksburg in chapter 8).

Despite the dire predictions of naysayers, Lincoln and Grant kept pounding until victory was won.

SKILL 2: UNLEASH THE POTENTIAL OF FOCUSED THINKING

As a brigadier general, Grant was stationed at Paducah, Kentucky, in the beginning of the war under General John C. Fremont, commander of the western theater of operations. Fremont paid Grant a supremely high honor by appointing the legendary General Charles Ferguson Smith to serve under him. Smith had been commandant at West Point when Grant was a cadet.

There was no one in the regular army for whom Grant had higher regard. "His personal courage was unquestioned, his judgment and professional acquirements were unsurpassed, and he had the confidence of those he commanded as well as those over him," Grant wrote in his memoirs.[197]

Whenever necessary, Grant issued orders to Smith with the greatest respect and deference. Smith showed no resentment; rather, he was proud of his former student. Together they were a formidable force of focused thinking and concentrated action.

"The harmonious relationship between Grant and Smith was one of the high points of the Union campaign on the Mississippi," observes biographer Jean Edward Smith. "Grant watched Smith closely, studied his manner, and generally assigned him the toughest tasks."

The Union army was blessed to have this dynamic duo. Both were smart, aggressive commanders. "The two shared a common outlook," Smith explains. "Grant's instinct was to carry the fight to the enemy. Smith put it more eloquently. 'Battle is the ultimate to which the whole life's labor of an officer should be directed. He may live to the age of retirement without seeing a battle; still, he must always be getting ready for it exactly as if he knew the hour of the day it is to break upon him. And then, whether it come late or early, he must be willing to fight—he *must* fight.'"[198]

Tragically, General Smith died from an infection that set in after scraping his leg while climbing into a boat. In a letter of sympathy written to Smith's wife, Grant declared his respect for his mentor and friend. "I can bear honest testimony to his great worth as a soldier and friend. Where an entire nation condoles with you in your bereavement, no one can do so with more heartfelt grief than myself."[199]

General Sherman shared in both the grief and the respect. Years later he wrote that if Smith had lived, "no one would have ever heard of Grant or myself."[200]

Skill 3: Discover the Joy of Creative Thinking

Once Grant came east, his primary objective was to crush Lee in Virginia, while Sherman moved against General Joe Johnston's forces in Georgia. Above everything else, Grant had to put all the Union forces to work and make certain that everyone labored in harmony.

Grant succeeded where previous Union commanders had failed—even though they had the same superior numbers and supplies—due to his creative thinking and strategic vision.

Skill 4: Recognize the Importance of Realistic Thinking

After Grant's stunning victory at Vicksburg, President Abraham Lincoln sent him a remarkable letter of congratulations. Lincoln had differed with Grant about the strategy of the campaign, but at the same time, he defended his favorite general against the attacks of jealous rivals. When Grant pursued his own plan with rousing success, Lincoln humbly praised Grant's realistic thinking.

In December 1866, more than a year after Lincoln's death, Joseph Gillespie, a legal colleague of Lincoln's from Illinois, mentioned the congratulatory letter when writing to Lincoln's law partner: "It required no effort on his part to admit another man's superiority, and his admission that General Grant was right and he was wrong about operations in Vicksburg was not intended for effect as some suppose but was perfectly in character."

Major General Grant
My dear General

I do not remember that you and I ever met personally. I write
this now as a grateful acknowledgment for the almost inestima-
ble service you have done the country. I wish to say a word further. When you first reached the vicinity of Vicksburg, I thought
you should do, what you finally did—march the troops across
the neck, run the batteries with the transports, and thus go below; and I never had any faith, except a general hope that you
knew better than I, that the Yazoo Pass expedition, and the like,
could succeed. When you got below, and took Port-Gibson,
Grand Gulf, and vicinity, I thought you should go down the river
and join Gen. Banks; and when you turned Northward East of
the Big Black, I feared it was a mistake. I now wish to make the
personal acknowledgment that you were right, and I was wrong.

Yours very truly
A. Lincoln[201]

Lincoln did not meet Grant in person until the following year
when he elevated him to the rank of lieutenant general. But he
wrote about him in glowing terms in a May 26, 1863, letter to
his friend Isaac Arnold: "His campaign from the beginning of this
month up to the twenty second day of it, is one of the most brilliant
in the world."[202]

Because Grant was on the ground observing the topography
and troop deployments around Vicksburg—and due to his military
training and years of experience—he had a much more realistic
understanding of the situation than Lincoln did sitting in the White
House. Lincoln was mature enough to recognize that fact in the
end. Modern-day leaders would do well to recognize the experience and education in their employees and supporters and tap into
that for the good of their business—a much more realistic approach
to leadership.

SKILL 5: RELEASE THE POWER OF STRATEGIC THINKING

The carnage at Cold Harbor caused Grant to rethink his strategy for defeating Lee and capturing Richmond. "I now find, after more than thirty days of trial, the enemy deems it of first importance to run no risks with the armies they now have," he wrote Halleck. "They act purely on the defensive, behind breastworks, or feebly on the offensive immediately in front of them and where, in case of repulse, they can instantly retire behind them. Without a greater sacrifice of human life than I am willing to make, all cannot be accomplished that I had designed outside of the city."[203]

Grant began to mature plans he had in mind from the beginning of the Overland Campaign—to boldly move his army across the James River. "Once on the south side of the James River, I can cut off all sources of supply to the enemy except what is furnished by the canal"—the James River Canal, west of Richmond. Grant planned to attack the vital railways supplying Richmond from the south and west, then attack the canal and complete Lee's encirclement.[204]

The Army of Northern Virginia seemed to have acquired a new respect for the courage, endurance, and soldierly qualities of the Army of the Potomac—and for the leadership of Grant. They no longer wanted to fight them "one Confederate to five Yanks," as they had boasted earlier in the war.

"Lee's position was now so near Richmond and the intervening swamps of the Chickahominy so great an obstacle to the movement of troops in the face of an enemy, that I determined to make my next left flank move carry the Army of the Potomac south of the James River," Grant wrote in his memoirs. "Preparations for this were promptly commenced. The move was a hazardous one to make: the Chickahominy River, with its marshy and heavily timbered approaches, had to be crossed; all the bridges over it east of Lee were destroyed. ... The Army of the Potomac had to be got out of a position but a few hundred yards from the enemy at the widest place."[205]

From Cold Harbor on June 5, he wrote to Halleck at Washington concerning his strategy for victory:

> My idea from the start has been to beat Lee's Army, if possible, north of Richmond, then after destroying his lines of communications north of the James River to transfer the Army to the south side and besiege Lee in Richmond, or follow him south if he should retreat.
>
> I will continue to hold substantially the ground now occupied by the Army of the Potomac, taking advantage of any favorable circumstance that may present itself until the cavalry can be sent west to destroy the Virginia Central Railroad from about Beaver Dam for some twenty-five or thirty miles west. When this is effected I will move the army to the south side of the James River.[206]

To win the game, Grant had to change the strategy—and he was prepared to do that in a dramatic way. (More on the crossing of the James River in chapter 6.)

SKILL 6: FEEL THE ENERGY OF POSSIBILITY THINKING

An example of what John Maxwell calls "possibility thinking" can be seen in a remarkable exchange between Grant and his top subordinate, General Sherman, after Grant was named lieutenant general. The respect and admiration between the two men is palpable, and it shows why they achieved success in prosecuting the war.

Grant wrote to Sherman that while he had been eminently successful in the war up to that time, none felt more than he how much of the success was due to the energy and skill of those subordinate to him. He further credited Sherman with a large measure of the responsibility for his promotion to lieutenant general, writing, "How far your execution ... entitles you to the reward I am receiving you cannot know as well as I do."

Sherman immediately responded with the most praiseworthy letter he probably ever wrote:

> You do yourself injustice. You are now Washington's legitimate successor, and occupy a position of almost dangerous elevation; but if you can continue as heretofore to be yourself, simple, honest, and unpretending, you will enjoy through life the respect and love of friends, and the homage of millions of human beings who will award to you a large share for securing to them and their descendants a government of law and stability.
>
> I believe you are as brave, patriotic, and just, as the great prototype Washington; as unselfish, kind-hearted, and honest as a man should be; but the chief characteristic in your nature is the simple faith in success you have always manifested, which I can liken to nothing else than the faith a Christian has in his Saviour.[207]

SKILL 7: EMBRACE THE LESSONS OF REFLECTIVE THINKING

Grant spent a large amount of his time in reflective thinking, analysis, and constant improvement. After learning that he had incurable throat cancer, he went into a season of deep, quiet reflection that greatly worried his wife and children. But Sherman reminded Julia that, throughout the war, this was how Ulysses worked through problems and created strategies to defeat the enemy.

Grant's close and trusted associate, Colonel Horace Porter, gave a poignant portrait of Grant's habit of reflective thinking in his great work, *Campaigning with Grant*:

> Throughout this memorable year, the most important as well as the most harassing of his entire military career, General Grant never in any instance failed to manifest those traits which were the true elements of his greatness. He was always calm amid excitement, and patient under trials. ... When he could not control he endured, and in every great crisis he could "convince when others could not advise." His calmness of demeanor and unruffled temper were often a marvel even to those most familiar with him. In the midst of the most exciting scenes he rarely

raised his voice above its ordinary pitch or manifested the least irritability.

Whether encountered at noonday or awakened from sleep at midnight, his manner was always the same; whether receiving the report of an army commander or of a private soldier serving as a courier or a scout, he listened with equal deference and gave it the same strict attention. He could not only discipline others, but he could discipline himself ...

The only manifestation of anger he had indulged in during the campaign was upon the occasion ... when he found a teamster beating his horses near the Totopotomoy. He never criticized an officer harshly in the presence of others. If fault had to be found with him, it was never made an occasion to humiliate him or wound his feelings ...

It was an interesting study in human nature to watch the general's actions in camp. He would sit for hours in front of his tent, or just inside of it looking out, smoking a cigar very slowly, seldom with a paper or a map in his hands, and looking like the laziest man in camp. But at such periods his mind was working more actively than that of any one in the army. He talked less and thought more than any one in the service ...

He held subordinates to a strict accountability in the performance of such duties, and kept his own time for thought. It was this quiet but intense thinking, and the well-matured ideas which resulted from it, that led to the prompt and vigorous action which was constantly witnessed during this year, so pregnant with events.[208]

SKILL 8: QUESTION THE ACCEPTANCE OF POPULAR THINKING

When it came to civil rights, Ulysses S. Grant was decades ahead of his time—and certainly in opposition to much of the thinking of his day. When he won the presidency in the 1868 election, Republicans also won a majority in Congress. With control of all three branches of government, the Republicans pushed through the Fifteenth Amendment, guaranteeing the right to vote to Black men throughout the country. Grant had pushed hard for its passage, telling delegates from the first national Black political convention in Washington that, as president, he would ensure that "the colored people of the Nation may receive every protection which the law gives them."[209]

Grant also championed the creation of the new Justice Department and gave it the mandate to crush the Ku Klux Klan and similar White supremacist groups. Many Northerners, disgusted by Klan violence, lent their support to both the Fifteenth Amendment, which gave the vote to Black men in every state, and the First Reconstruction Act of 1867, which placed harsher restrictions on the South and closely regulated the formation of their new state governments.

Other legislation attacked the Klan more directly. Between 1870 and 1871, Congress passed the Enforcement Acts, which made it a crime to interfere with registration, voting, office holding, or jury service of Blacks. In 1871, Congress also passed the Ku Klux Klan Act, which allowed the government to act against terrorist organizations. Grant had lobbied hard for the bill's passage, and he traveled up Pennsylvania Avenue to sign the law on Capitol Hill. Under the leadership of Grant and Attorney General Amos Akerman, federal grand juries, many interracial, brought 3,384 indictments against the KKK, resulting in 1,143 convictions.[210]

By 1872, under Grant's leadership, both legally and militarily, the Ku Klux Klan had been almost completely destroyed in the South.[211]

Another triumph was the Civil Rights Act of 1875, which Grant endorsed and signed into law. It outlawed racial segregation in public accommodations, schools, transportation, and juries.[212] Sadly, the Supreme Court ruled the Civil Rights Act of 1875 unconstitutional in 1883, thereby sanctioning the notion of "separate but equal" facilities and transportation for the races. With that ruling, the nation descended into eighty years of Jim Crow segregation. Not until the Civil Rights Act of 1964 were many of the 1875 Act's protections for Blacks restored.[213]

SKILL 9: ENCOURAGE THE PARTICIPATION OF SHARED THINKING

After the army under General Sherman triumphed over Atlanta, the question arose of where the Union forces should go next. The embarrassed and severely weakened Confederate Army of Tennessee under General John Bell Hood had moved west with the goal of cutting Sherman off from his supplies. Sherman was not intimidated. With Grant's blessings, he split his army, sending the capable General George Thomas west to deal with Hood. With the remaining sixty thousand soldiers, Sherman proposed to march across the state of Georgia, destroying everything in his path that could possibly aid the Confederate war effort.

Part of this plan was practical, as the Georgia countryside—much like the Shenandoah Valley—had supplied both food and munitions to help sustain the rebel armies. But Sherman's plan also had a powerful psychological aspect to it. With Lee tied to Richmond by Grant and Hood being pursued by Thomas, Sherman had an unopposed, well-equipped army that could tear through the South, disabling the Confederate infrastructure.

He wrote to Grant regarding his plan: "I can make this march and make Georgia howl."[214]

As he always did with important questions of strategy, Grant discussed it in detail with Sherman. Then he opened the discussion of Sherman's plan to the officers at headquarters for debate. Biographer Geoffrey Perret describes the democratic nature of the general in chief's headquarters:

> There were no councils of war at Grant's headquarters. Instead, he encouraged his staff to debate ideas—and tell him how wrong he was—in lengthy sessions around the campfire each night. Everyone could speak freely, whatever his rank. ... There was a tacit bargain at work, an unspoken agreement that those who lost an argument would support whatever decision Grant finally made just as loyally as those on the winning side.[215]

In this case, Rawlins opposed Sherman's plan, but Porter favored it. The two men took the lead in debating the proposed march to the sea. On one particular night, the debate lasted so long that a weary Grant retired to his tent. That didn't stop Rawlins and Porter from forcefully arguing their positions. Several minutes later, an exasperated Grant reemerged from his tent. "Oh, do go to bed, all of you! You're keeping the whole camp awake."[216]

Despite opposition by Rawlins and deep concerns by President Lincoln, Grant warmed to the idea. To have Sherman destroy the infrastructure of Georgia as Sheridan was doing in the Shenandoah Valley jived with Grant's view of prosecuting the war to its conclusion.

Grant approved the plan.

Sherman's army destroyed every manufacturer that could support the war effort and all railroad lines around Atlanta for fifty miles in every direction. Union soldiers heated the railroad ties in the middle and then bent them around a tree, making them unusable to the Confederates. In time, these twisted rails became known as "Sherman's neckties."

In December, Sherman's army reached Savannah on the seacoast, after reducing the countryside to a vast wasteland. Sherman wired the president: "I beg to present you, as a Christmas gift, the city of Savannah."[217]

SKILL 10: EXPERIENCE THE SATISFACTION OF UNSELFISH THINKING

After Sherman's decisive victory in Atlanta, talk began in Washington of conferring the equal rank of lieutenant general on Sherman with the possibility of giving him supreme command over Grant. Some Northern politicians and reporters accused Grant of loafing at Petersburg while other officers, like Sherman, were busy doing the fighting.

Sherman would have none of it.

The fiery commander immediately disavowed this talk as foolishness and wrote a heartfelt letter to his chief and his friend: "I would rather have you in command than anybody else, for you are fair, honest, and have at heart the same purpose that should actuate all. I should emphatically decline any commission calculated to bring us into rivalry."

Grant graciously replied, "No one would be more pleased at your advancement than I, and if you should be placed in my position and I put subordinate, it would not change our relations in the least. I would make the same exertions to support you that you have ever done to support me, and I would do all in my power to make our cause win."[218]

SKILL 11: ENJOY THE RETURN OF BOTTOM-LINE THINKING

Grant remained focused on victory by conquest from the day after the bloody Battle of Shiloh until the end of the war at Appomattox. But as soon as Lee surrendered, Grant rushed to Washington to cancel orders for military supplies in order to stop the financial bleeding. Like Lincoln, Grant was painfully aware that the war was costing the country between $3.5 and 4 million a day.[219] Grant did not even stay for the formal surrender ceremonies in Appomattox, where the Confederate troops stacked their arms before the triumphant Union soldiers.

Arriving in Washington, DC, after an all-night voyage from City Point, Grant checked into the Willard Hotel unannounced and mostly unnoticed. The next morning he walked over to army headquarters to begin the process of winding down the war.

"He instructed Quartermaster General Montgomery Meigs to suspend the purchase of additional supplies," Jean Edward Smith explains, "ordered the immediate discharge of convalescent soldiers, canceled the charter of unnecessary vessels, and halted all drafting and recruiting as of that day."[220]

The war was over, and along with the president, Grant focused on the bottom-line thinking of closing out the unneeded military accounts. Grant showed mastery over Maxwell's eleven necessary skills nearly 150 years before they were published—and achieved success again and again in life.

GRANT'S LEADERSHIP PRINCIPLES

- Remember that opponents fear your strengths.
- Avoid retreating under fire; hold your ground or attack an opponent.
- Realize that the minutes and the details control events in a conflict.
- Employ big-picture thinking.
- Understand the potential of focused thinking.
- Succeed by utilizing creative thinking and strategic vision.
- Set aside significant time for strategic thinking and planning.
- Recognize the necessity of clearheaded, bottom-line thinking.

1. Jesse and Hannah Grant, parents of Ulysses S. Grant.

2. Birthplace of Hiram Ulysses Grant, Point Pleasant, Ohio.

3. Brevet Second Lieutenant Ulysses S. Grant, 1843, soon after West Point graduation.

4. Julia Grant with sons Frederick and Ulysses Jr., 1854.

5. Julia Grant with daughter, Nellie, youngest son Jesse, and her father, Colonel Frederick Dent.

6. Grant & Perkins leather store, Galena, Illinois, where Ulysses worked the year prior to outbreak of the Civil War.

7. Ulysses S. Grant and his favorite horse, Cincinnati.

8. John Rawlins, Grant's Galena friend who became his chief of staff. Rawlins, along with Julia Grant, helped Ulysses stay sober through most of the Civil War.

9. General William Tecumseh Sherman, Grant's West Point friend who became his chief military subordinate.

10

11. Colonel Horace Porter, trusted member of Grant's army staff and later a close friend and supporter. Porter became president of the Grant Monument association and led the drive to finish the fundraising and begin construction of Grant's tomb.

11

10. Abraham Lincoln, the president who became a close friend of Ulysses S. Grant. Grant adopted Lincoln's views on racial relations and enforced them during his own presidency.

12

12. General James Longstreet, Grant's West Point friend who attended his wedding and later became a rival commander in the Army of Northern Virginia. Longstreet supported Grant in his presidential run and was one of the few former Confederates to join the Republican Party.

13. Ulysses S. Grant soon after the defeat at the Battle of Cold Harbor.

14. Grant's good friend and publisher Mark Twain, in his later years.

15. The Grant family home, Whitehaven, in Saint Louis, Missouri.

Chapter Six

PREPARE FOR THE NEW DAY THAT WILL COME

If the rebellion is not perfectly and thoroughly crushed it will be the fault and through the weakness of the people North. Be of good cheer and rest assured that all will come out right.
– Ulysses S. Grant

One of Grant's greatest strengths was his never-ending optimism regarding the future. Despite the misery he suffered in the years prior to the outbreak of the Civil War, he believed a new day would come for him, and he continued to work toward that inevitable conclusion. Much of his bad luck during those years was just that— bad luck. He was a hard worker, and his farmland yielded crops, but he couldn't control the economy.

A farmer must wait for harvest time to make his money, but in the meantime, food still must be placed on the table. To survive, Grant sold firewood on the streets of St. Louis—a necessary occupation that stole time from farming. "I regard every load of wood taken, when the services of both myself and team are required on the farm, is a direct loss of more than the value of the load." As a result, his wheat crop yielded only seventy-five bushels instead of the four or five hundred he had expected.[221]

Grant still held out hope for his potato, sweet potato, melon, and cabbage crops. But the Panic of 1857 led to sharp declines in commodity prices, bringing an end to Grant's farming days.

"In the last months of 1857, many people concluded that the failure of Ohio Life and Trust Company on August 24, 1857, had set in motion a series of events that created the Panic of 1857," writes Johnny Fulfer. This sharp economic downturn was the first financial crisis to spread rapidly throughout the country because of the invention of the telegraph. "News of the financial crisis that occurred just 20 years prior (the Panic of 1837) could only travel as fast as the postal service. After Samuel F. B. Morse invented the telegraph in 1844, news of the panic spread rapidly, creating a confidence crisis for investors throughout the United States and Europe."[222]

In an article for *Hunt's Merchants' Magazine*, Michigan lawyer Ezra Seaman observed that the crisis "soon extended [from Ohio Life] to other banking companies." Banks began to liquidate their investments, Seaman wrote, selling off their once-prized railroad stocks and bonds. This panic "caused a rapid and unprecedented decline in the stocks and securities, and particularly in the bonds and stocks of railroads owing large debts."[223]

Like millions of people around the world, Grant was adversely affected by this economic decline. An army friend was shocked when he saw Grant selling firewood in St. Louis around that time and asked him what he was doing. "I'm trying to settle the problem of poverty," Grant responded with a slight smile.[224]

Grant leased the farm and moved to St. Louis, where he unsuccessfully tried his hand at real estate. When Julia first suggested that Ulysses seek employment from his father, Jesse, he resisted. But when all other prospects dried up in St. Louis, he had no other choice but to seek a job in his prosperous father's leather goods business. Julia reminded him that his father "had always been not only willing but anxious to serve him."[225] Ulysses soon set out for Covington, Kentucky, to appeal to his domineering father.

Grant's father, Jesse Root Grant, had built his tannery into a prosperous business covering several Midwestern states. He was worth more than $100,000—or nearly $3 million today—and employed approximately fifty people. Ulysses arrived in Covington at a critical time. Now in his mid-sixties, Jesse Grant had turned over much of the business to his son Simpson. While Simpson was a capable businessman, he had contracted tuberculosis and was then staying with his parents to recuperate. The youngest Grant son, Orvil, was operating their leather goods store in Galena, Illinois. Sadly, Orvil had a problem with alcohol, and he wasn't very dependable.

Ulysses's youngest son, Jesse Grant, later recalled that the elder Jesse and Simpson had agreed to send his father "to the Galena store to stay until something else might turn up in his favor, and told him he must confine his wants within $800 a year."[226]

While not overly enthusiastic about his situation, Grant worked diligently in the store. While his confidence had been tested during the lean years in St. Louis, his natural optimism had never been defeated. He retained a certain amount of self-esteem, believing better things would come his way if he worked hard.

"He was a sensitive and retiring man," Fred Grant remembered of his father during the Galena days, "but behind his modesty was a fair estimate of his own worth. He tolerated no disrespect and was most determined."[227]

A relative, Melancthon T. Burke, worked with Grant in Galena and admired his experiences in Mexico and on the West Coast. "We all looked up to him as an older man and a soldier," said Burke. "He knew much more than we in matters of the world, and we recognized it."[228]

Grant's friend George W. Fishback saw that Grant's stature would inevitably rise, explaining that he "no doubt foresaw the threatened Civil War and felt that as an old defender of the Flag he had better take his chances among his people in the Northern States."[229]

With the outbreak of war, President Lincoln called for seventy-five thousand volunteers to put down the rebellion. Grant was confident he could secure a commission as a colonel, yet despite multiple inquiries, he was turned down again and again due to his reputation as a drunk.

Soon the need for trained officers became overwhelming, so Grant's past was ignored. He was given a temporary position in the Illinois militia as a mustering officer. As a result of his quartermaster experience, Grant quickly demonstrated his value. "It was soon bruited about that anyone could ask him a question and receive a clear, concise, and definitive answer."[230]

At that time, Illinois Governor Yates was faced with a problem. One of the regiments Grant had mustered in as thirty-day enlistments had spent their time raising hell and ignoring their timid commander. Half of the original twelve hundred men had gone home in frustration. The other half refused to serve under their hapless leader. The men ignored all discipline, raided local henhouses, got drunk every night, and burned down the guardhouse. Yates realized the regiment was far too undisciplined for an amateur commander. Longing for true leadership, regimental officers appealed to Yates to call on the professional soldier who had mustered them into service, Ulysses S. Grant.

Reluctantly, Yates sent a telegram to Grant offering him the command of the Seventh District Regiment—soon to become the Twenty-First Illinois Infantry Regiment of volunteers. Grant immediately wired his acceptance. Grant's preparation and professionalism opened the door to the new day that he knew would come.

FORT DONELSON AND UNCONDITIONAL SURRENDER

In 1887, only two years after the death of Ulysses S. Grant, a young English boy had only one request for his thirteenth birthday. Across the ocean in Great Britain, Winston Churchill was the boy, and he requested a copy of the *Personal Memoirs of Ulysses S. Grant*.[231] The book became one of his prized possessions.

Years later, in January 1943, Franklin Roosevelt and Winston Churchill met in secret near Casablanca, Morocco, for their second wartime summit. At the final press conference on January 24, Roosevelt announced to the world that the Allies would not stop until they had the "unconditional surrender" of Germany, Italy, and Japan.[232]

"Suddenly the Press Conference was on," Roosevelt later explained, "and Winston and I had had no time to prepare for it, and the thought popped into my mind that they had called Grant 'Old Unconditional Surrender,' and the next thing I knew I had said it.

"Some of you Britishers know the old story—we had a general called U. S. Grant. ... but in my, and the Prime Minister's, early days he was called 'Unconditional Surrender' Grant. The elimination of German, Japanese, and Italian war power means the unconditional surrender by Germany, Italy, and Japan. That means a reasonable assurance of future world peace."[233]

"Again, and again, and again Churchill will refer to Grant," explains Ronald White. Earlier, Roosevelt had contemplated writing a conciliatory letter to the German leadership offering negotiations to end the war. "Churchill writes to Roosevelt and said, 'No, no, no, no! Don't you remember what Grant said? We will fight it out on this line if it takes all summer. That's what the Allied forces ought to do right now.'"[234]

At the time, the pronouncement stirred a flurry of debate among the Allies and the generals, with the consensus of opinion being that it was a disastrous policy that would goad the Axis powers into a fight to the death. In the end, it proved to be the only policy the Allies could take—and the war was won. Once again, the famous words of General Grant caused a stir in the midst of a great war.[235]

The origin of the famous ultimatum was uttered by Grant during the Battle of Fort Donelson.

Grant knew that whoever controlled this strategic fort controlled the state of Tennessee, so he coordinated with his second in command, Brigadier General C. F. Smith, to prepare the attack. He also coordinated with Commodore Andrew Hull Foote to organize the necessary naval flotilla. But Grant's superior, General Henry Halleck, was jealous of him and purposely held him back from making the attack. Despite this bureaucratic interference, Grant continued to make all the necessary preparations, confident that an opportunity would eventually come.

That opening occurred in the form of an edict from President Lincoln. Exasperated that his generals were not moving in the field against the enemy, Lincoln issued the "President's General War Order No. 1," directing commanders to advance land and naval forces within a month. This was the opportunity General Grant had been waiting for. He had not been idle during the waiting period, and when the shackles were removed, Grant moved forward at full speed, attacking Fort Henry on the Tennessee River.

The Tennessee River had flooded, so the navy basically floated into Fort Henry to take it with relative ease. Ignoring Halleck's caution, Grant immediately pressed on to the heavily defended Fort Donelson, fifteen miles east on the Cumberland River.

More than twenty-four thousand Confederate soldiers guarded the fort—as opposed to Grant's force of sixteen thousand. But that didn't deter him.[236] Arriving at Fort Donelson, Grant positioned his troops in a semicircle. At the same time, Commodore Foote arrived with his gunboats, after steaming down the Tennessee River from Fort Henry and up the Cumberland River to Fort Donelson. Grant surrounded the fort and conducted several probing attacks. On February 14, Flag Officer Andrew H. Foot attacked from the river, but his fleet was badly damaged by the fort's water batteries and forced to retreat.

At dawn on the morning of February 15, the Confederates launched a surprise attack against the Union right. The Federal troops under General John Alexander McClernand held their positions until their ammunition ran low. Turning to run from the oncoming rebels, it seemed the Yankee line was about to collapse. At that moment, General Grant appeared on the scene.

"He was almost unattended," wrote General Lew Wallace, who was there with McClernand. "In his [Grant's] hand there were some papers, which looked like telegrams. Wholly unexcited, he saluted and received the salutations of his subordinates."

Wallace—who later authored the famous *Ben Hur: A Tale of the Christ*—recorded his insights on the importance of the moment for Ulysses S. Grant: "In every great man's career there is a crisis exactly similar to that which now overtook General Grant, and it cannot be better described than as a crucial test of his nature. A mediocre person would have accepted the news as an argument for persistence in his resolution to enter upon a siege. Had General

Grant done so, it is very probable his history would have been then and there concluded. His admirers and detractors alike are invited to study him at this precise juncture."

Wallace described how Grant's face flushed slightly at the news of the right wing's collapse. "With a sudden grip he crushed the papers in his hand. But in an instant these signs of disappointment or hesitation—as the reader pleases—cleared away. In his ordinary quiet voice he said, addressing himself to both officers, 'Gentlemen, the position on the right must be retaken.' With that he turned and galloped off."[237]

With his typical calm demeanor, Grant went to work. He saw to it that more ammunition was rushed to McClernand, who rallied his men and retook the ground on the right. He ordered General Charles Smith to attack on the left. Smith and his forces broke through the rebel lines and were poised to capture the Confederates the next day.

The next morning the Confederate commander—Grant's old West Point friend, Simon Bolivar Buckner—requested an armistice to negotiate terms. Grant responded with the message that would make him famous—and would be repeated by Roosevelt during World War II: "No terms except complete and unconditional surrender can be accepted. I propose to move immediately upon your works."[238]

The media quickly attached this demand to Grant's initials, dubbing him "Unconditional Surrender" Grant. As a result of his success at Donelson, Grant was promoted to major general and became a hero throughout the North, which was starving for a victory. Grant received the surrender of Buckner's entire army.

Following the victory at Fort Donelson, Grant produced a string of battlefield victories and forced the surrender of three enemy armies, something no other general officer in American history ever accomplished—not George Washington, Winfield Scott, Dwight Eisenhower, or Douglas MacArthur.[239]

Making the Tough Call

After two months of some of the most brutal fighting in human history, Grant had only one final obstacle and it was monumental—get into position for his ultimate strike on Lee.

Grant had just experienced one of the greatest defeats of the war at Cold Harbor with a total of thirteen thousand killed, wounded, or missing—with a loss of only twenty-five hundred on the Confederate side.[240] He now had to make the tough call. All of his predecessors would have most likely retreated and regrouped after a month of fighting where forty thousand Union soldiers were killed, wounded, sick, or missing. But Grant was not a retreating general, and he soon recovered from one of his worst losses to lead the Army of the Potomac in one of its greatest moments—the crossing of the James River.

Every leader faces difficult decisions, and this is where they either distinguish themselves and triumph or retreat and flounder. Leadership expert John C. Maxwell says, "Every change, every challenge, and every crisis requires a tough call, and the way those are handled is what separates leaders from everyone else."[241]

Maxwell says that at a time of crisis, a leader needs to recognize the need for making the tough call, which is marked by three things:

1. The tough call demands risk.

General Grant's first move toward his objective was to march his army south and then cross the formidable James—a tidal river more than eighty feet deep. He had already called for pontoon bridge materials to be sent from Fortress Monroe at the mouth of Chesapeake Bay. He also asked the navy to send vessels from all directions to help ferry troops and supplies to the south side of the river.

To cross the James and position the Army of the Potomac in a place where they could bring the war to a close, Grant had to split his army into four units—which made each group vulnerable to being beaten by a larger enemy force "in detail." This was an extremely daring and dangerous thing for a commander to do.

At its narrowest, ten miles east of City Point, the James River was more than two thousand feet wide. It had a tidal range of four feet. No one knew whether a twenty-one-hundred-foot pontoon bridge could ride out that kind of buckling rise and fall.

No army had ever built a pontoon bridge more than a thousand feet long.

Grant then took the greatest risk of his military career—and perhaps of the entire war—by allowing his army to be divided for an extended period of time as they crossed this formidable obstacle. If Lee had discovered the location of the Army of the Potomac, he could have moved in force to cut off and destroy large numbers of the Northern troops. That could have evened the odds in the war and possibly destroyed Lincoln's chances for reelection.

Another danger was the Confederate flotilla at Richmond, including three ironclads with long-range, heavy-caliber guns. From their position, only twenty-five miles upstream, they could have shelled the steamers that carried the infantry across the river. Or they could have sent fireships downstream to wreck the pontoon bridge. For two days and one night, the Army of the Potomac was divided and vulnerable to attack.

No one in the history of war had ever moved a force of 115,000 men across a tidal river so close to the guns of enemy naval forces.[242] Grant risked everything—the Overland Campaign, Lincoln's reelection, possibly the war itself. The stakes couldn't have been higher.

In permitting Grant to cross the James, Lee was completely deceived—first by Sheridan and his cavalry, who diverted his attention to the north as Grant and the bulk of the army were moving south; next by Warren's corps who deployed to the west of Cold Harbor, making it seem as if the entire army was heading that way; and then ultimately by Grant's ingenious strategy and direction.

"Thus the last, and perhaps the best chances of Confederate success," General Alexander lamented, "were not lost in the repulse of Gettysburg, nor in any combat of arms. They were lost during the three days of lying in camp believing that Grant was hemmed in by the broad part of the James below City Point, and had nowhere to go but to come and attack us."[243]

2. A tough call brings with it an inward battle.

In the final months of his life, General Grant built a strong relationship with his medical doctors, and particularly Dr. George Shrady. On one occasion, Grant confided in Shrady that before every battle he calculated the dreadful cost in killed and wounded. For him, it was the price to be considered before the bargain could be closed. "He more than once informed me that the carnage in some of his engagements was a positive horror to him," Shrady recalled, "and could be excused to his conscience only on the score of the awful necessity of the situation."

The accusation of Grant as a "butcher" was ironic for a man who had shied away from a military career and who couldn't stand the sight of blood. In fact, his greatest ambition upon graduating West Point was to become an assistant mathematics professor. "I never went into a battle willingly or with enthusiasm," he remarked. "I was always glad when a battle was over."[244]

3. A tough call will distinguish you as a leader.

Former New York City mayor Rudy Giuliani once said, "When the right person is the leader, he does even better during tough times."[245] That was certainly the case for Ulysses S. Grant after the disastrous Cold Harbor battle.

Some of the troops sensed Grant's intentions. Two days after the battle at Cold Harbor, Union Cavalry Captain Charles Frances Adams told Richard Henry Dana Jr.: "I think Grant will be forced to adopt his Vicksburg tactics—he will have to uncover Washington, cross the James, move up the south bank and then throw himself on the Confederate line of communications and supplies."[246]

As he had done at Vicksburg, Grant sent out his cavalry to divert the attention of the enemy commander. The other objective of this move was to sever the railroads and canal supplying Richmond. On

June 7, Sheridan set out on the raid around Richmond to destroy enemy railroads and canals, and most importantly at that moment, to draw the Confederate cavalry away from the main army, bringing near blindness to Grant's movements in the south.

On June 9, a Federal detail was set to work fortifying a line to the left and rear on ground overlooking the Chickahominy. Engineers worked to bridge the necessary points on the river, and a large force worked to repair and "corduroy" the roads through the swampy bottoms.[247]

All this activity could have suggested one of Grant's famous moves by the left flank. The problem, as Lee saw it, was that Grant was running out of room. If he moved much further left, he would be forced to confront the Confederates straight on, using the same roads General McClellan had used two years earlier.

But Lee did not know that the navy had deployed a small armada well out of his sight on the lower James, including ironclad gunboats to guard against rebel raiders. The pontoons Grant ordered arrived at Wilcox's Landing from Fortress Monroe, along with a large supply of bridging lumber.

Behind the screen of Federal cavalry and Warren's Fifth Corps, Grant evacuated his line one corps at a time.

The sky on that fateful morning was a cloudless blue as the troops approached the river. Steamers waiting at the shore greeted the soldiers with short blasts on their whistles. At the pier, bands played martial tunes to keep spirits high—though soldiers were instructed to march out of step as they crossed to keep the bridge from swaying.[248]

Grant rode to a hill near the riverbank on the north side of the James to watch the grand procession—a line of blue stretching for twenty-five miles. Clasping his hands behind his back, the commanding general of all the armies of the United States drank in the mesmerizing scene below him. Banners snapped in the breeze coming off the river, steam rose from the vessels, and the sun reflected off the ripples of the river, the cannon, and thousands of gun barrels.

As he watched with wonder the crossing of the massive Army of the Potomac, Assistant Secretary of War Charles Dana breathlessly wired Stanton: "All goes on like a miracle."[249]

The muffled sound of cannon far off to the north announced that Warren's corps and Wilson's cavalry at the other end of the column continued to hold Lee in check and in confusion.[250] By midnight on June 16, the army, all the trains, the artillery, and the herds of cattle had been safely transferred to the south side of the James. There were no casualties, except those which occurred as Warren's corps and the cavalry held off the enemy.[251]

Lee still had no idea that Grant's army had slipped across the James. The operation was so successful one Confederate general later dubbed it "the most brilliant stroke in all the campaigns of the war."[252]

Confederate General Alexander described how the rebels could have attacked and annihilated the isolated Fifth Corps on the afternoon of June 13 had they known they were part of a grand ruse. "The only trouble about that was that we were entirely ignorant of the fact that it was isolated. On the contrary ... Warren's corps had taken up its line so near to Riddell's Shop as to give us the idea that it was the advance corps of Grant's whole army pushing toward Richmond on the road from Long Bridge."[253]

Grant believed in ultimate success—his own and that of the Union over the Confederacy. In his most difficult times after resigning from the army, he knew that if he worked with diligence, he eventually would find success. Grant planned and prepared—sometimes months in advance and sometimes even years in advance—for the day of success he knew would come. He carried this same thinking into his leadership of the western armies, then into his leadership over all the armies of the United States.

GRANT'S LEADERSHIP PRINCIPLES

- Maintain a never-ending optimism regarding the future.
- Identify potential risks to your organization, then provide the resources necessary to protect against that threat.
- When necessary, make the tough call to lead your organization into the future—even if it means sacrifice and challenges in the short run.
- To win the game, you sometimes need to change the game through creative, strategic thinking.

Chapter Seven

CHOOSE YOUR ACTIONS FOR MAXIMUM EFFECT

If he had studied to be undramatic, he could not have succeeded better. – General Lew Wallace

"One of the most famous images of Grant is a photograph taken at the Battle of Cold Harbor in 1864," writes Andrew Knighton. "Wearing an infantryman's coat with his [general's] stars pinned on the shoulder, a plain hat, and a week's worth of beard, he is seen leaning casually against a post, a distant look in his eyes." The unassuming look was characteristic of Grant's style.

"Grant did not go in for big speeches or dramatic gestures. There was a minimalism to what he did in front of the soldiers, earning their respect through calmness rather than showmanship. It was the perfect style for the man leading an army of the people in a democratic state."[254]

THE EXAMPLE OF ZACHARY TAYLOR

Grant learned the concept of servant leadership early in his career. In the Mexican War, he observed the care General Zachary Taylor gave to his men. In preparation for battle, Taylor paid attention to the most basic needs of his troops, even ensuring their canteens were filled with water. From Taylor, Grant learned the importance of both meticulous planning and preparation for battle. Taylor also demonstrated the importance of flexible leadership. He showed Grant how an army must be able to react to changes on the battlefield, requiring instantaneous adjustments to the commander's plan.

General George Gordon Meade saw hints of General Taylor in his Civil War general in chief: "Grant is not a striking man, is very reticent, has never mixed with the world, and has but little manner, indeed is somewhat ill at ease in the presence of strangers; hence a first impression is never favorable. ... At the same time, he has natural qualities of a high order, and is a man whom, the more you see and know him, the better you like him. He puts me in mind of old Taylor, and sometimes I fancy he models himself on old Zac."[255]

Grant adopted many of the servant leadership attributes he had observed in General Zachary Taylor during the Mexican War.

Taylor reciprocated this respect. As he prepared to advance his army into Mexico in 1846, Taylor observed Grant overseeing his command in clearing underwater obstacles near the beach. His men were having difficulty understanding Grant's instructions, so the second lieutenant entered the water himself to demonstrate what needed to be done. Other officers viewing the scene scoffed at Grant and criticized him for lowering himself to work side by side with his men. Taylor quickly corrected them. "I wish I had more officers like Grant who would stand ready to set a personal example when needed."[256]

As a result of his continued diligence, Grant's status grew with his men and in the eyes of the commanding general. Soon he was assigned to the important quartermaster post.

Grant noted that General Taylor knew the names of all the officers under his command as well as the names of several of the enlisted men. Unlike the chief commander, Major General Winfield Scott, Taylor often wore casual dress in the field and carried himself with a humble demeanor. He regularly mingled with his troops, taking the pulse of the men and gathering information he otherwise would not have known. Taylor earned the nickname "Old Rough and Ready" for his willingness to get dirty in the trenches alongside his men.

When President Polk transferred command of the majority of the army to Scott in the middle of the war, Taylor paid one last visit to his troops. One soldier wrote of that remarkable day: "He is a very pleasant old man and very sociable not only to officers but to buck privates also. He is not a proud man at all. When he came to see us he rode a mule and looked like an old man a going to mill. He left us and bid goodbye as though he had always been acquainted with us and told us to be good boys and fight like men if needs be and then left."[257]

In these encounters, Taylor listened to his soldiers but seldom talked. When he spoke, he was direct and brief. Taylor was calm under fire, displaying bravery that bolstered his troops. Grant took note of his first commander's calm demeanor and the more casual manner of his attire. He learned a different set of lessons from his next commander.

FUSS AND FEATHERS

In his style, manners, and dress, Grant's new commander, Major General Winfield Scott, was nearly Taylor's opposite. More formal and flamboyant, Scott's pomp and pageantry earned him the nickname "Old Fuss and Feathers." Grant respected both leading generals and was honored when he received praise years later from General Scott.

In mid-November of 1864, after Lincoln's reelection was secured, Grant took time to visit his family, who were living in Burlington, New Jersey. During that time, he also traveled to New York to pay tribute to his old commanding officer, Winfield Scott.

Grant had first seen the great general twenty-five years earlier as a West Point cadet. "With his commanding figure, his quite colossal size and showy uniform," Grant later wrote, "I thought him the finest specimen of manhood my eyes had ever beheld, and the most to be envied." At that time, he allowed himself to fantasize that one day he would have the honor of leading all the armies of the United States. Very few people would have envisioned Grant the cadet ever achieving that dream.

But he did.

During the Civil War, Scott kept a close watch on the Mexican War lieutenant, passing along short notes of encouragement and advice. "Not only had he spoken highly of Grant's service at Molino del Rey," writes Brooks Simpson, "Scott assured Elihu Washburne, but he had also told others that the new lieutenant general 'had richly earned his present rank.'"

Grant was humbled by these generous comments and responded that Scott's remarks about him had been "more flattering to me than I probably deserve." But his former commander clarified that this was not mere flattery when he presented Grant with a copy of his newly published memoirs with the inscription: "From the oldest to the ablest General in the world."

"High praise indeed," Simpson explains, "especially from someone who once counted Robert E. Lee as a prized staff officer."[258]

It is interesting to note that on the first day of the Overland Campaign, as Grant and the Army of the Potomac crossed the Rapidan and entered the Wilderness, he wore his best dress uniform. "General Grant was dressed in a uniform coat and waistcoat, the coat being unbuttoned," remembered Colonel Horace Porter. "On his hands were a pair of yellowish-brown thread gloves. He wore a pair of plain top-boots, reaching to his knees, and was equipped with a regulation sword, spurs, and sash. On his head was a slouch hat of black felt with a plain gold cord around it. His orderly carried strapped behind his saddle the general's overcoat, which was that of a private soldier of cavalry."[259]

This was one of the only times General Grant leaned more toward the attire of General Scott than General Taylor during the entire Civil War. He never told anyone why he dressed so formally that day, but one can speculate that at this critical moment—as he was about to confront Robert E. Lee—Ulysses S. Grant allowed the pomp of Winfield Scott to add solemnity to the occasion.

GRANT'S STRATEGY: BEGIN WITH THE END IN MIND

One reason for Grant's success is that in his planning and thinking, he always began with the end in mind. "Grant could look beyond the current battle or campaign, and devise a strategy to win a decisive victory in an entire theater of war," observes Sean P. Murray. "To do this he had to project into the mind of his adversary and predict how they were going to react. He also understood the value of logistics and supplies. Grant would often gain the advantage by cleverly sustaining and supplying his Army as it moved quickly across varied terrain to gain an upper hand. These movements would surprise the enemy and put them in a compromising position."[260]

"Before Grant became chief general, the Union's military effort had been fragmented and disjointed," notes Ron Chernow, "deprived of a single supervisory mind to govern the whole enterprise. 'Eastern and Western armies were fighting independent battles, working together like a balky team where no two ever pull together,' Grant recalled. Now he mapped out an overarching design that encompassed all Union Armies."[261]

This concept of coordinated warfare had been championed by President Lincoln since the early days of the war, but his generals never embraced it. In a meeting where Grant explained to Lincoln the workings of the supporting columns in his Virginia strategy, a delighted Lincoln exclaimed, "Oh, yes! I see that. As we say out West, if a man can't skin he must hold a leg while someone else does."[262]

Lincoln had finally found a general he could trust, and the two men soon established a solid relationship. The contrast between the quiet, respectful Grant and the bombastic, criticizing McClellan became clear to Lincoln.[263]

In Stephen Covey's groundbreaking book, *The 7 Habits of Highly Effective People*, habit number two is "Begin with the End in Mind." He writes, "Start with a clear understanding of your destination. … It means to know where you're going so that you better understand where you are now and so that the steps you take are always in the right direction. … 'Begin with the end in mind' is based on the principle that *all things are created twice.* There's a mental or first creation, and a physical or second creation, to all things."[264]

GRANT'S POLITICAL FRIENDS

Grant was raised to respect authority, and he gave deference to those in command over him—even when it was difficult, as in the

case of General Halleck or President Johnson. This position of respect stood in marked contrast to most of Grant's predecessors in
the role of general in chief—especially the arrogant McClellan.

On July 5, 1863, two days after the bloody Battle of Gettysburg,
Robert E. Lee retreated to Virginia with his badly damaged army.
Gettysburg was a decisive Union victory, and for the moment, Meade was a national hero. Meanwhile, in Washington, an elated President Lincoln knew that the war could come to an end more quickly
if Meade mounted an offensive and crushed the severely wounded
Army of Northern Virginia. But inexplicably, and much to the annoyance of Lincoln, Meade did not decisively follow through.

Meade seemed to be satisfied with the victory at Gettysburg
and only halfheartedly followed Lee south, allowing the Confederates to cross the Potomac River without a fight. In fact, Meade
ordered his troops to "drive from our soil every vestige of the presence of the invader." When Lincoln read this in the telegraph office,
he was shocked. "Drive the invader from our soil!" he cried. "My
God! Is that all? ... This is a dreadful reminiscence of McClellan,"
Lincoln told John Hay. "The same spirit that moved McClellan to
claim a great victory because Pennsylvania and Maryland were safe.
The hearts of ten million people sunk within them when McClellan
raised that shout last fall [at Antietam]. Will our generals never get
that idea out of their heads? The whole country is our soil."[265]

In contrast, Grant was intent on complete annihilation of the
Confederate armies, with the goal of a renewed union. He understood that to put down the rebellion meant total war. He planned
his strategy with that outcome at the forefront of his thinking.

In early 1864, Congress passed a bill reviving the rank of lieutenant general, which had been last held by George Washington.
Grant's local congressman and political cheerleader, Elihu Washburne, championed the bill in the House of Representatives, warning that the war would never end "until we had a fighting general to
lead our armies."[266]

While the bill passed with overwhelming support in the House
and Senate, President Lincoln was reticent to support it. With the

presidential election looming later that year, Lincoln was in no hurry to elevate a potential political rival. As Brooks Simpson explains, "He had already suffered through several generals who fantasized about replacing him in the White House. Even now George B. McClellan was readying himself for the Democratic nomination. Would Grant do likewise?"[267]

Some find it surprising, but Ulysses S. Grant was rather adept in the art of politics. When one of his former generals, Frank Blair, wrote to the major general to ask about the rumors of his political ambitions, Grant understood where the question originated. Aware that Lincoln was close to the Blair family, who were powerful political leaders in the Republican Party, he knew Blair was likely inquiring on behalf of the president.

Grant framed his response with careful political eloquence. "Everyone who knows me knows I have no political aspirations either now or for the future," he wrote to Blair. The general disliked seeing his name "associated with politics either as an aspirant for office or as a partisan." He then made it clear that he understood the reason for the exchange. "Show this letter to no one unless it be the president himself."[268]

When Lincoln asked Washburne to also inquire about Grant's political plans, the congressman produced a letter from Grant to a mutual friend. "Nobody could induce me to think of being a presidential candidate, particularly so long as there is a possibility of having Mr. Lincoln reelected."[269] This response finally placed Lincoln at ease, and he became an enthusiastic supporter of the lieutenant general bill.

As long as Abraham Lincoln was president, Grant was happy to support him as general in chief. When Andrew Johnson became president after Lincoln's assassination, the situation changed dramatically for Grant. In the eyes of the country, Grant became the stabilizing factor in the midst of Johnson's volatile and sometimes erratic behavior. When the country reached the point of crisis during Johnson's impeachment, Grant was a bulwark of strength and stability.

In 1868, it became apparent to the majority of people in the country that Grant was the only person who could step into the presidency after eight long years of struggle and instability. Grant recognized the seeming historical inevitability of the moment and accepted the Republican nomination for president. His campaign slogan was a declaration of his deepest desire for America: "Let us have peace."

GRANT'S WISE AND HISTORIC LEADERSHIP AT APPOMATTOX

The outcome Grant envisioned in the spring of 1864 unfolded nearly a year later when the Confederacy finally imploded in the spring of 1865. When Petersburg and Richmond fell on April 2, 1865, Lee and the Army of Northern Virginia had nearly an eight-hour head start on Grant and his armies in their escape to the west. Grant dispatched Sheridan and his cavalry to race ahead to keep Lee from turning south to link up with Joseph Johnston's Confederate army in North Carolina.

Grant directed the Army of the James to follow closely behind the cavalry, staying south of Lee and north of Johnston as a buffer between the two. General Meade and the Army of the Potomac followed at the rear of Lee's forces, engaging them in battle whenever possible and gathering the rebel deserters, stragglers, and wounded who hadn't escaped into the woods.

Due to Grant's leadership, Lee and the Army of Northern Virginia were being systematically surrounded.

Sheridan's cavalry troopers finally got ahead of Lee at Appomattox Station, capturing vital supply trains filled with rations on the morning of April 9. Lee's forces had dwindled to only twenty-eight thousand troops.[270] Hemmed in on all sides, Lee ordered General John B. Gordon to make one final, desperate attempt to break through Sheridan's cavalry line.

Gordon hit Sheridan's dismounted troopers at dawn and pushed them back, which gave the rebels a glimmer of hope as they pressed westward. The Confederate soldiers' spirits rose as Union troops appeared to retreat, but the Southerners' hearts sank when they reached the crest of the hill and viewed the valley below.

Just as the sun was rising over Appomattox on that unseasonably cold, damp Palm Sunday, a wall of blue appeared out of the darkness fanning out behind the cavalry—General Edward Ord and his Army of the James with thirty thousand men. Ord's infantry had marched all night and were bone-tired. Yet as they trudged through the darkness, they understood their sacrifice could help to finally corner Lee.[271]

The day these Union boys had fought so valiantly for over the last four years had finally arrived.

Gordon and his men watched in shock as Ord's columns poured onto the battlefield. The rebels reflexively halted, then fell back toward Appomattox Court House. Gordon realized they were completely surrounded. The situation was hopeless. At 7:30 a.m., he informed Lee that he could do nothing further.

Lee sent word to General Grant and General Meade that the time had come for him to surrender.

Despite his mud-spattered boots and clothing, Ulysses S. Grant projected an air of confident authority as he approached the Appomattox home of Wilmer McLean, the place selected for the official surrender. This victory was his triumph. Some said Grant merely wore down the Confederacy by sacrificing superior numbers and resources in a series of bloody battles. But these critics overlook the fact that all of the Union generals before Grant had access to the same troop superiority and northern resources, but they refused to bring them to bear.

General Grant had devised and deployed a strategy that coordinated all the Federal forces, unleashing the strength of the United States, not against cities but against the armies of the Confederacy. He directed Yankee forces in a manner that blocked Confederate leadership from sending soldiers from one army to another to reinforce their weak points. He unleashed a "total warfare" strategy in places like the Shenandoah Valley and the heart of Georgia to destroy industrial and civilian support of the military. And, as he had done so effectively in Vicksburg, Grant moved methodically to cut off supplies to the rebel armies by destroying railroads and canals.

Having directed Union forces to do these things, he held on with a bulldog grip—and he "chewed and choked," as Lincoln observed, until the rebels fell to their knees.[272]

Following the advice of President Lincoln and Frederick Douglass, Grant didn't utilize Black soldiers only for manual labor or guard duty, but once they had proved themselves to him, he placed them in combat to fight for their own freedom—and they made excellent soldiers. They understood from the day the rebels fired on Fort Sumter what the war was really about.

Brigadier General Joshua Lawrence Chamberlain, one of the heroes of Gettysburg, stood awestruck on the main street of Appomattox as Grant trotted by on his horse. He described the scene: "Slouched hat without cord; common soldier's blouse, unbuttoned, on which, however, the three stars; high boots, mud-splashed to the top; trousers tucked inside; no sword, but the sword hand deep in the pocket; sitting his saddle with the ease of a born master, taking no notice of anything, all his faculties gathered into intense thought and mighty calm. He seemed greater than I had ever seen him, a look as of another world about him. No wonder I forgot altogether to salute him. Anything like that would have been too little. He rode on to meet Lee at the Court House."[273]

The two commanders stood in striking contrast. Lee dressed in a bright new uniform, with a sash and a jeweled sword, appearing as the patrician from the revolutionary era; Grant in his mud-spattered uniform, looking like the common American of the unknown future. Lee stood tall and erect; Grant was relatively short, and he slouched as a result of years of labor on his St. Louis farm. Lee was the son of one of General Washington's top commanders in the Revolutionary War; Grant was the son of an unknown tanner from the western frontier.[274]

"Lee was tall, large in form, fine in person, handsome in feature, grave and dignified in bearing—if anything, a little too formal," Adam Badeau recorded of the encounter. "There was a suggestion of effort in his deportment, something that showed he was determined to die gracefully, a hint of Caesar muffling himself in his mantle."

The man who conquered this grand figure and his army couldn't have been more different. "Grant as usual was simple and composed, but with none of the grand air about him," Badeau remembered. "No elation was visible in his manner or appearance. His voice was as calm as ever, and his eye betrayed no emotion. He spoke and acted as plainly as if he were transacting an ordinary matter of business.

"No one would have suspected that he was about to receive the surrender of an army, or that one of the most terrible wars of modern times had been brought to a triumphant close by the quiet man without a sword who was conversing calmly, but rather grimly, with the elaborate gentleman in grey and gold."[275]

General Grant stepped into the hall, and Colonel Babcock opened the door of the room on the left. The general passed in as Lee arose and stepped forward. Grant extended his hand, saying respectfully, "General Lee." The two shook hands cordially.[276]

Colonel Porter painted the scene for posterity:

> We entered, and found General Grant seated in an old office arm-chair in the center of the room and Lee sitting in a plain arm-chair with a cane seat beside a square, marble-topped table near the front window, in the corner opposite the door by which we entered, and facing General Grant. ... The contrast between the two commanders was singularly striking, and could not fail to attract marked attention as they sat, six or eight feet apart, facing each other.
>
> General Grant, then nearly forty-three years of age, was five feet eight inches in height, with shoulders slightly stooped. His hair and full beard were nut-brown, without a trace of gray in them. He had on his single-breasted blouse of dark-blue flannel, unbuttoned in front and showing a waistcoat underneath. He wore an ordinary pair of top-boots, with his trousers inside, and without spurs. The boots and portions of his clothes were spattered with mud. He had worn a pair of thread gloves of a

dark-yellow color, which he had taken off on entering the room. His felt 'sugar-loaf,' stiff-brimmed hat was resting on his lap. He had no sword or sash, and a pair of shoulder-straps was all there was about him to designate his rank. In fact, aside from these, his uniform was that of a private soldier.

Lee, on the other hand, was six feet and one inch in height, and erect for one of his age, for he was Grant's senior by sixteen years. His hair and full beard were a silver-gray, and thick, except that the hair had become a little thin in front. He wore a new uniform of Confederate gray, buttoned to the throat, and a handsome sword and sash. The sword was of exceedingly fine workmanship, and the hilt was studded with jewels. It had been presented to him by some ladies in England who sympathized with the cause he represented. His top-boots were comparatively new, and had on them near the top some ornamental stitching of red silk. Like his uniform, they were clean. On the boots were handsome spurs with large rowels. A felt hat which in color matched pretty closely that of his uniform, and a pair of long, gray buckskin gauntlets, lay beside him on the table.[277]

For the first time during the war, the two great commanders met face-to-face. Grant carried out the directive of President Lincoln to offer magnanimous terms of surrender. The Southerners would be paroled so they could return peacefully to their homes and farms. At Lee's request, Grant allowed officers to keep their sidearms and any soldier who owned a horse would keep it. It was spring and most of these men would soon be planting crops—horses and sidearms would allow them to get a start on their post-war lives.

Grant wrote out these reasonable terms of surrender, and after some minor adjustments, he and Lee signed them. Artillery and small arms were to be turned over and stacked in a formal surrender ceremony. When Union soldiers cheered upon Lee's exit from the McLean house, Grant quieted them. "The war is over. The rebels are our countrymen again."[278]

An important and historic part of the surrender agreement promised that "each officer and man will be allowed to return to their homes, not to be disturbed by United States authority so long as they observe their paroles and the laws in force where they reside."[279] This final line, added spontaneously by Grant, effectively provided a pardon for all surrendering Confederate soldiers and officers.

Southerners were always grateful to Grant for these compassionate terms of surrender. Years later, former Confederate generals served as honorary pallbearers at Grant's New York City funeral. Aged Confederate soldiers dressed in their gray uniforms gathered in their units to march alongside their former foes in the miles-long funeral procession through Manhattan.

Grant's symbolic and magnanimous actions at Appomattox bore fruit for years to come.

The war was over. Not only the war but also the entire colonial and revolutionary era came to a close at that moment. Two men of the western frontier—Grant under the leadership and support of Abraham Lincoln—made it happen. The baton had been handed from the son of the aristocratic Englishman to the son of a common American frontier businessman. Slavery was forever eradicated in the United States of America.

It was a new birth of freedom.

GRANT'S LEADERSHIP PRINCIPLES

- Earn respect through calmness rather than showmanship.
- Understand the importance of meticulous planning and preparation.
- Practice flexible leadership, realizing that an organization must be able to react to changes in the environment.
- Never forget that success for your organization requires your total commitment.
- Despite reticence to step into certain areas of responsibility, recognize the historic inevitability of key moments of change and accept the higher level of responsibility as your destiny.

Chapter Eight

APPLY CONSTANT PRESSURE
UNTIL BREAKTHROUGH

The art of war is simple enough. Find out where your enemy is. Get at him as soon as you can. Strike him as hard as you can, and keep moving on. – Ulysses S. Grant

Immediately after the victory at the Battle of Shiloh, newspapers such as *The New York Times* introduced Ulysses S. Grant to the public. "He is a man of plain exterior, light hair, blue eyes, five feet nine in height, plain and retiring in his manners, firm and decisive in character, esteemed by his soldiers, never wastes a word with any one, but pays strict attention to his military duties. ... His personal bravery and dash is undoubted. ... He is one of the hard-fighting school of Generals."

Grant first demonstrated his "hard-fighting" ways at Fort Donelson, but he displayed his tenacity most brilliantly in the Vicksburg campaign.

VICKSBURG

After the costly victory at Shiloh, Grant recognized that his next objective must be Vicksburg. But taking the "Gibraltar of the West" would be difficult. The city was surrounded by swamps and bayous to the north and tall bluffs and the Mississippi River to the west. The eastern approaches were all well defended by the rebels. The only vulnerable point was to the south, but how would he get his troops below the city and across the mile-wide Mississippi River?

During the winter of 1862–63, Grant launched several experimental schemes against the stronghold with the dual purpose of seeking a breakthrough to the fortified city and also keeping his troops occupied. Union soldiers cut trees below the water line to open possible pathways for navy gunboats. Others built dikes and dams to raise or lower water levels. They even attempted to dig a new channel to divert the flow of the Mississippi beyond the range of the Vicksburg cannons. None of these experiments worked, but they provided the men with labor to keep them in shape and focused on the war effort—a fact that many in the press and in the government failed to understand.

As his soldiers toiled on, Grant devised a strategy for the coming spring campaign—a major push set to begin when the roads finally dried. Up to this point, Union forces threatening Vicksburg had been hindered by the enemy, by swamps and bayous, by topography, and by the great Mississippi itself. Grant needed an audacious plan to end the stalemate.

After the army's multiple attempts to get at Vicksburg during the winter, the public, the media, and politicians turned against Grant. "I think [he] has hardly a friend left, except myself," said Lincoln. "What I want, and what the people want, is generals who will fight battles and win victories. Grant has done this and I propose to stand by him."[280]

Sitting high on a bluff above the Mississippi River, Vicksburg seemed almost impenetrable. A naval bombardment in 1862 by Admiral Farragut had shelled the city from the river, but without infantry support, he was unable to dislodge the Confederates.[281]

On December 29 of that year, General William Tecumseh Sherman attacked Vicksburg with thirty-two thousand Federal troops at the Battle of Chickasaw Bluffs. The Yankees outnumbered the rebels six to one. However, the Confederates became aware of Sherman's plans and reinforced Vicksburg with another seven thousand men. The rebels occupied a defensive line, and they were stationed in trenches high above the Yankees on the bluff. On that December day, Sherman ordered his men to advance across the open ground under a hail of artillery fire. Only one Union brigade reached the bluff, but they came under sustained fire and suffered heavy casualties. The Union lost two thousand men in the battle while the Confederates lost only two hundred.[282]

Grant was convinced he had to find a way to transport his troops to the dry ground to the south of the city. To do so, he would have to persuade the Yankee naval commanders to run their boats past the guns on the bluffs overlooking the Mississippi. Then he would march his army southward down the dry west bank of the Mississippi, moving below Vicksburg. From there, naval vessels would ferry his army across the Mississippi somewhere to the south of the Confederate stronghold.

Grant's subordinates—Sherman, McPherson, and Logan—feared the scheme was too risky. Sherman strongly objected when Grant explained that once on the east side of the Mississippi, the army would move so fast it would be cut off from food and supplies and would have to survive off the land. This idea went against everything the officers had learned at West Point, and Sherman made his opposition known to his friend. Grant respectfully noted Sherman's objections, then went ahead with the plan anyway.

As spring approached and the muddy roads dried, Grant was ready to move.

"Admiral Porter was the first one to whom I mentioned it," Grant later wrote. "The co-operation of the navy was absolutely essential to the success (even to the contemplation) of such an enterprise. I had no more authority to command Porter than he had to command me. It was necessary to have part of his fleet below Vicksburg if the troops went there. Steamers to use as ferries were also essential. The navy was the only escort and protection for these steamers, all of which in getting below had to run about fourteen miles of batteries. Porter fell into the plan at once."[283]

Admiral David Dixon Porter prepared his ships for the hazardous passage in front of the Vicksburg guns. He made it clear to Grant that the ironclads could not return upstream against the strong Mississippi currents under fire from Vicksburg's artillery. Whatever vessels survived the gauntlet would remain south of the fortified city. To protect his vulnerable boilers, Porter directed his sailors to stack bales of cotton and hay, along with sacks of grain, all around them.[284]

On April 16, as the moon shined brightly over the Mississippi, Porter's flotilla of gunboats and transport barges set out on their harrowing journey. Beginning at 10:00 p.m., Porter led seven iron-clad gunboats and four steamers downstream. Coal barges and excess vessels were lashed to the sides of the main ships to provide additional protection, and later, extra room for transporting troops and supplies.[285]

Grant's wife, Julia, and their son Fred arrived just in time to witness the navy's running of the Vicksburg guns. Ulysses, Julia, and Fred, along with members of the general's staff, boarded a steamer at Milliken's Bend, on the Louisiana side of the Mississippi. Near midnight they dropped anchor at a safe distance just north of Vicksburg, close enough to view the engagement.

When Porter's ships came into sight in the moonlight, rebel lookouts alerted the garrison. Confederate cannons opened up on the Union boats, and Porter immediately returned fire. In the midst of the exploding cannon shells, houses and cabins along the Vicksburg shoreline either burst into flame or were purposely set on fire, providing even more light for Confederate gunners.[286]

Artillery shells arced through the sky in both directions as deafening explosions shook the earth. Union vessels pressed forward under Confederate bombardment for two hours. The Southerners fired 525 rounds, landing sixty-eight hits. Despite this hellish fire, only one steamboat was lost after taking a direct hit to the engine room.[287] The other two steamers and most of the barges sustained only minor damage and no loss of life.[288]

MOVING THE ARMY

On the morning of April 30, Grant marched his forces down the western bank of the Mississippi and began to transport his troops across to Bruinsburg. McClernand's troops had marched across the top of a levee under cover of night, unobserved. "By the time it was light the enemy saw our whole fleet," Grant recalled, "iron-clads, gunboats, river steamers and barges, quietly moving down the river three miles below them, black, or rather blue, with National troops."[289]

Troops crammed aboard gunboats, river steamers, coal barges, and the occasional bayou flatboat. Even the *Benton*, Porter's flagship, served as a ferry. Porter and Grant oversaw the transports, one division at a time. By dusk McClernand's entire corps had completed the mile-wide amphibious crossing, as had a division of McPherson's corps. Twenty-three thousand Union men had crossed the river to begin the land-based assault on Port Gibson.[290]

With a strong foothold on the eastern side of the great Mississippi River, Grant experienced a rare moment of joy in the midst of the campaign.

~

FROM *PERSONAL MEMOIRS*

When this was effected I felt a degree of relief scarcely ever equaled since. Vicksburg was not yet taken it is true, nor were its defenders demoralized by any of our previous moves. I was now in the enemy's country, with a vast river and the stronghold of Vicksburg between me and my base of supplies. But I was on dry ground on the same side of the river with the enemy. All the campaigns, labors, hardships and exposures from the month of December previous to this time that had been made and endured, were for the accomplishment of this one object.[291]

~

PRESSING INLAND

Once ashore, Grant pushed McClernand two miles inland to high, dry ground and then onward toward the town of Port Gibson, where a bridge crossed Big Bayou Pierre, leading to Grand Gulf. Grant saw this small but strategic hamlet as the perfect supply base on the Mississippi.

As McClernand moved to take the bridge at Port Gibson, Grant oversaw the transport of troops and vital supplies across the Mississippi deep into the night. Aided by the light of huge bonfires, McPherson's soldiers were transported until a 3:00 a.m. collision between two transports halted the operation until daylight.

McClernand's troops had advanced inland until they collided with a Confederate force of five thousand men, and the Battle of Port Gibson commenced.[292] Grant arrived shortly after and oversaw the battle as it raged from early morning until nightfall. After months of labor on Grant's various experiments, the Union forces were ready for a brawl. They soon pushed the Confederates back into the city.

When night fell, the exhausted rebels abandoned Port Gibson. The next morning, Grant and his soldiers occupied the deserted town and began establishing a supply depot. Grant sent a dispatch to Halleck in Washington, informing him that the battle was waged "over the most broken country I ever saw … a series of irregular ridges divided by deep and impassable ravines, grown up with heavy timber, undergrowth and cane."[293]

Grant moved to place his troops between Pemberton and any possible Confederate reinforcements. The strategy was to keep the rebel forces divided, then to defeat them in detail. Grant doggedly followed the plan he had developed during the winter months, deploying his troops with celerity.

General Sherman counseled his friend to wait for the wagon trains, but Grant knew that the speed of an army made all the difference in a battle. Grant's strategy proved correct. Choosing speed over security, he directed his army to live off the land. This gave the Union forces the advantage of surprise.

It worked.

After the Confederates were defeated at Champion Hill, they withdrew into their stronghold at Vicksburg. In three weeks of battle, Grant's men marched 180 miles, won five battles, and captured some six thousand prisoners, all the while fighting a combined rebel force larger than their own.[294]

The Siege

On the morning of May 18, Grant crossed the Big Black River and met Sherman. Greeting each other with knowing smiles, they turned their horses and rode together toward the strategic position on the Yazoo River northeast of Vicksburg, where they could establish another base for supplies from the Mississippi.[295] This was the same hill above Haynes Bluff that Sherman's troops had failed to take back in December—and where he feigned an assault from below only days before.

Grant savored the moment sitting on his charger next to Sherman.

~

From *Personal Memoirs*

In a few minutes Sherman had the pleasure of looking down from the spot coveted so much by him the December before on the ground where his command had lain so helpless for offensive action. He turned to me, saying that up to this minute he had felt no positive assurance of success. This, however, he said was the end of one of the greatest campaigns in history and I ought to make a report of it at once. Vicksburg was not yet captured, and there was no telling what might happen before it was taken; but whether captured or not, this was a complete and successful campaign.[296]

~

The two generals took a rare break from the battle to smoke cigars and gaze down from the rolling hills upon the land below with the Mississippi River in the distance. "Well, Grant," Sherman said with a smile, "you are entitled to every bit of the credit for this campaign. I opposed it. Why hell, I wrote you a letter about it. But here we are. Until this moment I never thought your expedition a success," Sherman told his old friend. "I never could see the end clearly until now. But this is a campaign. This is a success, if we never take the town. Well done, General."[297]

The expression in Grant's face remained mostly unchanged, other than a slight lift of one side of his smile and a twinkle in his eyes—signs that those closest to the general recognized as an outward hint of delight. "Sherman, your untiring energy and great efficiency during the campaign entitles you to a full share of all the credit due for its success," Grant replied.[298]

With his army encircling the beleaguered city, Grant informed Admiral Porter that the reduction of Vicksburg was underway. "My men are now investing Vicksburg. Sherman's forces run from the Mississippi River above the city two miles east. McPherson is to his left, and McClernand to the left of McPherson." Grant informed Porter that the Confederates were severely weakened by the recent battles. "The enemy have not been able to return to the city with one half of his forces. If you can run down and throw shell in just back of the lower part of the city, it would aid us and demoralize an already badly beaten enemy."[299]

By June 28, rebel deserters were informing Grant's division commanders that only six days' rations remained in the town. Pemberton had his eye on the Fourth of July. He planned to fire a salute to the Confederacy on Independence Day, then surrender. Grant believed the deserters.

Grant resolved that if Pemberton did not quit by then, he would end the siege his own way. The Union commander had well-fed and rested soldiers, 220 artillery pieces, dozens of mortars, and boatloads of ammunition. Porter's gunboats would join in the barrage from the river. If Pemberton failed to surrender, the army would assault the stronghold on July 6 and fight until it collapsed.

By July 1, Pemberton saw his last hopes vanish. "Unless the siege of Vicksburg is raised, or supplies are thrown in," he warned his commanders, "it will become necessary very shortly to evacuate the place." With his garrison verging on mutiny, Pemberton reluctantly concluded he could not withstand the rumored assault.

Pemberton later wrote in his report: "If it should be asked why the 4th of July was selected as the day for surrender, the answer is obvious. I believed that upon that day I should obtain better terms.

Well aware of the vanity of our foe, I knew they would attach vast importance to the entrance on the 4th of July into the stronghold of the great river, and that, to gratify their national vanity, they would yield then what could not be extorted from them at any other time."[300]

With only one day of rations remaining and his men too weak or sickly to attempt a breakout, Pemberton finally gave in. At 10:00 a.m. on July 3, white flags appeared all along Confederate lines. Pemberton sent a message to Grant, asking for an armistice and the appointment of three commissioners from each side, who would negotiate the terms of capitulation. "I make this proposition to save the further effusion of blood."

Grant sent back much the same reply he had given General Simon Bolivar Buckner more than a year earlier at Fort Donelson. "The useless effusion of blood you propose stopping can be ended at any time you choose, by the unconditional surrender of the city."

Pemberton continued to seek better terms throughout the night, but Grant knew the Southerners were beaten. He issued an ultimatum: If the town did not surrender by 9:00 a.m. on July 4, he would consider his demands rejected.[301]

The besieging Union troops were eating breakfast the next morning when a messenger arrived at Grant's tent. The general was at a table, writing. Fred was sitting on his army cot, nursing a leg wound he had received from a stray shot at Champion's Hill. Grant opened the note the messenger handed to him, read it, sighed deeply, and looked up at his son. "Vicksburg has surrendered."[302]

For his brilliant victory at Vicksburg, Grant was promoted to the highest rank in the United States military at the time—major general in the regular army.[303] Grant's success at Vicksburg astonished President Lincoln.

General David Petraeus, commander of US forces in Iraq and Afghanistan, agrees with Lincoln's assessment of Grant: "He was near genius as a tactical leader, an operational leader, and a strategic leader. ... He's really an extraordinary hero in that sense. Just the sheer will, the indomitable determination, the quiet fortitude and so forth that I found very instructive, again, literally during the surge in Iraq."[304]

THE OVERLAND CAMPAIGN—WAR OF ATTRITION UNDER A NATIONAL STRATEGY

Grant carried his philosophy of applying constant pressure to the enemy east when he was promoted to general in chief over all the Union armies. Grant's strategy was straightforward, and it was on a national scale. "I therefore determined … to hammer continuously against the armed force of the enemy and his resources, until by mere attrition, if in no other way, there should be nothing left to him but an equal submission with the loyal section of our common country to the constitution and laws of the land."[305]

Grant planned to deliver four simultaneous blows to keep the Confederates fighting—causing them to lose men, materials, money, and morale. At the same time, his strategy kept the armies separated so they could not be reinforced in a time of crisis. That allowed the Union forces to whittle down the strength of the Southern troops until they were too weak to continue fighting. The Confederates collapsed first in Atlanta, then Mobile, the Shenandoah Valley, Nashville, and finally Appomattox.

"The previous history of the Army of the Potomac had been to advance and fight a battle, then either to retreat or lie still," noted Charles Dana of the War Department, who traveled with the Army of the Potomac and sent constant updates to Secretary of War Stanton and President Lincoln. "Grant did not intend to proceed in that way. As soon as he had fought a battle and had not routed Lee, he meant to move nearer to Richmond and fight another battle.

"As the army began to realize that we were really moving south, and at that moment were probably much nearer Richmond than was our enemy, the spirits of men and officers rose to the highest pitch of animation. On every hand I heard the cry: 'On to Richmond!'"[306]

These soldiers were all too aware of the horrors and hardships that waited for them down that road. They knew that many would not live to see the end of the war. But all of this was up ahead, and that was now the direction in which they were moving. "I do not know that during the entire war," declared one soldier, "I had such a real feeling of delight and satisfaction as in the night when we came to the road leading to Spotsylvania Court House and turned right."[307]

Grant communicated to Lincoln that the fighting had been fierce, with great losses on both sides. He was whittling away at Lee's forces—troops the Confederacy could not replace.

Lincoln was overjoyed. "It is the dogged pertinacity of Grant that wins," the commander in chief told his assistant, John Hay. After Grant assured the president that he would bring the Confederates to their knees, Lincoln commented to one of Grant's staff that once he "gets possession of a place, he holds on to it as if he had inherited it."[308]

CHEW AND CHOKE

While the Army of the Potomac and the Army of the James started their siege of Petersburg, many in the North were resisting the draft. During the summer of 1863, thousands of enlistments were expiring for Union soldiers, and they were going home. Grant had difficulty replacing soldiers who were wounded or whose enlistments had expired.

Amid growing tensions in Northern cities, General Halleck wrote to Grant warning of possible draft riots in New York, Pennsylvania, Indiana, and Kentucky. Halleck thought it would be necessary to withdraw combat troops from around Richmond to quell the riots and maintain order. "Are not the appearances such that we ought to take in sail and prepare the ship for a storm?"

Grant couldn't have disagreed more. He dug in his heels and refused to compromise.

In his view, draft riots were police work that should be left to the state governors and local militias. "If we are to draw troops from the field to keep the loyal states in the harness it will prove difficult to suppress the rebellion in the disloyal states." If forced to move troops from Petersburg, Grant warned that Lee could send soldiers to defend Atlanta, just as he had reinforced Bragg at Chickamauga the year before—and that "would insure the defeat of Sherman."

After reading Grant's reply on August 17, President Lincoln immediately telegraphed his agreement with his commanding general. "I have seen your dispatch expressing your unwillingness to break your hold where you are. Neither am I willing. Hold on with a bull-dog grip, and chew and choke as much as possible."[309]

Reading the president's message at his City Point headquarters, Grant broke into loud laughter—something he seldom did. When surprised staffers asked what had amused him, he showed them the president's telegram. "The president has more nerve than any of his advisers," he chuckled.[310]

Despite the dire predictions of naysayers, Lincoln and Grant kept pounding until victory was won. That November, Lincoln won reelection. Richmond fell the following April, and Lee surrendered at Appomattox.

Grant first demonstrated his "hard-fighting" ways at Fort Donelson, but he displayed his strategic leadership like never before in the brilliant campaigns to take Vicksburg and then to crush the Army of Northern Virginia. These were Grant's twin moments of military brilliance. In both cases, he demonstrated the tenacity necessary for any great leader to succeed in the most difficult of circumstances.

GRANT'S LEADERSHIP PRINCIPLES

- Once a strategy is established, stay the course unless circumstances change to the point where that strategy must be reevaluated.
- Once a strategy is established, maintain the vision of the organization, even in the face of opposition by key subordinates.

- Constant pressure must be applied for a strategy to be implemented and success gained.
- Recognize that it takes—as Abraham Lincoln observed in Ulysses S. Grant—"dogged pertinacity" to accomplish great things.

Chapter Nine

THINK CREATIVELY, THEN TAKE CALCULATED RISKS

I don't underrate the value of military knowledge, but if men make war in slavish observance of rules, they will fail. – Ulysses S. Grant

During my research for this book, I visited the Ulysses S. Grant Presidential Library on the campus of Mississippi State University. One of the many fascinating exhibits in the museum included two paintings Grant created while he was a cadet at West Point.

I was impressed! They were good and showed a remarkable artistic eye.

This skill served him extremely well when he became a general because it gave Grant a valuable ability to understand topography. Subordinates observed that after he looked at a map of a battlefield or territory once or twice, it remained etched in his mind. He rarely had to refer to the map again.

GRANT AT WEST POINT

Grant is often criticized for ranking twenty-first out of thirty-nine cadets in his 1843 West Point graduating class. The class, however, began with seventy-seven students. Grant made it through the grueling entrance exam—the test that Thomas "Stonewall" Jackson took gripped with fear and drenched with sweat.[311] Then Ulysses survived a curriculum designed as much for training engineers as for creating military officers. In this, Grant had an advantage, though; in addition to his artistic ability, he was also quite skilled in mathematics.

"I did not take hold of my studies with avidity," Grant wrote in *Personal Memoirs*. "In fact I rarely ever read over a lesson the second time during my entire cadetship."[312]

In his youth, Grant didn't have much interest in certain subjects. He was bored with the study of French and found the military tactics of the time—mostly Napoleonic techniques—somewhat rigid and stifling. He did the necessary studying to pass his tests, but he wasn't an enthusiastic student.

He later changed his mind on the importance of studying French in the pursuit of a military education and made sure that his son Fred had a thorough grasp of the language to help prepare him for his own West Point education.

In addition to math and painting, Grant loved novels—another glimpse into his personality. "There is a fine library connected with the Academy from which cadets can get books to read in their quarters," Ulysses wrote in his memoirs. "I devoted more time to these, than to books relating to the course of studies. Much of the time, I am sorry to say, was devoted to novels, but not those of a trashy sort."[313]

As mentioned earlier, Grant excelled above everyone else in his class in horsemanship. One cadet remarked, "It was as good as any circus to see Grant ride."[314] During the West Point graduation ceremonies, Grant was offered the chance to display his riding skills. At the direction of the riding master, Sergeant Henry Herschberger, Ulysses mounted York, a spirited horse that many in his class wouldn't dare ride. Grant was not intimidated. As his classmates, dignitaries, and spectators looked on, Sergeant Herschberger "strode to the jumping bar, lifted it higher than his head, fixed in place, then facing the class barked, 'Cadet Grant!'"

A new student at the Academy, James B. Fry (who later became a Union general), described the slender cadet dashing forward on the big sorrel, wheeling and galloping toward the far end of the hall. Grant "turned York, and then the two of them came thundering down toward the bar, faster, faster—then into the air and over." Still in awe years later, Fry wrote, "It seemed as if man and beast had been welded together." The crowd rose to cheer this remarkable feat of horsemanship. Proud of his protégé, Sergeant Herschberger barked, "Well done, sir! Class dismissed."

According to early Grant biographer Albert D. Richardson, the height of Grant's jump was a record that stood at West Point for twenty-five years.[315]

This dashing display of horsemanship was the beginning of the illustrious military career of Ulysses S. Grant.

With such amazing equestrian skills, it seemed obvious he would be given a position in the cavalry. But his grades and his class ranking destined him for service in the infantry instead. Many of his fellow cadets would not have seen in Grant's particular mix of talents the skills necessary to become a great leader. Most were shocked when he rose so high so quickly once the Civil War broke out.

THE POWER OF SOFT SKILLS

Many of the abilities Grant possessed—artistic acumen, appreciation for literature, horsemanship, and a tendency to spend much of his time listening rather than talking—are called "soft skills" by leadership experts today. Many people are just beginning to realize the power of soft skills in making a great leader.

In his book, *The Softer Side of Leadership*, Eugene Habecker writes, "Business leaders continue to understand that hard skills are no longer enough." He quotes Tim Sanders: "The most profound transformation in business ... is the downfall of the barracudas, sharks, and piranhas and the ascendancy of nice, smart people with a passion for what they do."[316]

This description fits Grant like a glove. Unlike the aloof Halleck, the arrogant McClelland, the brooding Meade, or the bombastic Hooker, Grant was "one of the guys." He ate dinner in the mess tent with the rest of the officers, listening to the stories of the day and occasionally adding a zinger to the conversation.

THE SECRET OF CREATIVITY

Habecker, who served as a university president, shares a light-bulb moment that occurred when he recognized a major missing piece to his life puzzle. In a lecture Habecker attended, Dr. Walter Massey, president of the Art Institute of Chicago, linked effective leadership to creativity and artistic expression, identifying the need for creativity as a distinctive leadership soft skill.

"At some time in my life," Habecker realized, "I had subordinated the 'soft' stuff, to the 'hard' stuff, in essence, the analytical, intellectual side of me. At some time in my life, I had concluded that only the 'hard' skills mattered in management and leadership, and if the 'soft' skills were in play, they were far less relevant and certainly less important. ... In the words of another, I had to come face to face with this question: 'If you want your team members to think outside the box, why are you coloring inside the lines?'

"Here I was learning from Dr. Massey that leaders without an authentic creative side may ultimately be unprepared, if not inadequate, for the contemporary demands of leadership. Why? Because of our inability to color outside the lines, or to think outside of the proverbial box, we may be unable to see, let alone understand, the multifold new opportunities that are everywhere, all around us."[317]

The soft-side skills Grant possessed often allowed him to out-think his opponents, which enabled him to outfight them.

Habecker refers to a *Fast Company* interview between then-Disney Television president Anne Sweeney and British educational theorist Ken Robinson in which they examined the relationship between art, creativity, and the business world. Sweeney observed, "Actually companies need people who can think differently and adapt and be creative. ... Imagination [is] the most extraordinary set of powers that we take for granted: the ability to bring into mind the things that are not present."

She went on to explain how, in doing portraiture art, she sometimes has to deconstruct a painting to get a better perspective on what she's trying to accomplish: "And in some ways, [deconstructing faces and putting them back together], that has helped me at work in deconstructing problems: looking at them from different angles."[318]

In *Thinking for a Change,* John C. Maxwell explains that creative thinkers often don't fear failure as much as others do. "The difference between average people and achieving people is their perception of and response to failure. ... Why is that so crucial? Because creativity equals failure. ... Creativity requires a willingness to look stupid. It means getting out on a limb—knowing that the limb often breaks! Creative people know these things and still keep searching for new ideas. They just don't let the ideas that don't work prevent them from coming up with more ideas that do work."[319]

When necessary, Grant was both flexible and adaptable. He was willing to think creatively in order to win. It's interesting that Grant did not excel in military strategy at West Point, but that weakness actually became an asset during the Civil War. Grant had learned enough about military tactics at West Point and in the Mexican War to understand the basics of troop movements, terrain, the placement of artillery, and so on. But he resisted the trap that many of his fellow West Point graduates fell into, which was to rely on what their textbooks told them rather than mixing the theory with the practicalities they faced on the actual battlefield.

Grant learned just enough to allow him to be knowledgeable yet flexible, which helped him adapt to situations as they evolved in the Civil War.

Grant never stopped thinking strategically, even in the lean St. Louis years. During his time as a bill collector, Grant followed the growing division between North and South in the newspapers. His friend John W. Emerson remembered Grant "sitting alone at his desk with his hand holding a newspaper hanging listlessly by his side, with every evidence of deep thought, suggesting sadness."[320] Others observed this habit of deep thought in Grant and, like Emerson, mistook it for daydreaming. Grant thought deeply about the political situation in the nation—and he thought strategically about what would occur if hostilities led to war.

As if sharpening his skills in anticipation of an outbreak of hostilities, Grant analyzed battles then raging in Italy. After studying maps in the newspaper, he would exclaim, "This movement was a mistake. If I commanded the army, I would do thus and so."[321] The other St. Louis employees either snickered or smiled sympathetically for the poor captain with delusions of grandeur.

Little did they know.

"I don't underrate the value of military knowledge," Grant explained, "but if men make war in slavish observance of rules, they will fail." He understood that every war was different, explaining that while generals "were working out problems of an ideal character, problems that would have looked well on a blackboard, practical facts were neglected. To that extent I consider remembrances of old campaigns a disadvantage. Even Napoleon showed that, for my impression is that his first success came because he made war in his own way, and not in imitation of others."

"War is progressive," Grant declared, "because all the instruments and elements of war are progressive." His victory at Vicksburg reinforced this conclusion, convincing him "that there are no fixed laws of war which are not subject to the conditions of the country, the climate, and the habits of the people."

Grant concluded that "every war I knew anything about had made laws for itself."[322]

CREATIVE DECEPTION

Another of Grant's often-overlooked attributes was his ability to creatively deceive his opponents to shield the movements of his troops. This talent was used with full effect in the false raids he orchestrated at Vicksburg in the west and the smoke screen he deployed before crossing the James River in the east.

As Grant prepared to march his army down the western side of the Mississippi River during the Vicksburg Campaign, he ordered a cavalry raid under the leadership of Colonel Benjamin H. Grierson as a diversion. These dashing troopers traveled from Tennessee to Louisiana through the length of eastern Mississippi, causing havoc all along the way. On April 17, Grierson and his seventeen hundred horsemen rode out of LaGrange, Tennessee, with a six-gun battery, capturing the attention of the Confederate commander at Vicksburg, General John C. Pemberton. Ignoring Grant's massive troop movements in Louisiana, Pemberton instead sent his soldiers to block Grierson before he reached the railroad.

On April 27, Pemberton sent seventeen messages to Mississippi commands about Grierson's raiders, but not a single dispatch concerning Grant's maneuvers on the west bank of the Mississippi River. By April 29, Pemberton had been so deceived by the false raid that he ordered his entire cavalry to pursue Grierson. At the same time, he inexplicably ignored panicked dispatches from lookouts south of Vicksburg, who observed major troop movements on the western side of the river.

Grierson's dazzling raiders finally rode out of Mississippi on May 2, reaching the safety of Union lines at Baton Rouge. The raid was so successful that the cavalry inflicted one hundred enemy casualties and captured more than five hundred prisoners. Grierson's troops suffered fewer than twenty-five casualties.[323]

At the same time, Grierson was causing panic in Mississippi, Colonel Abel D. Streight led what was called a "poorly mounted horse and mule brigade" from Middle Tennessee into Alabama, diverting the attention of infamous Confederate cavalry leader Nathan Bedford Forrest, keeping him away from the Vicksburg Theater.[324]

Grant ordered Sherman and his troops to carry out a fourth diversion at Chickasaw Bayou, just north of Vicksburg, the same spot they had unsuccessfully attacked only a few months previous. While Grant moved south with McClernand and McPherson, Sherman's Fifteenth Corps moved on Vicksburg. On April 29, while eight naval gunboats bombarded the Confederate forts at nearby Haynes Bluff, Sherman debarked ten regiments and launched an assault— but it was all a ruse. [325]

At the same time, Confederate Brigadier General John S. Bowen saw the Union navy ships gathering across the river from Grand

Gulf, a few miles south of Vicksburg, preparing to transport the Union troops. Bowen urgently requested reinforcements from Pemberton. But Grant's fourfold deception had completely fooled the Vicksburg commander, who remained focused on Grierson and Sherman. Due to fear of an invasion elsewhere, he refused to send reinforcements south toward Grand Gulf until late on April 29. By then the Confederates were too late to halt the amphibious crossing.

In his memoirs, Grant wrote about his use of subterfuge to deceive the enemy: "My object was to compel Pemberton to keep as much force about Vicksburg as I could, until I could secure a good footing on high land east of the river. The move was eminently successful and, as we afterwards learned, created great confusion about Vicksburg and doubts about our real design."[326]

On the morning of April 30, Grant began the transport of his troops across the river at Bruinsburg, Mississippi. General Sherman counseled him to wait for the wagon trains, but Grant understood that the speed of an army made all the difference in a battle. "I do not calculate upon the possibility of supplying the army with full rations from Grand Gulf," Grant wrote to Sherman. "I know it will be impossible without constructing additional roads. What I do expect is to get up what rations of hard bread, coffee, and salt we can, and make the country furnish the balance."[327]

An important lesson Grant learned from General Zachary Taylor in the Mexican War was the concept of an army living off of the land until the supply train could be reestablished. Grant's strategy proved correct. Choosing the speed of movement over the security of his wagon trains, Grant directed his army to live off the fat of the Mississippi countryside. In three weeks of battle, Grant's men marched 180 miles, won five battles, and captured some six thousand prisoners, all the while fighting a combined rebel force larger than their own.[328]

On the steamy Mississippi morning of July 4, 1863, Confederate General Pemberton surrendered thirty-one thousand men and

172 pieces of artillery. Through creativity and ingenuity, Grant had captured his second major Confederate army.

Later that day, Grant rode to the levee to meet Admiral Porter, whose new flagship, the *Black Hawk*, was ablaze with multicolored banners and streamers. The crew wore their dress white pants and blue jackets. Porter opened his wine locker to toast the victory, and Grant joined briefly in the celebration.

Soon the general quietly strolled to a corner of the vessel where he sat alone, calmly enjoying a fresh cigar. Years later, Porter remembered the poignant scene. "No one, to see him sitting there with that calm exterior amid all the jollity ... would ever have taken him for the great general who had accomplished one of the most stupendous military feats on record."[329]

The United States rewarded Ulysses S. Grant for the victory at Vicksburg by promoting him to the rank of major general in the regular army, the highest honor the nation could bestow.[330] When Lincoln heard of the fall of Vicksburg on July 7, he rejoiced as he proclaimed: "Grant is my man, and I am his, the rest of the war."[331]

The Union troops forced the capitulation of one of the largest Confederate armies—the second rebel army to surrender to Grant.

"Grant is the greatest soldier of our time if not all time," Sherman later declared. "He fixes in his mind what is the true objective and abandons all minor ones. If his plan goes wrong he is never disconcerted but promptly devises a new one and is sure to win in the end."[332]

Creative Writer: The Memoirs

During the conflagration of the Civil War, Grant emerged to guide the United States first to victory and then to the beginnings of reconciliation. As a general, he defeated the rebellion. As lieutenant general of the army, he became a stabilizing presence in the midst of the Andrew Johnson impeachment. As a candidate for president, he created and embodied the slogan that represented the heart cry from millions of Americans: "Let us have peace."

As incredible as these events were, perhaps the most dramatic and creative season in Grant's life came in his final two years. After leaving the White House without a pension—no president enjoyed that benefit until Harry S. Truman—he lost all his money in Ward's massive Ponzi scheme. Then, only a few months later, he received the devastating news that he was dying of throat cancer.

Military memoirs were popular in the decades following the Civil War. Some were credible, making a helpful contribution to the history of the war—like the memoirs of William Tecumseh Sherman, James Longstreet, or Philip Sheridan. But many were self-serving vanity pieces, tending to minimize the faults of the author, embellish his accomplishments, and take potshots at political enemies.

Raised by his devout Methodist mother, Hannah Grant, to carry himself in humility, General Grant found many of these memoirs distasteful. He had rebuffed every attempt to persuade him to write his own reminiscence. "Oh, I'm not going to write any book," he told a Saint Louis reporter not long after leaving the White House. "There are books enough already."[333]

In January 1881, Mark Twain paid a visit to Grant at his 2 Wall Street office, accompanied by his friend, author, and literary critic William Dean Howells. During the conversation, Twain suggested that Grant write a book about his life and career. Twain planned to start his own publishing house and hoped to release Grant's memoirs.[334]

"The same suggestion you make has been frequently made by others," Grant responded, "but never entertained for a moment. In the first place I have always distrusted my ability to write anything that would satisfy myself, and the public would be much more difficult to please. In the second place I am not possessed of the kind of industry necessary to undertake such a work."

Grant could see that Clemens was disappointed, so he tried to mollify his friend in a note: "If I ever settle down in a house of my own I may make notes which some one of my children may use after I am gone." He would do nothing before then, however. "I am very much obliged to you for your kind suggestions and for the friendship which inspires them and will always appreciate both."[335]

But in the wake of the Grant & Ward failure and his cancer diagnosis, the general had second thoughts about writing a book. Julia faced a life of struggle if Grant died in his current financial condition. To ensure that his wife was cared for after his death, Grant set out to write his memoirs in the midst of excruciating pain and exhaustion.

Twain agreed to publish the book and organized an amazing nationwide subscription sales campaign. As Twain read through the completed first volume, he recognized that he had a literary and historical masterpiece on his hands. He concluded that Grant's writings were on par with Caesar's Commentaries:

> The same high merits distinguished both books—clarity of statement, directness, simplicity, manifest truthfulness, fairness and justice toward friend and foe alike and avoidance of flowery speech. General Grant's book is a great, unique, and unapproachable literary masterpiece. There is no higher literature than these modern, simple memoirs. Their style is flawless—no man can improve upon it. [336]

While Grant busied himself daily as much as his strength would allow, Twain became concerned that the general was losing valuable time on fact-checking. "Only one-half or two-thirds of the second and last volume was as yet written," Twain later wrote. "However, he was more anxious that what was written should be *absolutely correct* than that the book should be finished in an incorrect form and then find himself unable to correct it.

"His memory was superb," Twain marveled, "and nearly any other man with such a memory would have been satisfied to trust it. Not so the general. No matter how sure he was of the fact or the date, he would never let it go until he had verified it with the official records. This constant and painstaking searching for the records cost a great deal of time, but it was not wasted. Everything stated as a fact in General Grant's book may be accepted with entire confidence as being thoroughly trustworthy."[337]

Everything that could be done to speed along the process had been done. Twain realized that he had to trust Grant's will to finish and win his race with death. Like Doctors Douglas and Shrady, Twain began to see that the will to complete the book and restore his family's financial security was actually keeping Grant alive, which became abundantly clear as Grant grew weaker.

In the evening, Ulysses often meditated and made notes. "He never dictated at night," his daughter-in-law Ida remembered, "as he was much too weak, but several of us would look through books to verify dates and little bits of fact. Sometimes Colonel Fred Grant and I would do this together."[338]

For Grant, the struggle was no longer simply to provide an income for his family after the bankruptcy of Grant & Ward. The writing of his memoirs gave him reason to soldier on in ways he could not have imagined when he began the task. As his body weakened, Grant became aware of how his writing gave him a reason to continue living.

He spoke of this in a letter to his daughter, Nellie: "It would be very hard for me to be confined to the house if it was not that I have become interested in the work which I have undertaken. It will take several months yet to complete the writing of my campaigns. If you ever take the time to read it you will find out what a boy and man I was before you knew me. I do not know whether my book will be interesting to other people or not, but all the publishers want to get it, and I have had larger offers than have ever been made for a book before."[339]

The book also gave General Grant the opportunity to correct the errors that had begun to be communicated by the Lost Cause school of writers, historians, and professors. In the closing of his memoirs, Grant made clear that the war was about slavery—from beginning to end.

Grant completed the book on July 19, 1885, and died four days later, on July 23. *Personal Memoirs of U.S. Grant* became the second-biggest seller of the nineteenth century, earning nearly $450,000—equivalent to more than $10 million today. In this inspiring act of selflessness and love, Grant restored his family's fortune. On both counts, Grant triumphed.

The soft skills that Grant possessed—artistic acumen, appreciation for literature, horsemanship, and a tendency to spend much of his time listening rather than talking—gave him an edge in the mid-nineteenth century. They will provide a competitive edge to any leader who is wise enough to employ them today.

GRANT'S LEADERSHIP PRINCIPLES

- Be both flexible and adaptable as you guide your organization.
- Be willing to think creatively in order to succeed.
- There are no fixed leadership laws that are not subject to the conditions of the country, the climate, and the habits of the people.
- Every major challenge makes laws for itself, so adapt and change to meet the challenge.
- Protect your inventions, ideas, and fruitful methods.
- Focus your attention on the true objective and abandon all minor concerns.
- If a plan goes wrong, promptly devise a new one.
- Communicate both verbally and in writing with clarity, directness, simplicity, manifest truthfulness, fairness, and justice toward friend and foe alike.

Chapter Ten

KEEP THE SUPPLY LINES OPEN

I do not calculate the possibility of supplying the army with full rations from Grand Gulf. ...What I do expect, however, is to get up what rations of hard bread, coffee, and salt we can, and make the country furnish the balance. – Ulysses S. Grant

In 1863, General Halleck had ordered General William S. Rosecrans to attack the Confederates under General Braxton Bragg at Chattanooga, Tennessee. Things went well for the Union forces at first, as the rebels were driven from the city and across the state line into Georgia. The Confederates halted about fifteen miles south of Chattanooga, then took a decisive stand at Chickamauga Creek and turned the tide of battle. After three of the bloodiest days in the war, the defeated Union Army of the Cumberland retreated back to Chattanooga.

The one Northern commander who stood his ground, covering the Federal retreat, was General George Thomas—earning for himself the nickname "The Rock of Chickamauga."

Following up on their victory, the Confederates took the high ground around Chattanooga, besieging the Union Army of the Cumberland in the city, pounding it with artillery, and cutting off the Union's supplies. Perplexed by the erratic behavior of the Union commander, General Rosecrans, Lincoln said that he was "confused and stunned like a duck hit on the head."[340]

Facing the destruction of the Army of the Cumberland, President Lincoln called on Ulysses S. Grant, fresh off his victory at Vicksburg, to save the day. Secretary of War Stanton met Grant on the train en route to Chattanooga—their first face-to-face meeting. Stanton gave Grant the authority to either retain or dismiss General Rosecrans. Grant didn't hesitate. He immediately replaced

Rosecrans with Thomas—a Virginian who had remained loyal to the Union.

As soon as Grant arrived in Chattanooga, he met with General Thomas and General "Baldy" Smith, the chief engineer, to assess the situation. Sitting in front of a roaring fire, the officers showed Grant the various troop positions on a map. After listening for some time, Grant fired "volleys of questions at the officers who had been on the scene," observed Horace Porter, then on the staff of General Thomas.

"So intelligent were his inquiries," said Porter, "and so pertinent his suggestions, that he made a profound impression upon everyone by the quickness of his perception and the knowledge which he had already acquired regarding important details of the army's condition. His questions showed from the outset that his mind was dwelling not only upon the prompt opening of a line of supplies, but upon taking the offensive against the enemy."[341]

"Coming to us with the laurels he had gained in Vicksburg," Horace Porter later wrote, "we naturally expected to meet a well-equipped soldier, but hardly anyone was prepared to find one who had the grasp, the promptness of decision, and the general administrative capacity which he displayed at the very start."[342]

Grant immediately recognized the first priority was to break the Confederate blockade of the Tennessee River and establish a supply line to bring food, forage, and supplies to the Army of the Cumberland. Smith guided Grant to a place on the river where an old wagon road ran to Brown's Ferry, and the forest blocked the view from nearby Confederate pickets. Smith suggested that a pontoon bridge built across the river would open a route to bring badly needed supplies to the besieged Union army. Grant approved the plan and empowered Smith, chief engineer of the Army of the Cumberland at the time, to lead the operation.

"At three a.m. on October 27, William Hazen's and John Turchin's brigades began sliding nine miles down the Tennessee in pontoon boats," writes biographer Ronald C. White, "seven of the miles passing enemy-held positions. Under a full moon, with Confederate picket fires close by, another brigade slipped along the road Grant had used earlier, bringing heavy weapons with bridge-building supplies. Both groups reached Brown's Ferry with rebels firing only a few wild shots. Once the pontoon bridge was completed, the cracker line opened."[343]

"The much-needed supplies, which had been hurried forward to Bridgeport [Alabama] in anticipation of this movement, soon reached the army, and the rejoicing among the troops manifested itself in lively demonstrations of delight," wrote Horace Porter. "Every man now felt that he was no longer to remain on the defensive, but was being supplied and equipped for a forward movement against his old foe."[344]

"It is hard for anyone not an eye-witness to realize the relief this brought," Grant observed. Soon food and supplies were rushing across the pontoon bridge—vegetables, hardtack, new clothing, ammunition, and more as "cheerfulness prevailed not before enjoyed in many weeks."[345]

Grant then devised a plan to attack the rebel forces.

General Sherman soon arrived with the Army of the Tennessee and was joined by troops under General Hooker. Sitting in on a strategy conference with the top commanders, General Oliver Otis Howard said he had never witnessed a military planning meeting that was so relaxed. Grant, Thomas, and Sherman led the discussion. As usual, Sherman bubbled over with ideas, while Thomas provided critical information on the roads, rivers, and mountains surrounding the city. Grant mostly listened as the other generals offered proposals.

Grant's battle plan directed Thomas and his Army of the Cumberland to hold General Bragg in place in the center at the foot of Missionary Ridge while Sherman and Hooker did the bulk of the work by rolling up the Confederates on the left and the right. But having suffered a humiliating defeat at Chickamauga, the troops under Thomas were not in the mood to play second fiddle, and they showed it with their courageous actions.[346]

"Immediately a rare sight in military history commenced," White explains. "Almost twenty-four thousand men in blue massed forward in assault formation, in a two-mile-long line, double deep with skirmishers in front—larger by far than Pickett's charge at Gettysburg—and it began to sweep across the plain of the geographic amphitheater at the base of Missionary Ridge. ... To everyone's surprise, Thomas's troops quickly captured the rifle pits, braving a hail of fire, shells bursting above and around them. ... As Union soldiers rushed forward, they could not believe what they saw. The defenders, panicking, abandoned their positions and started to retreat up the ridge."[347]

Observing the battle from a nearby mountainside, a surprised General Grant asked Thomas who had given the order to charge. Thomas couldn't answer, but he was thrilled with the result of his soldiers' gallant charge.

"Through field glasses Grant looked on in wonder as Thomas's men, with regimental flags flying, confronted an obstacle course of ravines, cut timber, and, farther up, loose rock. Yet, in what seemed like no time at all, they reached the crest, which they found poorly defended. ... Grant asked for his horse, and as he rode up to the crest of the ridge, the common soldiers recognized him and clung to his stirrups, raising their voices in cheers. He lifted his hat and halted again and again to thank the men."[348]

A captured Confederate soldier wrote that as he and his fellow prisoners were herded to the rear, they were suddenly halted to allow a group of Union generals and their staffs to pass by. "When General Grant reached the line of ragged, filthy, bloody, despairing prisoners strung out on each side of the bridge, he lifted his hat and held it over his head until he passed the last man of that living funeral cortege. He was the only officer in that whole train who recognized us as being on the face of the earth."[349]

EXPANDING THE SOURCE OF SUPPLY

As the war ground on, General Grant realized that maintaining supply lines was limiting his actions against the enemy. "By tying himself to the rivers to ensure supplies, he was limiting his ability to maneuver," writes Andrew Knighton. "In response, he developed a model of baseless war. Early experiments showed him that his army could easily live off the land in the fertile American south. Supplying himself through foraging and raiding on a vast scale became the hallmark of his campaigns, freeing his troops to move where he wanted."[350]

"Grant understood he was fighting a new sort of war. His leadership was marked by an understanding of how to relate differently to his men, the enemy, and the land."[351]

Soon after the victory at Chattanooga, Grant was promoted to lieutenant general and given command over all Union forces. He immediately went to work formulating a national strategy with the goal of complete conquest over the rebellion. To secure victory, he knew he had to achieve three key objectives: (1) fully equip the Union forces; (2) direct the Federal armies to fight the Confederates without ceasing in order to keep the rebel forces separated—he could not allow Jefferson Davis or Robert E. Lee to dispatch troops to various areas in times of emergency; (3) most importantly, Grant had to defeat Lee and the Army of Northern Virginia.

In *Personal Memoirs*, Grant explained the importance of keeping the Union forces in constant attack mode to whittle down the Confederate troops and supplies:

> From an early period in the rebellion I had been impressed with the idea that active and continuous operations of all the troops that could be brought into the field, regardless of season and weather, were necessary to a speedy termination of the war. The resources of the enemy and his numerical strength were far inferior to ours; but as an offset to this, we had a vast territory, with a population hostile to the government, to garrison, and long lines of river and railroad communications to protect, to enable us to supply the operating armies.
>
> The armies in the East and West acted independently and without concert, like a balky team, no two ever pulling together, enabling the enemy to use to great advantage his interior lines of communication for transporting troops from East to West, rein-

forcing the army most vigorously pressed, and to furlough large numbers, during seasons of inactivity on our part, to go to their homes and do the work of producing, for the support of their armies. It was a question whether our numerical strength and resources were not more than balanced by these disadvantages and the enemy's superior position.[352]

Grant worked continuously with Quartermaster Rufus Ingalls and General George Meade to keep the Army of the Potomac fully equipped. At the same time, he was relentless in his requests to Secretary of State Edwin Stanton to replenish the ranks of the army. From the beginning of the Overland Campaign in May until the Siege of Petersburg, the Army of the Potomac had lost sixty thousand men killed, wounded, or missing.[353]

The other pressing problem for Grant in the summer of 1864 was that those who had signed three-year enlistment papers in 1861 were approaching the end of their promised service. "Needing more men," writes Brooks Simpson, "Grant pushed again for an effective draft. Bounty-jumping volunteers were worthless; conscription would bring a better grade of recruit into the army. 'We ought to have the whole number of men called for by the President in the shortest possible time,' he told Stanton. 'Prompt action in filling our Armies will have more effect upon the enemy than a victory over them. They profess to believe, and make their men believe, there is such a party North in favor of recognizing southern independence that the draft can not be enforced. Let them be undeceived.'"[354]

In addition to pushing for the draft, Grant had partially replenished his army by pulling soldiers from the defenses around Washington, DC. The units were called "the heavies" because of the large siege guns they manned around the capital. At the same time, he ordered a reevaluation of forces across the continent and instructed commanders to send any unengaged troops to Petersburg.

Yet despite these manpower challenges, Grant remained optimistic.

"You people up North must be of good cheer," the general wrote Chicago acquaintance Russell Jones. "Recollect that we have the bulk of the Rebel Army in two grand Armies both besieged and both conscious that they cannot stand a single battle outside their fortifications with the Armies confronting them. The last man in the Confederacy is now in the Army."

"They are becoming discouraged," Grant assured his friend. "Their men deserting, dying and being killed and captured every day. We lose too but can replace our losses." Grant assured him that everything would come out right.[355]

CUTTING THE ENEMY'S SUPPLY

Just as Grant sought to keep his own supply lines open, he knew the best way to defeat the enemy was by cutting off his supplies. After settling in for a siege at Petersburg, Grant understood that he had to extend his lines as far as he could, knowing Lee would be forced to extend his smaller force to defend the Confederate capital, mile for mile. Grant continued to push the Union lines to the west in an attempt to cut off the vital supplies coming into Richmond and Petersburg by rail and canal.

"Grant wanted to make Lee stretch his thinly staffed lines to the bursting point," writes Ron Chernow. "Lee worried more about the steady provision of supplies for his men than an attack by Grant's army. Grant's overriding objective was to strike at the five railroads that crisscrossed Petersburg and fed Richmond. Starting on June 22, he threw cavalry units against the South Side and Danville Railroads."[356] Grant continued pushing his forces west to take these vital arteries. Conversely, the Confederates fought desperately to keep these lifelines open, knowing they could lose the war if Grant succeeded in cutting them off.

At the same time, the Union navy blockade was choking off supplies coming into the Confederacy by sea. The Anaconda Plan was working, slowly squeezing the life out of the rebellion.

Years ago, I was a faculty advisor for a group called Students in Free Enterprise (SIFE). Every year our goal was to win the national championship in Kansas City, Missouri, and several years we made it to the semifinals. The event always included great speakers from the business and leadership world. One year a senior executive from Walmart told the story of how he had come up the ladder within the Walmart organization and that he worked closely with founder Sam Walton.

This executive said that when the senior leadership of Walmart traveled, Sam Walton always took the team to visit one or more of the competitor's stores in the area. The other managers talked about the parking lot or the cleanliness of the store or the bathrooms. But Sam focused on the prices of the goods and remarked on how the competition was able to undercut them on certain products. The executives left these field trips with assignments to check on those suppliers to see if they could get an even better deal.

Sam Walton worked tirelessly to keep his supply lines open while doing everything he could to cut off his enemy's lifeline—and it worked. Walmart Stores became the world's largest corporation in revenue as well as the biggest private employer in the world. When Sam Walton died in 1992, he was the richest man in America.[357]

The Beginning of the End

A vital Confederate supply line was cut in January 1865 with the capture of Fort Fisher, the Confederate fortress guarding the port of Wilmington, North Carolina, the South's final port of entry. When Lee received word that Fort Fisher had fallen into Yankee hands, he knew the end was drawing near for the Confederacy. The Army of Northern Virginia was running short of food, clothing, shoes, ammunition, and medicine. Desperate letters from equally hungry loved ones drove a rash of desertions.

During the winter months, as the Union army was eventually strengthened with manpower and refitted with equipment and ammunition, the Confederate army was evaporating. Nearly 40 percent of rebel soldiers east of the Mississippi had deserted during the fall and early winter.[358]

Lee's army continued to melt away. On February 25, the Southern commander wrote: "Hundreds of men were deserting nightly to the Union Lines."[359] The situation in the rebel army became so desperate around Petersburg and Richmond that in January, Lee and Davis agreed to exchange their African-American prisoners— something they had sworn they would never do.

Referring to the new Southern law for conscripting boys from fourteen to eighteen, calling them junior reserves, and men from forty-five to sixty, calling them senior reserves, General Butler used the now-common phrase that the Confederates were "robbing both the cradle and the grave."[360]

Sherman's and Sheridan's victorious campaigns—along with the recent Union victory that closed Wilmington Harbor—had their intended effect. With all Southern ports closed to blockade runners, the scarcity of food and supplies not only affected Lee's army but also brought privations to the South's civilians. Soldiers in the trenches started receiving desperate letters from home, begging them to leave the army and tend to their families.[361] By the end of 1864, less than half of the Confederacy's soldiers were present in their units.

Grant was extremely anxious to end the war sooner rather than later. To do that, he needed to keep General Lee's and General Joseph Johnston's armies divided. Sherman's forces worked to keep Johnston away from Virginia, and Grant's troops labored to keep Lee from swinging west and south to hook up with Johnston in North Carolina. If the Federals could keep these two rebel armies separated, then the end was truly in sight. If not, the war could go on and on.

The pressure on Grant was acute.

But the pressure on Lee was even greater, prompting him to ask the Confederate Congress to pass a bill allowing the recruiting of slaves into the army. "We must decide whether the Negro will fight for us, or against us," Lee wrote. Residents of Richmond were shocked to see a new Confederate battalion made up of slaves and White hospital convalescents marching up Main Street while a band played "Dixie."[362]

Progress was also being made by the Union cavalry, led by the fiery General Sheridan. Galloping through central Virginia, the Yankees tore up and twisted railroad ties back toward Lynchburg. A division continued on to the vital James River Canal to destroy locks, levies, and culverts. Mills, factories, grain silos, and anything else that could contribute to the Confederate war effort were destroyed as well.

Sheridan decided to fight his way along the railroad and canal as he moved as close to Richmond as possible. More than two thousand escaped slaves joined his column, assisting in the destruction of the railroad and the canal. Convinced the war was nearing its close, Sheridan wanted his cavalry "to be in at the death."[363]

As the Federals tightened the vise on the rebels, General Grant had two choices: hold Lee while Sherman mopped up the rest of the Confederate armies, or force Lee out of his entrenchments and destroy the remainder of the Army of Northern Virginia in open battle. Sheridan believed the second option was the best way to end the war.

On March 22, 1865, Grant wrote to Sherman, who was then at Goldsboro, North Carolina: "Since Sheridan's very successful raid north of the James, the enemy are left dependent on the Southside and Danville roads for all their supplies. These I hope to cut next week. His instructions will be to strike the Southside road as near Petersburg as he can, and destroy it so that it cannot be repaired for three or four days, and push on to the Danville road, as near to the Appomattox as he can get."[364]

"When this movement commences I shall move out by my left with all the force I can," Grant told Sherman, "holding present entrenched lines. I shall start with no distinct view further than holding Lee's forces from following Sheridan. But I shall be along myself and will take advantage of any thing that turns up."[365]

The pressure on Lee was unbearable. To save his army, he had to abandon Petersburg and allow Richmond to fall. In an attempt to persuade Grant to concentrate his forces in the center of the

Petersburg line so he could escape around his right, Lee launched a major attack at dawn on March 25, temporarily overrunning Fort Stedman.

It didn't work.

The Union lines on either side of the breakthrough held firm, allowing Ninth Corps Commander John G. Park and Second Corps Commander Andrew A. Humphreys to mount a counterattack that pushed the rebels back. Thousands of abandoned Confederates surrendered.

Grant then ordered Sheridan to take his cavalry and sweep west, beyond Lee's right, tearing up his remaining railroads. "I mean to end the business here," he told Sheridan.[366]

On the evening of March 29, Grant told Sheridan to ride around the Confederate right and into the enemy rear. Reports from the front led Grant to believe that Lee's right was stretched so thin that a direct frontal assault could break the line completely. The commanding general dispatched the Fifth Corps to join Sheridan in the attack at Five Forks.

By the end of the following day, Grant received good news from Horace Porter, who had accompanied Sheridan in the attack at Five Forks. "Jumping off his mount," writes Brooks Simpson, "the excited aid rushed to Grant, hugged him and blurted out the news that Sheridan had smashed the Confederate lines. The Southside Railroad was doomed; so was the Confederate defense of Richmond and Petersburg. Staff members started shouting and celebrating."[367]

Grant immediately ordered a general assault all along the lines to begin at first light. By day's end, Petersburg and Richmond had fallen. In the end, General Scott's Anaconda Plan that blockaded the seaports, along with Grant's "chewing and choking," brought the Confederacy to its knees.

The modern leader must ensure an unimpeded cash flow while also ensuring that his or her organization is equipped with the best technology to get the job done—all the while remaining within wise budgetary restraints. And the modern equivalent of cutting off the enemy's supplies would follow Sam Walton's strategy, including continual attention to the marketing endeavors of the competition and constantly looking for ways to outsell your enemy.

GRANT'S LEADERSHIP PRINCIPLES

- Maintain cash flow, necessary supplies, and updated technology.
- Ensure that your organization is always fully equipped.
- Properly compensate and thank your colleagues and subordinates for their contributions.
- Show respect for your competition, and do not underestimate their abilities or possible paradigm shifts.

16. President Ulysses S. Grant, 1870.

17. The Grant family at their summer cottage at Long Branch, New Jersey.

18. The Grant summer cottage, Long Branch, New Jersey.

19. General Fred Grant in his later years. Fred was at his father's side through the crucial Battle of Vicksburg. Notice the World War I era airplane in the background.

20. Ulysses S. "Buck" Grant, Jr., in his later years.

21. Grant's beloved daughter, Nellie.

22. Ulysses and Julia's youngest son, Jesse Grant.

23. Grant with Li Hung-chang, China's northern viceroy during Grant's two-year world tour. Grant helped to broker a peace treaty between China and Japan over disputed islands.

24. Dr. George F. Shrady became one of Grant's friends and confidants during the final year of his life.

25. Sculptor Karl Ger-
hardt, a friend of Mark
Twain, who sculpted
the famous bust and
death mask of Ulysses S.
Grant.

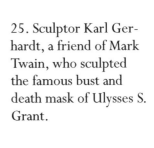

26. Ulysses S. Grant
writing his memoirs at
Mt. McGregor, 1885.

27. The death mask of
Ulysses S. Grant by Karl
Gerhardt, 1885.

Chapter Eleven

DO WHAT IS RIGHT—EVEN IF IT'S NOT POPULAR

> As soon as slavery fired upon the flag ... we all felt, even those who did not object to slaves, that slavery must be destroyed. We felt that it was a stain to the Union that men should be bought and sold like cattle. – Ulysses S. Grant

Ulysses S. Grant roomed with Frederick Dent of St. Louis for three years at West Point. Dent later introduced Ulysses to his sister, Julia, Grant's future wife. Like many of the 250 West Point cadets, Fred admired Grant's character. He described Grant as "the clearest headed young man I ever saw. ... He always wanted to do what was right, and we all had great respect for him."[368]

Another lifelong friend was fellow cadet James Longstreet, the man who became the chief lieutenant to Robert E. Lee. After the Civil War, Longstreet was reviled by many in the South because of his willingness to maintain his own independent thinking, which included a certain amount of criticism for Lee and some praise for Ulysses S. Grant. Longstreet remembered Grant from their time together at West Point, describing his "girlish modesty; a hesitancy in presenting his own claims; a taciturnity born of his modesty; but a thoroughness in the accomplishment of whatever task was assign [sic] him."[369]

Stories from Grant's youth give a glimpse into the character of the man who emerged. With a command over horses from the age of five, Ulysses was earning money by hauling wood with a horse and cart at the age of eight. Within a year, he had raised enough cash to purchase a colt from a nearby farmer named Ralston. With his heart set on the animal, he listened carefully to his father's instructions for negotiating the sale. First, offer $20, as that was all his father thought it was worth. If Ralston refused, offer $22.50. If that wasn't enough, go up to $25.

When young Ulysses arrived at the farm, Ralston asked how much his father said he should offer. The innocent boy repeated his father's instructions, word for word. "Papa says I may offer you $20 for the colt, but if you won't take that, I am to offer $22.50. And if you won't take that, to give you $25."[370]

Ulysses rode the colt home, minus the twenty-five dollars.

Years later, after working with Grant to publish the general's memoirs, Mark Twain shared his observations on the character of the former president and general: "He was a very great man and superlatively good."[371] During Grant's final illness, Twain observed him up close under the worst possible circumstances. Writing about Grant during that time, Twain said, "The sick-room brought out the points of General Grant's character. His exceeding gentleness, kindness, forbearance, lovingness, charity. … He was the most lovable great child in the world."[372]

ENDING SLAVERY

For Ulysses, ending slavery happened in his own heart before it became his political position. As slavery tore the country apart, Grant became increasingly convinced that the institution was, in fact, immoral. Years earlier, his father-in-law, Colonel Dent, had given him a thirty-five-year-old slave named William Jones to help him work his farm. It was the only time Grant had owned a slave, and he worked side by side with Jones, trying to make his farm a success. When the farm failed, Grant was at his lowest point financially. He could have sold Jones and made more than a thousand dollars—a large sum of money in those days. Instead, and much to the surprise of his St. Louis neighbors, Grant set Jones free.

On March 29, 1859, Grant appeared at the circuit court in St. Louis and filed papers that declared, "I do hereby manumit, emancipate & set free said William from slavery forever."[373] With the growing crisis over slavery, Grant made a bold statement to his father-in-law, his wife, and his St. Louis neighbors on the divisive issue.

Only months later, Grant moved north to work at his father's leather goods store in Illinois. Perhaps he saw the inevitability of the war and wanted to make himself available for service in the Federal army.

When the Southern states seceded from the Union after the attack on Fort Sumter, Lincoln issued a proclamation to recruit seventy-five thousand state militiamen for ninety days. As a West Point graduate, Grant knew he would likely be pulled into the struggle. His friend, Ely Parker, asked if Grant planned to enter the conflict on the side of the Union. "He replied that he honored his country, and that having received his education at the expense of the Government, it was entitled to his services."[374]

Writing to his father in April 1861 to inform him of his decision to leave the leather goods store and join the army, Ulysses explained that earlier political differences between them ended with the firing on Fort Sumter. "Whatever may have been my political opinions before I have but one sentiment now. That is we have a Government, and laws and a flag and they must all be sustained. There are but two parties now, Traitors & Patriots, and I want hereafter to be ranked with the latter."[375]

Grant's views on slavery continued to evolve as the war progressed, and he grew to respect and adopt President Lincoln's policies. These views were solidified during his time as president, as he took a bold stand to protect Black civil rights.[376] He was the last president until John F. Kennedy to intervene in the civil rights of African Americans in the South. Grant insisted on keeping federal military forces in the South through the end of his presidency to protect the freed slaves and to enforce the victory won in the Civil War.

The First Signs of Freedom

After President Lincoln's Emancipation Proclamation took effect on January 1, 1863, Southern slaves started escaping from their plantations and gathering around Union armies for protection. As Federal forces pressed forward, secessionist slaveholders fled their plantations, releasing even more slaves. At first, Grant sent Black refugees northward, having heard jobs were available in Northern cities. "The Lincoln administration, sensitive to Democratic charges that emancipated blacks would swarm over the north in search of jobs," writes Brooks Simpson, "a frank and effective appeal to the racist sentiments of many northern whites—put a halt to that."

Grant needed to concentrate on military matters, and the refugee crisis was an understandable but unwelcome distraction. It tapped the resources not only of the commander but also of the army as a whole. The continued flood of refugees threatened to overwhelm resources, spread disease, and cause confusion. Out of necessity, Grant devised a plan that benefited both the displaced former slaves and the military.

Grant decided to establish encampments for Black families where the former slaves worked the abandoned plantations, raising cotton, corn, and other crops that could then be used by the Union armies. The freedmen were paid a fair wage for their labor. Grant placed Chaplain John Eaton of the Twenty-Seventh Ohio Regiment in charge of the program. The general explained to Eaton that his proposal attempted to satisfy the demands of military necessity and "the dictates of mere humanity."

Some Whites at that time believed that former slaves would not work of their own free will. Grant disagreed. His experience working with the Dent slaves in Missouri led him to believe this prejudice to be false. "It also suggested that the best way to counter racist stereotypes was to provide concrete examples of how freed blacks would respond to opportunity," writes Simpson. "Give blacks the chance to earn a living, either by helping the military authorities or by working on plantations, and they would prove to whites that they would work on their own, eroding racist assumptions."

Chaplain Eaton was moved by both the morality and the compassion behind Grant's plan. "Never before in those early and bewildering days had I heard the problem of the future of the Negro attacked so vigorously and with such humanity combined with practical good sense," he remembered.

"Grant's plan embodied the important assumption that the only way to challenge racism was to repudiate stereotypes and ignorance," Simpson concludes. "It may have reflected paternalistic notions, especially in its insistence that whites oversee newly freed blacks, but it solved immediate problems of subsistence and survival and served the needs of the Union military."[377]

SLAVERY MUST BE DESTROYED

After leaving the White House, a politically mature Ulysses S. Grant traveled the world for two years. In addition to a full schedule of sightseeing, Grant agreed to meet with heads of state from Great Britain to Japan. In this unofficial role as America's chief diplomat, Grant was so successful that President Rutherford B. Hayes agreed to send US naval ships to shuttle him from nation to nation. Chronicling the trip at the request of the general was thirty-seven-year-old journalist John Russell Young. Grant asked the reporter to serve as historian, sending telegraphic dispatches to the *New York Herald* describing the journey so readers could follow the general's adventures around the globe.

Young captured the conversation between Grant and German Chancellor Otto von Bismarck at his residence when they spoke of the American Civil War:

> "What always seemed so sad to me about your last great war was that you were fighting your own people," Bismarck observed. "That is always so terrible in wars, so very hard."
>
> "But it had to be done," Grant replied.
>
> "Yes," said the prince, "you had to save the Union just as we had to save Germany."
>
> "Not only save the Union, but destroy slavery," Grant answered. [378]

SAVING LEE'S LIFE

At Appomattox, General Grant reflected the policy of leniency conveyed by President Lincoln toward the surrendered Confederate soldiers and included this language in his written terms of surrender. As Lee and several officers looked on, Grant wrote the terms in longhand, occasionally puffing on his lit cigar. The general followed the spirit of Lincoln's command to "let them up easy"—a phrase taken from Lincoln's background as a champion wrestler.[379] As pointed out in an earlier chapter, Grant included a compassionate final sentence, declaring that paroled Confederate soldiers and officers were "not to be disturbed by the United States authority so long as they observed their paroles and the laws in force where they reside."

This leniency on Grant's part was severely tested when Confederate Generals Lee, Johnston, and Longstreet were subsequently indicted in June 1865 for treason by a federal grand jury in Norfolk, Virginia. The new president, Andrew Johnson, was a Southerner who had remained loyal to the Union, and he wanted to punish the Southerners who had rebelled. Having received Grant's written promise of clemency, Lee reached out to the general to intervene.

As general in chief of the United States Army, Grant used his clout and wrote to Secretary of War Stanton, reminding him of the terms of surrender. Stanton, however, agreed with President Johnson in desiring to see retribution and punishment for Confederate leaders. While he delivered Grant's message to the cabinet, Stanton did so with little enthusiasm, and Grant's request was denied.

For Grant, the issue was a matter of honor—the promise being made, it must be kept. But it was also a matter of vital post-war diplomacy. The act of hanging Lee, Longstreet, and Johnston could reignite hostilities, which would then be fought as a guerilla war lasting for decades. Grant decided he needed to meet directly with President Johnson.

Johnson reiterated his intention to allow the executions. At this point, the general lost his temper—quite uncharacteristic for Grant. "I have made certain terms with Lee," Grant proclaimed, "the best and only terms. If I had told him and his army that their liberty would be invaded, that they would be open to arrest, trial, and execution for treason, Lee would have never surrendered, and we should have lost many lives in destroying him. My terms of surrender were according to military law, and so long as General Lee observes his parole, I will never consent to his arrest. I will resign the command of the army rather than execute any order to arrest Lee or any of his commanders so long as they obey the law."[380]

Johnson was cornered. Grant was enormously popular, and the president needed the general's support to govern in those tenuous times immediately following the war. Johnson conceded to the general's demand, and the matter was settled. Grant communicated to Lee that the terms of the surrender would stand, but he never mentioned his role in saving the Southern commander's life.

RECONSTRUCTION AND CRUSHING THE KLAN

When he became president, Grant promised that his domestic policy would be a continuation of Lincoln's vision for Reconstruction. As Grant's second term began, Reconstruction was becoming increasingly unpopular. Former Confederates in the South chafed under the occupation by Federal troops needed to enforce the law. At the same time, Northern Whites were exhausted by the struggle that had gripped the country for more than twelve years.

Yet despite pressure to back down, Grant remained resolute in his fight for equal rights for all people—in every part of the country—under the Constitution.

One of the most important accomplishments of the Grant presidency was his valiant crusade to crush the Ku Klux Klan. White supremacy came roaring back during the Andrew Johnson administration, so when Grant became president in 1868, he faced Southern politicians who were protecting segregation and Southern law enforcement officers who were ignoring federal law regarding people of color.

"Through the Klan, white supremacists tried to overturn the Civil War's outcome and restore the status quo ante," writes Ron

Chernow. "No southern sheriff would arrest the hooded night riders who terrorized black citizens and no southern jury would convict them. Grant had to cope with a complete collapse of evenhanded law enforcement in the erstwhile Confederate states."

With presidential power in his hands, Grant responded with the dual force of the army and the federal court system. From the time of George Washington, there had been an attorney general, but Grant oversaw the establishment of the Department of Justice.

With Grant's support, the 15th Amendment to the Constitution was passed, which guaranteed Black men the right to vote. Grant also supported and signed the landmark Civil Rights Act of 1875, which outlawed racial discrimination in public accommodations.

Sadly, three of his four appointees to the Supreme Court voted to overturn this landmark civil rights act in 1883—a move that angered and saddened Grant. This action, along with the withdrawal of Federal troops from the South by President Rutherford B. Hayes, triggered the eighty-year reign of terror for African Americans under Jim Crow laws.

Despite overwhelming political pressure, Grant never relented in his advocacy for equality for African Americans.

GRANT, VANDERBILT, AND REPAYING HIS DEBTS

After losing the Republican nomination to James Garfield in 1880, Grant was looking for work. He had forfeited his army pension to run for president, and there was no retirement fund for former presidents. So once again, Ulysses S. Grant was out of work.

After serving as an aide to his father in the White House, Buck Grant had launched an investment firm with a talented young man who had gained a reputation among financiers as "the young Napoleon of Wall Street"—twenty-nine-year-old Ferdinand Ward.[381] Buck and Ward approached the general with the hope that he would join the firm to help attract more of "the carriage trade."

After several days of discussions, Ulysses agreed to become an equal partner with Buck, Ward, and James D. Fish, president of the Marine National Bank. Ulysses knew and trusted Fish, who had underwritten part of Grant's world tour. Fish was a respected businessman who could cover any shortfalls the firm might incur. Buck trusted Ward—and, in time, so did his father.

General Grant invested $100,000 of his own money into the business. Buck borrowed another $100,000 from his millionaire father-in-law, former Senator Chaffee of Colorado, to secure his partnership.[382] Ward persuaded Chaffee, who had also settled in New York, to invest another $400,000 from his vast fortune.

In their negotiations, Grant made it abundantly clear to Ward that there should be no government contracts. "There are some men who get government contracts year in and year out, and whether they manage their affairs dishonestly to make a profit or not, they are sometimes supposed to, and I did not think it was any place for me."[383]

Ward understood that the general public had no clue how government contracts were issued or maintained. He deceitfully used Grant's connections with the government and the military as leverage in duping unwary investors. The insinuation was made that the firm was loaded down with government contracts because of the general's connections, tempting potential clients to get in on the action.

Ward intimated that he and the Grants were willing to let certain favored investors in on particularly promising deals. The firm was lending money on these contracts, he whispered, but they were doing so discreetly. He stealthily assured his customers that with the general's influence and contacts, hefty returns on their investments would bring in handsome returns.[384]

Sadly, the general and Buck knew nothing of Ward's deceptive game.

General Grant was given an elegant office on the second floor of the Grant & Ward building at 2 Wall Street, where he also conducted business as the president of the fledgling Mexican Southern Railway. The former president arrived at the office by carriage each day to lend his influence, handshake, and sometimes his signature to Ward's various escapades.[385]

Every morning Ferdinand Ward placed twenty-five thick Havana cigars on the general's desk.

Ward stopped by the senior Grant's office three or four times a day with papers for the general to sign, which Grant did, most often without reading. At the end of each month, Ward answered any questions Buck or the general asked about the books. Grant informally perused the monthly statements. This was the extent of the general's oversight of the business. He never questioned the daily operation of the firm, though he thoroughly enjoyed the life of leisure that it provided.[386]

Grant was eventually led to believe he was worth more than a million dollars. "As a family we are much better off than ever we were before," Ulysses wrote his daughter, Nellie.[387] Ulysses gave his wife, Julia, $1,000 a month to spend as she wished—an extravagant amount of money for the time. Julia employed a full staff of servants and stocked the kitchen full of food. Ulysses attended weekly poker parties with the captains of politics, industry, and finance. The Grants purchased the best horses, ate at the finest restaurants, and attended festive parties around New York.[388]

Grant's trust in Ferdinand Ward had grown to the point that he eventually sent the two Arabian horses he received from the Ottoman sultan to be housed in Ward's stables.[389] "I was told that the pedigrees of all of them ran back from five to seven hundred years (in breed)," Grant explained.[390]

Just as she had done as First Lady, Julia loved living the life of a socialite at the center of Gilded Age New York. The Grant home became like a miniature version of the White House, welcoming celebrities, politicians, and visiting heads of state. The Grants hosted lavish parties, welcoming the crème de la crème of New York society. Julia was a frequent visitor at theater premiers and the Metropolitan Opera.

It seemed the Grant family had arrived.

Then on Sunday morning, May 4, Ferdinand Ward arrived unannounced at the Grant home. The general greeted his young partner pleasantly, almost like a member of the family.[391] A nervous-looking

Ward explained that the city chamberlain of New York had made a sudden and unforeseen withdrawal from the Marine Bank. This move imperiled Grant & Ward's ability to conduct business.[392] Unless $400,000 could be raised immediately, the Marine Bank would not be able to open its doors for business on Monday morning.

Grant knew their partner, James D. Fish, was president of the Marine Bank, but he had trouble making the connection. "Why are you concerned about the Marine Bank?"

"We have six hundred and sixty thousand dollars on deposit there," Ward answered. "It would embarrass us very much if the bank should close its doors. I have been able to round up commitments for $250,000, but if we cannot raise an additional $150,000 before the following morning, Grant & Ward could be in trouble."[393]

A suddenly sober Grant assured his young partner he would do what he could to help in this crisis.

Riding in his carriage, Grant called on several of his wealthy friends. These men were sympathetic but unable to help. Finally, he drove to the home of William H. Vanderbilt, head of the massive New York Central Railroad. The palatial Vanderbilt estate extended the entire block of Fifth Avenue between Fifty-First and Fifty-Second Streets. Grant explained the state of affairs as Vanderbilt listened graciously.

When the general concluded, Vanderbilt spoke frankly. "I care nothing about the Marine Bank. To tell the truth, I care very little about Grant & Ward. But to accommodate you personally, I will draw my check for the amount you ask. I consider it a personal loan to you, and not to any other party." Asking for nothing as collateral, Vanderbilt wrote the check.

Grant returned home and handed the check to Ward, who thanked him extravagantly. With Vanderbilt's check in hand, everything would be fine, Ward assured him.[394]

When a friend called on Grant that evening, the general was not at all bothered by the day's events. Grant invited him to a poker game that Tuesday night. "Ward is certainly coming, and the party is made."[395]

When word spread through Wall Street that Vanderbilt, a man with an estimated worth of $200 million, had given him $150,000 to cover a shortfall, Grant believed everything would be all right. The following morning, Monday, May 5, that assumption seemed to be correct. Ward told Ulysses and Buck that he had deposited Vanderbilt's check at Fish's Marine Bank. Grant spent the day uneventfully and went home in the afternoon, thinking everything had returned to normal.[396]

Unknown to the general, that same day, a frantic Ward begged Buck to secure another $500,000 loan from Vanderbilt. "I am very much afraid that the end has come and that, unless something is done to-night, everything will be over tomorrow. ... This is our last hope, Buck, so do all you can."

In reality, Ward had borrowed enormous amounts from Marine Bank, despite having nearly nothing on deposit there. When New York City pulled $1 million from its Marine National account, the bank called in its loans to Grant & Ward to cover the shortfall. Bank president James Fish frantically ran to the bank association armed with cash and securities to use as collateral as he begged for a colossal rescue loan.[397] But the deficit was too great.

On the morning of Tuesday, May 6, the Marine Bank failed, pulling Grant & Ward down with it. Ward and Fish went to prison for their part in the Ponzi scheme. Ulysses and Buck were exonerated—having been deceived by their scheming business partners— but they were both ruined financially, and their reputations were seriously tarnished.

In the midst of the swindle, Grant had placed too much trust in young Ward, signing his name to business investments and loans, most often without reading the terms. Grant was legally obligated for all of this debt, in addition to the $150,000 check from Vanderbilt.

Grant vowed to repay every penny of his debt while also taking care of his wife and children. He took account of everything he owned, including the White Haven farm in Missouri, formerly owned by his father-in-law and purchased by Grant in the final years of the Civil War. It had been his dream to one day retire to this farm to raise thoroughbred racehorses. He had designed and built an excellent horse stable on the property, although he rarely made it to St. Louis to work with his animals. The Grants also owned homes in Galena, Philadelphia, the summer cottage in Long Branch, and two undeveloped parcels of land in Chicago.

The value of all these properties combined did not cover the $150,000 needed to repay Vanderbilt. So the Grant family collected the general's wartime mementos and the gifts Ulysses and Julia received on their world tour to help cover the debt. The family boxed up all of Grant's war trophies, campaign maps, cigar boxes, gold medals, honorary commemorations, letters, notebooks, papers, uniforms, and boots.

Ulysses and Julia added to this collection all the cabinets, gold coins, jade, porcelain vases, teakwood cabinets, jewelry, and mementos from their world tour. All of this was calculated at precisely $155,417.20, which was $150,000 plus interest. These items were loaded into wooden crates and shipped off to the Vanderbilt mansion.

William Vanderbilt had been out of the country on a trip to Europe and was perplexed when he returned and found the wooden crates stacked in his foyer. Vanderbilt swiftly dispatched his lawyer to call on the Grants and reassure them that this "personal loan" should not be a matter of concern. He considered the loan to Grant as a loss in the course of business and did not intend to press the matter. He asked that all the boxed-up items be returned.

But for Ulysses and Julia, repaying this debt was a matter of honor. Grant insisted that Vanderbilt lodge a judgment against him for the full amount of the loan. Vanderbilt argued the matter in vain. Finally, to satisfy the former president's dignity, he reluctantly agreed. In a moment of sad irony, two titans of the Gilded Age—one in business, the other in politics and the military—appeared in a New York City courtroom, and the judgment was entered.

Vanderbilt was more embarrassed than Grant.[398]

Vanderbilt reluctantly took title to the contents of the house— Grant's Civil War and presidential memorabilia, along with the gifts showered upon him by heads of state during his trip around the world. With Vanderbilt's approval, Julia later gave all these objects and Grant's large collection of books to the federal government to be cared for by the Smithsonian Institute and the Library of Congress.[399]

As his death approached, Ulysses gave instructions to his son Fred regarding his debts. Writing to Julia, he explained, "I have known for a long time that my end was approaching with certainty ... the end is not far off. ... My will disposes of my property. ... I have left with Fred a memorandum giving some details of how the proceeds of my book are to be drawn from the publisher."[400]

In the end, Julia paid all the debts Ulysses had unwittingly signed on to as a part of Grant & Ward—and she had plenty left over to live on until the end of her days.

Mark Twain's literary marketing army had gone door to door across America, selling more than 312,000 two-volume sets of the *Personal Memoirs of Ulysses S. Grant* at prices from $3.50 to $12, depending on the binding—624,000 books total. Each copy included a facsimile of a handwritten note from Grant himself.

Seven months after her husband's death, Twain presented Julia Grant with the largest single royalty in the history of publishing up to that time: $200,000. In the end, Grant's widow received nearly $450,000—equal to more than $10 million today. No previous book had ever sold so many copies in such a short period of time. Grant's book rivaled the popularity of another nineteenth-century sensation, *Uncle Tom's Cabin*.[401]

Grant's *Personal Memoirs* became a treasure of American literature and is recognized as one of the enduring masterpieces of military autobiography.[402]

With a final flourish of character—in the midst of grueling pain—Grant did what was right. He secured the financial future for his beloved Julia and their children. Through Julia, he paid off all his debts. Through the book, he confronted the Lost Cause school of Southern politicians and historians who tried to convince the public that the war was about states' rights and not about slavery. And he wrote a masterpiece of American literature that endures to this day.

GRANT'S LEADERSHIP PRINCIPLES

- Constantly strive to do what is right.
- Defend what is right, even in the midst of opposition and persecution.
- Insist on equality and fairness in your dealings with other people and organizations.

Chapter Twelve

VICTORY OVER ADDICTION

If I begin to drink, I must keep on drinking. – Ulysses S. Grant

Exceptional leaders are often vulnerable to addictions—sex, money, power, fame, drugs—and in the case of Ulysses S. Grant, alcohol.

To this day, many people believe the myth that Grant was a drunk throughout his life—or, as they called it in his time, a "drunkard," which implies self-serving, destructive, and immoral behavior. In all likelihood, Ulysses S. Grant was an alcoholic.

Author Ron Chernow recognized that Grant sometimes struggled due to the consequences of his drinking. Chernow felt compelled to thoroughly examine the historical record to help modern readers understand how alcohol influenced the life of this great American leader. After extensive research, Chernow brought the evidence to his brother, a medical doctor, for his expert opinion. His conclusion? "This is a textbook case of alcoholism."[403]

"Because Grant's drinking has been scrutinized in purely moralistic terms," writes Chernow, "his admirers have felt the need to defend him from the charge as vigorously as detractors have rushed to pin it on him. The drinking issue, both real and imaginary, so permeated Grant's career that a thoroughgoing account is needed to settle the matter."

Chernow then states his thesis: "Grant was an alcoholic with an astonishingly consistent pattern of drinking, recognized by friend and foe alike: a solitary binge drinker who would not touch a drop of alcohol, then succumb at three- or four-month intervals, usually on the road. As a rule, he underwent a radical personality change and could not stop himself once he started to imbibe. ... Alcohol was not a recreation selfishly indulged, but a forbidden impulse against which he struggled for most of his life. He joined a temperance lodge in early adulthood and lent the movement open support in later years."[404]

Twenty-first-century leaders can learn much from Grant's struggle with addiction, even if they don't have a similar struggle. The key issues regarding Grant's drinking to be considered are: (1) abuse of alcohol led to him being brought up on charges and then being pushed out of the army in 1854; (2) reports of Grant's earlier drunken behavior hindered him for a time from returning to the military at the outbreak of the Civil War; (3) Grant's reputation as a drunkard dogged him throughout the Civil War and almost relegated him to the place of a footnote in history; and (4) through the love and enduring support of his wife, through accountability to key friends and colleagues, through dogged self-discipline, and through faith in a higher power, Grant gained the victory over his addiction and rose to become one of the greatest American leaders.

Grant's battle with alcoholism took place fifty to seventy years before the establishment of the modern Alcoholics Anonymous organization in 1935—and long before much of the science was established showing that alcoholism is a chronic disease. And yet the parallels between Grant's story and modern addiction treatment methods are striking.

DEFINING THE ALCOHOLIC

According to the Journal of the American Medical Association, one in eight American adults, or 12.7 percent of the US population, now meets diagnostic criteria for alcohol use disorder.[405] According to the National Institute on Alcohol Abuse and Alcoholism, "an estimated 88,000 people die from alcohol-related causes annually, making alcohol the third leading preventable cause of death in the United States."[406]

Tragically, alcohol is a factor in more than half of the country's homicides, suicides, and traffic accidents. Alcohol abuse also plays a role in many social and domestic problems, from job absenteeism and crimes against property to spousal and child abuse.[407]

Alcoholism was identified in 1956 as an illness by the American Medical Association (AMA). It alters the portion of the brain that controls a person's motivation and ability to make healthy choices. The most destructive form is chronic alcoholism, which is emotionally, socially, and physically devastating to the sufferer and his or her loved ones. Alcoholism emerges from alcohol abuse when there is a pattern of drinking despite negative consequences.[408]

THE BEGINNING

The first reports of Grant's problem with alcohol came while he served with the army in Mexico—a season in his life that included long stretches of idleness, boredom, and loneliness. People immediately noticed a negative change in Grant when he drank. A fellow soldier from Ohio wrote home in May 1848, explaining that Grant was "altered very much: he is a short thick man with a beard reaching half way down his waist and I fear he drinks too much."[409]

Another friend, Richard Dawson, later wrote to a biographer that Grant "got to drinking heavily during or right after the war." Dawson shared that he encountered Grant, who "was in bad shape from the effects of drinking, and suffering from *mania a potu* [delirium tremens] and some other troubles of the campaign."[410]

Sadly, Ulysses wasn't the only member of the Grant clan who struggled with alcohol addiction. His younger brother, Orvil, suffered from the same disease. Years later, in 1880, Orvil embarrassed Ulysses by appearing on the street outside the auditorium during the Republican National Convention, where the elder Grant was being considered as the nominee for a third term. One Grant supporter wrote: "Brother Orville' [*sic*] is here & you ought to see him. A perfect wreck from liquor, and in a ragged, drunken, collarless [state], almost without shoes, & his clothes in the most disgusting condition." Orvil succumbed to alcoholism one year later, at age forty-six.[411]

TEMPERANCE

After the Mexican War, Ulysses returned to St. Louis, where he and Julia were wed in August 1848. Soon after they were married, they moved to the remote outpost of Madison Barracks on the shores of Lake Ontario, where they enjoyed their time together in their snug military cabin. As long as he was with Julia, Ulysses never touched a drop of alcohol.

In March 1849, Ulysses was transferred to Detroit, where he continued as regimental quartermaster. In the early fall of that year, Julia became pregnant and decided to return to St. Louis to have the baby. During Julia's prolonged absence, Ulysses fell back into his drinking habits. The surprising thing to those who observed him under the influence was that it didn't take much to get him "stupid drunk"—a phrase used by many to describe his alcoholic behavior over the years. "The problem was neither the amount nor the frequency with which he drank, but the dramatic behavioral changes induced," observes Chernow.[412]

HIGHER POWER

On May 30, 1850, Julia gave birth to their first child, Frederick Dent Grant. Perhaps it was becoming a father that motivated him, but during this time, Grant decided to speak to his Methodist pastor, Dr. George Taylor, about his drinking.

"I think that Dr. Taylor helped Grant a great deal," said Colonel James E. Pitman. "It was said that he had a long talk with Grant at that time and told him that he could not safely use liquor in any form and Grant acknowledged this and took the pledge and thereafter used no liquor at all in Detroit."[413]

One of the signature tenets of the modern Alcohol Anonymous movement is a belief in a higher power—however one defines what that is. Apparently, along with an incredibly loving and supportive wife, Grant's strong belief in the God of the Bible and his adherence to Christianity helped him in his struggle with alcohol.

In what Alcoholics Anonymous calls "The Big Book," a solution for the person struggling with addiction is given:

> Almost none of us liked the self-searching, the leveling of our pride, the confession of shortcomings which the process requires for its successful consummation. But we saw that it really worked in others, and we had come to believe in the hopelessness and futility of life as we had been living it. When, therefore, we were approached by those in whom the problem had been solved, there was nothing left for us but to pick up the simple kit of spiritual tools laid at our feet. We have found much of heaven and we have been rocketed into a fourth dimension of existence of which we had not even dreamed.
>
> The great fact is just this, and nothing less, that we have had deep and effective spiritual experiences which have revolutionized our whole attitude toward life, toward our fellows and toward God's universe. The central fact of our lives today is the absolute certainty that our Creator has entered into our hearts and lives in a way which is indeed miraculous. He has commenced to accomplish those things for us which we could never do by ourselves.[414]

TEMPERANCE GROUPS

In June 1851, Grant's unit was transferred to Sackets Harbor, New York. Julia decided to take the baby during this time to visit both sets of grandparents in Ohio and Missouri. Lonely and miserable without Julia and Fred, Ulysses was greatly tempted to imbibe. But somehow he resisted the temptation this time, perhaps due to his conversations with Dr. Taylor. Instead of falling back into drinking, he embraced the growing temperance movement.

He told a friend, "I heard John B. Gough lecture in Detroit the other night, and I have become convinced that there is no safety from ruin by drink except from abstaining from liquor altogether."[415]

Gough, a former actor and reformed drinker, traveled the country as a spokesman for "the Washingtonian movement," which encouraged followers to sign a pledge of abstinence from alcohol.

Gough spoke before more than nine million people in his lifetime, telling the story of how he had lost his wife and child as a result of his drunkenness. No doubt Gough's tale caught the attention of U. S. Grant, who loved his wife and child more than anything else in the world.[416]

With newfound fervor, Grant helped to organize a Sons of Temperance lodge, taking the pledge not to "make, buy, sell, or use, as a beverage, any Spiritous or Malt Liquors, Wine, or Cider." Meetings were held weekly at the Presbyterian church, and Grant attended regularly. He took part in lodge activities, dressed in the red, white, and blue regalia of the movement, and even marched in temperance parades.[417]

Grant's friend, Walter Camp, explained that Grant "gave hearty encouragement to the order in the village by his presence. ... I heard him refuse to join in a drinking bout once. ... It took courage in those days to wear the white apron of the Sons of Temperance, but Lieutenant Grant was prepared to show his character."[418]

Publicly, Julia Grant refused to admit her husband's drinking problem, remaining fiercely protective of his reputation. However, an early biographer chronicled the fact that "Grant attended the weekly meetings with Julia's hearty approval. She hung his parchment proudly in their home."[419]

Off the Wagon

One of the greatest crises in Grant's life came in May 1852 when his unit was ordered to the West Coast. Julia was pregnant with their second child, and the perils of an ocean journey, coupled with a mule-and-train ride across cholera-plagued Panama, proved too dangerous to risk. Once again, Ulysses would be alone in a distant military post—only this time, there was no continental railroad to allow Julia to eventually come to him. With his measly military salary, he didn't know when he would see Julia, Fred, and the soon-to-be-born baby.

It didn't take Ulysses long to fall off the wagon. During the first leg of the journey, Grant's regiment was crowded onto an overbooked ship that lacked sufficient bedding or bathrooms for the passengers. The vessel, which was built for 330 travelers, was packed with nearly 1,100 souls. In addition, Grant's commanding officer, Lieutenant Colonel Benjamin L. E. Bonneville, was a flamboyant character fond of stirring up trouble between the soldiers—arguments Grant was forced to arbitrate. These stresses, along with his anticipation of an unknown future away from his family, prompted Ulysses to turn to the bottle for comfort.

The ship's captain, James Findlay Schenck, immediately took a liking to Grant in light of his peacemaking abilities. Grant "seemed to me to be a man of an uncommon order of intelligence."[420] Schenck gave Grant permission to freely imbibe from the liquor cabinet located in his cabin. The captain said he "urged him frequently never to be backward in using it as though it were his own, and he never was. Every night after I had turned in, I would hear him once or twice, sometimes more, open the door quietly and walk softly over the floor so as not to disturb me; then I would hear the clink of the glass and a gurgle, and he would walk softly back."[421]

After a horrifying trip across Panama, where many lives were lost to cholera, Grant's regiment arrived on the West Coast. Once settled at his post, Grant joined the other officers in daily drinking to fight off boredom. The consumption of alcohol in remote garrisons is common to every army throughout history. Grant's drinking on the western frontier was not unique in any way. Second Lieutenant George Crook reported that all of the officers he met were drunk at least once a day, "and mostly until the wee hours of the morning."[422]

The problem in Grant's case was that at five feet seven and 135 pounds, a little liquor went a long way. Commissary General Robert McFeely remembered that a couple of swallows slurred his speech, and two drinks made him drunk. Grant's close friend, Lieutenant Henry Hodges, reported that Ulysses understood he had a problem and worked to gain the victory over it. "He would perhaps go on two or three sprees a year, but was always open to reason, and when spoken to on the subject would own up and promise to stop drinking, which he did."[423]

SCIENCE AND ADDICTION

Alcoholics Anonymous likens the disease to an allergy—a description that fits the behavior of Ulysses S. Grant well:

> We believe … that the action of alcohol on these chronic alcoholics is a manifestation of an allergy; that the phenomenon of craving is limited to this class and never occurs in the average temperate drinker. These allergic types can never safely use alcohol in any form at all; and once having formed the habit and found they cannot break it, once having lost their self-confidence, their reliance upon things human, their problems pile up on them and then become astonishingly difficult to solve.[424]

Research has shown the validity of this theory. By the mid-1970s, "evidence that alcoholism is genetically influenced became so strong that it was time to start looking for what might be inherited," said Dr. Marc Schuckit of the University of California at San Diego, chief of the alcoholism research unit at the Veterans Administration Hospital in La Jolla. In an article published in *The New York Times*, Sandra Blakeslee reported that researchers started to see that alcoholism is analogous to diabetes or hay fever. "Some people are born at risk. But such genetic vulnerability unfolds in specific environmental contexts. As always, nature and nurture interact."[425]

During his time at Fort Vancouver in Washington Territory, officers noticed that Grant's speech became slurred after only a few drinks. "Liquor seemed a virulent poison to him, and yet he had a fierce desire for it," recalled Lieutenant McFeely. "One glass would show on him, and two or three would make him stupid."[426]

The contrast between the controlled, Methodist-raised Ulysses and the alcohol-affected Grant was striking to other officers who knew him over the years. Alcohol loosened his inhibitions, releasing the jovial side of the man few others had ever seen. Many fellow officers described him using the same term as McFeely—Grant was "stupidly" or "foolishly" drunk.[427]

At this point, Grant made a mistake that almost derailed him years later. As quartermaster, one of his responsibilities was to supply pack animals and other provisions for officers surveying a railroad route through the Cascade Mountains—these engineering teams laid the groundwork for what became the Northern Pacific Railroad. In July 1853, a surveying team arrived, led by twenty-six-year-old Brevet Captain George B. McClellan—who later became the commanding general of the Union armies during the Civil War. According to Henry C. Hodges, while the expedition was being outfitted, "Grant got on one of his little sprees, which annoyed and offended McClellan exceedingly, and in my opinion he never quite forgave Grant for it."[428]

Grant was suffering from a severe cold at the time, which may have been part of the reason he was drinking—and yet he delivered two hundred horses and all the supplies on time. Despite this, McClellan was the type of officer that showed little patience for anything but peak performance. Grant's drunkenness at this critical moment helped to create a powerful enemy who would not easily forget the indiscretion.[429]

In August 1853, Grant received a letter from Secretary of War Jefferson Davis informing him he had been promoted to captain. Soon after this, he was transferred to isolated Fort Humboldt, 250 miles north of San Francisco. The only way to get to the remote location was by water, so the mail seemed to take forever to arrive. Julia, busy with two children, did not write as often as Grant wished, and he felt even more isolated and claustrophobic. Within a month of arriving, Grant had fallen into a deep depression. "You do not know how forsaken I feel here," he wrote to Julia.[430]

A contractor who supplied beef to Fort Humboldt, W. I. Reed, recognized Grant's descent into depression. "No greater misfortune could have happened to him than his enforced idleness. He had little work, no family with him, took no pleasure in the amusements of his fellow officers—dancing, billiards, hunting, fishing, and the like." The result could be predicted. "He took to liquor.

Not in enormous quantities, for he drank far less than the other officers."[431]

One of the greatest tragedies experienced by those who struggle with addiction is the disease's negative effect on their professional life. The loneliness and isolation of Fort Humboldt, combined with Grant's inability to make extra money to transport Julia and the boys west, created a poisonous mixture that triggered excessive drinking—and created a downward spiral.

The time of reckoning came for Grant when he was confronted by the commanding officer at Fort Humboldt, Colonel Robert C. Buchanan. An 1830 graduate from West Point, Buchanan had served with distinction in the Mexican War. However, many fellow officers and subordinates looked at Buchanan as a martinet who enjoyed punishing those who did not share his sense of military decorum.

According to Grant's body servant, A. P. Marble, "Colonel Buchanan was an efficient officer but strict in petty details to the verge of absurdity." Ulysses S. Grant had previously made a negative impression on Buchanan when he served under him at Jefferson Barracks in St. Louis. As a young soldier, Grant often returned late to barracks after visiting Julia and the Dent family at their nearby plantation. At that time, Buchanan fined Grant a bottle of wine for each infraction.

At Fort Humboldt, Grant found himself in an extremely difficult place. He came up with several schemes to make more money to bring his family west to be with him—planting potatoes, investing in a San Francisco business, and even having ice shipped in from Alaska. Nothing worked. Even the ice melted when the ship was delayed by mechanical problems. These setbacks caused him to seriously consider resigning from the army and returning to his family in St. Louis.

"I sometimes get so anxious to see you, and our little boys," Ulysses wrote to Julia in March 1854, "that I am almost tempted to resign and trust to Providence, and my own exertions, for a living where I can have you and them with me." Then the painful reality of their situation took over his thoughts. "Whenever I get to thinking upon the subject however, poverty, poverty, begins to stare me in the face and then I think what would I do if you and our little ones should want for the necessaries of life."[432]

Most soldiers drank to pass the time at this lonely outpost. "Commissary whisky of the vilest kind was to be had in unlimited quantities and all partook more or less," said one military wife.[433] After morning drills, many officers drank at a local saloon or general store.

In despair, Grant allowed his drinking to get the better of him during these dark days. Buchanan's adjutant, Lewis Cass Hunt, reported that Grant "used to go on long sprees till his whole nature would rebel and then he would be sick."[434]

Grant then received a warning for appearing tipsy on duty. Buchanan sent Lewis Cass Hunt to tell Grant that the commander would "withdraw the drinking charge if Grant didn't offend again—he had Grant write out his resignation, omitting the date." A journalist named Benjamin Perley Poore later confirmed Buchanan's warning to Grant: "You had better resign or reform," to which Grant responded, "I will resign if I don't reform."[435]

The final confrontation came one Sunday morning when Grant appeared at his company's pay table clearly under the influence of alcohol. Buchanan ordered Hunt to tell Grant that if he didn't resign, he would face a court-martial. Colonel Thomas M. Anderson later shared Hunt's account: "Grant put his face down in his hand for a long time and then commenced writing something. ... Grant said that he did not want his wife to know that he had ever been tried. ... Grant then signed his resignation and gave it to the commanding officer."[436]

His old West Point roommate, Rufus Ingalls, and other friends tried to convince Ulysses to fight the charges, convinced he would win in a court-martial. But Grant decided to resign. "His loneliness already had him on the brink of resigning," notes biographer H. W. Brands. "If he fought the charge and won, his victory would be a sentence to more of what was making him miserable. Even if he did win, the charge against him would be a matter of record. The army didn't forget, acquittals notwithstanding."

Ingalls, Grant's best friend at Fort Humboldt, thought a personal consideration mattered most: "He said he would not for the world have his wife know that he had been tried on such a charge."[437] Grant had taken the pledge of temperance for Julia and Fred back at Sackets Harbor. He would return to her to pick up the pieces and find a way to move on.

In a private conversation with Civil War chaplain John Eaton, Grant confessed that "the vice of intemperance had not a little to do with my decision to resign."[438]

"It was plain that the army life in Washington Territory and Oregon had been full of temptations, and it is more than probable that he followed the example of the other officers while there," Eaton later wrote.[439]

Grant was also quite forthright in a conversation with General Augustus Chetlain, where he admitted that "when I have nothing to do I get blue and depressed, I have a natural craving for a drink. When I was on the coast I got in a depressed condition and got to drinking."[440]

HARDSCRABBLE

After Grant resigned, he faced seven years of hardship as he tried to eke out a living. Although he was happy to be with his wife and children—a brood that eventually grew to three boys and one girl—he was never successful during that season. Nothing clicked.

During this time, he built a house with his bare hands, hewing logs from the nearby forest. The name he gave it reflected his circumstances—Hardscrabble Farm.

In the midst of these difficult years, Ulysses was happy to be with his wife—and he didn't drink when Julia was around. "During all the time I knew Grant, between his return from California in 1854 to the fall of Vicksburg, I never saw him intoxicated," wrote Julia's sister, Emma Dent.[441]

When Grant ran into his old army friends from nearby Jefferson Barracks, he clung to his pledge of sobriety. An old West Point classmate invited Grant to the Planter's House hotel bar in St. Louis. "I will go and look at you," Ulysses responded, "but I never drink anything myself."[442] His abstinence was confirmed during this time by Captain Don Carlos Buell, who reported that Grant "drank nothing but water." Major Joseph J. Reynolds agreed: "He will go into the bar with you, but he will not touch anything."[443]

Grant had stumbled onto an understanding of something we now know to be true—the only answer for the alcoholic is abstinence.

"All these, and many others, have one symptom in common," the AA Big Book explains. "They cannot start drinking without developing the phenomenon of craving. This phenomenon, as we have suggested, may be the manifestation of an allergy which differentiates these people, and sets them apart as a distinct entity. It has never been, by any treatment with which we are familiar, permanently eradicated. The only relief we have to suggest is entire abstinence."[444]

ACCOUNTABILITY

With the outbreak of the Civil War, Grant believed he would quickly receive a commission. Writing to the War Department in Washington, DC, he sought a position in the army: "I would say that in view of my present age, and length of service, I feel myself competent to command a regiment, if the President, in his judgment, should see fit to entrust one to me."[445]

His inquiry went unanswered. Despite several attempts to get back into the military, Grant's history of drinking came back to haunt him. A member of the adjutant general's office described him as "a dead-beat military man—a discharged officer of the regular army."[446]

Unable to secure a commission in Illinois, Grant looked for military work elsewhere. Traveling east, he visited George McClellan, who had become a major general of volunteers with headquarters in Cincinnati, Ohio. A clerk informed him that the general was out for the moment, and Grant was asked to sit in McClellan's outer office.

"For the next two days Grant waited and watched as staff officers worked away, writing with quill pens," writes biographer Brooks Simpson. "Perhaps he thought that McClellan would remember him, although McClellan's last impression of him—as a tipsy officer on the West Coast—would not have helped much."[447] After two frustrating days of fruitless waiting, Grant moved on.

In the end, Grant's diligence to serve wherever needed, along with the overwhelming need for West Point-trained officers, opened a place for him. Of the 1,108 officers on active duty at the start of the war, 313 resigned their commissions to join the Confederacy.[448] At the same time, many of the current officers were assigned to duty throughout the western United States and would not be recalled for war duty. Uncle Sam needed officers, and in the end, he called on Sam Grant (the nickname Ulysses received at West Point).

Grant received an invitation from Illinois Governor Richard Yates to become colonel of what would become the Twenty-First Illinois Regiment. Grant accepted the commission and never looked back.

During his time in Galena, Illinois, Grant built a friendship with a local lawyer and politician, John Rawlins, who represented the Grant family's leather goods shop. Grant was impressed with Rawlins's intellect and political instincts. Rawlins, in return, became convinced that Grant, with his military training and mind for strategy, would become a force to be reckoned with in the coming war. The two men entered the war with an understanding that each would benefit from his relationship with the other.

When Grant was promoted to brigadier general, he named Rawlins, a civilian with no military training, as his chief of staff. Rawlins agreed to take the position with one condition—that Grant abstain from drinking during the course of the war. Grant agreed.

This move proved to be a masterstroke as Rawlins displayed administrative ability, deep patriotism, and true loyalty to his commander.

By the end of 1861, Grant received increased responsibilities and thus prominence—and with that came jealousy from others eager to pull him down to advance their own careers. Since Grant had been given the label of "drunkard" in the army, his enemies tried to use it to slow, or even stop, his rise in the military.

Grant's local congressman, Elihu Washburne, was a close friend of President Lincoln and had worked to promote the hometown general. Disturbed by reports of Grant's drunkenness appearing in the Washington newspapers, Washburne wrote to their mutual friend, John Rawlins, anxious to know if there was any truth to the stories.

Rawlins's own father had abused alcohol and, as a result, had always struggled to provide for his family. Consequently, Rawlins developed a hatred for booze of any kind. Many staff officers and officials were privy to conversations between Grant and Rawlins that indicated the lawyer had become the general's conscience when it came to steering clear of alcohol. Some on Grant's staff were shocked by the candid, forthright manner with which Rawlins confronted Grant regarding liquor.

Rawlins prepared a long response to Washburne's questions and showed it to Grant before sending it. Grant read the letter slowly and then responded, "Yes, that's right; exactly right. Send it by all means."

"I would say unequivocally and emphatically," Rawlins wrote, "that the statement that General Grant is drinking very hard is utterly untrue and could have originated only in malice." He explained that there were times when Grant drank a glass of champagne or wine on social occasions, but never "did he drink enough to in any manner affect him." Then he added a touching sentiment that showed his growing friendship with Grant. "I regard his interest as my interest, all that concerns his reputation concerns me; I love him like a father."[449]

In April 1863, President Lincoln and Secretary of War Stanton sent Charles A. Dana, the assistant secretary of war, to investigate the rumors of Grant's drinking. In addition to reporting that Grant was not the stumbling drunk his political enemies were describing, Dana also included an insight into the accountability Rawlins provided to Grant.

"He is a lawyer by profession," Dana said of Rawlins, "a townsman of Grant's, and has a great influence over him, especially because he watches him day and night, and whenever he commits the folly of tasting liquor hastens to remind him that at the beginning of the war he gave him [Rawlins] his word of honor not to touch a drop as long as it lasted."[450]

Rawlins remained true to his word, scolding Grant for any diversion from his promise. In June 1863, Dr. Charles McMillan prescribed wine to help Grant with painful migraines—an ailment that dogged him throughout the war. On an inspection trip up the Yazoo River, Grant not only imbibed the wine but also got rip-roaring drunk. A letter penned immediately by John Rawlins confirms the story:

> The great solicitude I feel for the safety of this army leads me to mention what I had hoped never again to do—the subject of your drinking. ... I have heard that Dr. McMillan ... induced you, notwithstanding your pledge to me, to take a glass of wine. ... You have full control of your appetite and can let drinking alone. Had you not pledged me the sincerity of your honor early last March that you would drink no more during the war, and kept that pledge during your recent campaign, you would not today have stood first in the world's history as a successful military leader.[451]

Rawlins later wrote that he gave the letter to Grant. "Its admonitions were heeded," Rawlins reported, "and all went well."[452]

Grant may have been alarmed by these slips off the wagon. Understanding that such indiscretions could send him into obscurity again, Grant immediately called for Julia to come and be with him.

With the cooperative oversight of Rawlins and Julia, Grant stayed mostly sober through the rest of the war.

A Friend to Stand By

Grant also confided in his friend William Tecumseh Sherman about his drinking problem. "We all knew at the time that Genl. Grant would occasionally drink too much," Sherman later explained. "He always encouraged me to talk to him frankly of this and other things and I always noticed that he could with an hour's sleep wake up perfectly sober and bright, and when anything was pending he was invariably abstinent of drink."[453]

After his victories at Belmont and Fort Donelson, General Grant came to the attention of President Lincoln. Other Union armies were suffering one defeat after another, so Grant's victories were a glimmer of light to the beleaguered president. Then after the costly victory at Shiloh, many were calling for Grant's head. Some blamed his drinking for the high casualty count. But Grant had earned the president's trust, and at this critical moment, Lincoln stood behind his winning general.

Congressman Washburne later informed Grant, "When the torrent of obloquy and detraction was rolling over you ... after the battle of Shiloh, Mr. Lincoln stood like a wall of fire between you and it."[454]

A now-famous story appeared in the *New York Herald* on September 18, 1863, that shows how Lincoln had become a lightning rod for charges about Grant's drinking:

> After the failure of his first experimental explorations around Vicksburg, a committee of abolition war managers waited upon the President and demanded the General's removal, on the false charge that he was a whiskey drinker, and little better than a common drunkard. "Ah!" exclaimed Honest Old Abe, "you surprise me, gentlemen. But can you tell me where he gets his whiskey?" "We cannot, Mr. President. But why do you desire to know?" "Because, if I can only find out, I will send a barrel of this wonderful whiskey to every general in the army."[455]

Taking Responsibility

A turning point for those struggling with alcoholism is to face the reality of their addiction. Grant recognized his drinking problem and occasionally was forthright about it in public. After his victory at Vicksburg, the general was honored at a reception in St. Louis. Waiters kept placing wineglasses at Grant's side, but he ignored them throughout the night. "I dare not touch it," Grant told General Schofield. "Sometimes I can drink freely without any unpleasant effect; at others I could not take even a single glass of wine."

Writing of this later in his autobiography, Schofield commented: "A strong man indeed, who could thus know and govern his own weakness!"[456]

On another occasion, Grant visited General Delos B. Sacket and his friend, E. D. Keyes, at a Philadelphia hotel. "We conversed pleasantly on various subjects," wrote Keyes, "and when I offered to fill a glass with champagne for him, the general placed his hand over his glass saying, 'If I begin to drink, I must keep on drinking.'"[457]

When Grant sat for a portrait by the Norwegian painter and Union officer Ole Peter Hansen Balling, he asked the general why he served only water to visitors. "How could I permit a drop of liquor or wine in my camp," Grant responded, "with all newspaper slander I receive."[458]

As president of the United States, Grant allowed wine to flow freely at state dinners because it was a diplomatic custom, but the Grants never had alcohol when they dined in private. Admiral Daniel Ammen observed, "During all of these years I never saw General Grant in a condition that would give rise even to a suspicion that he had indulged too freely in liquor, and only on one occasion have I ever had a glass of liquor in the White House."[459]

In the end, Ulysses S. Grant was able to gain victory over his alcoholism—allowing him to also achieve success as commanding general over the Union army, as president of the United States, and as a best-selling author, whose *Personal Memoirs* have never been out of print. Alcohol tripped him up once, but he learned from this mistake and did not allow it to happen again. With the help of a loving wife, loyal friends, a trusting president, and his relationship with God, Ulysses S. Grant won his battle with addiction and became one of the greatest leaders we have ever known.

Modern leaders must be willing to take an honest look at any addictions they may have developed that can hinder them personally or professionally—or hinder or harm the organization. If necessary, the leader must take steps to check and overcome any destructive addictions to guard against the negative consequences that have hindered so many people who neglected this honest self-assessment.

GRANT'S LEADERSHIP PRINCIPLES

- Acknowledge destructive addictions.
- Overcome addictions by taking these steps:
    1. Rely on the love of a faithful spouse or partner;
    2. Place reliance in a higher power;
    3. Seek the help of ministers, counselors, and experts;
    4. Agree to be accountable to strong but firm friends;
    5. Accept the necessity of abstinence.

Chapter Thirteen

HAVE FAITH IN GOD
AND FAMILY

Hold fast to the Bible as the sheet-anchor of your liberties. ...
To the influence of this book we are indebted for all the progress
made in true civilization. – Ulysses S. Grant

The opening words of Grant's memoirs give us insight into his
worldview:

"Man proposes and God disposes." There are but few important
events in the affairs of men brought about by their own choice.[460]

Grant was quoting eleventh-century Christian philosopher
Thomas Aquinas. Ulysses drew strength from his Christian faith although, as in most aspects of his life, he was not overly vocal about it.

"I've come to believe that one of the missing components of
most American biographies is the whole religious or faith story,"
says biographer Ronald White in an interview with General David Petraeus. "So that in Lincoln I think there is a profound faith
story that comes to fruition in the second inaugural address—701
words, he mentions God 14 times, quotes the Bible four times,
invokes prayer three times. ... He's trying to discern the difficult
question, 'Where is God in the midst of the Civil War?'"

"Is there a faith story in Grant?" White asks. "Well, Grant is
the son of Methodism. Julia's grandfather is a Methodist minister.
When Grant is living in Galena, there's a young Methodist minister
that arrives whose name is John Heyl Vincent. ... Grant begins to
... listen to his sermons. As he's leaving Shiloh, Vincent writes to
him, and he writes back and says, 'I can still remember your feeling
discourses in the church in Galena.' ... Grant can't speak of his own
feelings—Methodism is a religion of the heart, of experience, and
Grant is drawn to this.

"When Grant returns to Galena after the Civil War, he's not a good public speaker and so he says, 'I'd like Reverend Vincent to speak for me.' Vincent would become the founder of the great Chautauqua of New York. In its second year, Grant is now mired in scandal. He's at his home resort in Long Branch, New Jersey, and Vincent sends out a call, wanting to broadcast this new endeavor. ... He said, 'Would you be willing to come for a weekend? It would mean so much to me and our movement.'

"Grant arrives with 20,000 other people in this small setting in southwestern New York. ... So I believe Vincent is the missing person in the religious story," White observes. "We don't say enough about this part of it. When you ask the question, 'What's the basis of his character?' I think his character is more from his mother than his father—the kind of values that are a part of his internal moral compass are basically kind of Methodist values."[461]

Faith Background

While doing research on Ulysses S. Grant for this book, I stumbled on a part of his heritage that I hadn't seen in the literature. When I visited Grant's birthplace at Point Pleasant, Ohio, just across the street from the banks of the Ohio River, I discovered something about his religious ancestry. A bronze plaque in the backyard commemorates one of Grant's ancestors who was a part of the Huguenot movement—a group of Bible-believing Christians in France who adopted the beliefs of the Protestant Reformation while rejecting many of the traditions of the Roman Catholic Church. This group suffered severe persecution, and many were martyred for their brave stance. The plaque reads:

TO THE MEMORY OF
JEAN DE LANNOY
1570—1604
THE HUGUENOT ANCESTOR OF
PRESIDENT ULYSSES S. GRANT
ERECTED BY
THE HUGUENOT SOCIETY OF OHIO
1972

Inside the small, white clapboard birth house is a wall hanging that chronicles the "THE HUGUENOT LINEAGE OF PRESIDENT ULYSSES S. GRANT." The chart shows that Huguenot Susannah Delano married Noah Grant, the great grandfather of Ulysses, in 1746. The chart also mentions that Noah, a captain in the French and Indian War, was reported lost on September 20, 1756, and never returned from the war.

The Huguenots' religious convictions and work ethic were undoubtedly passed down to Grant over the next few generations.

But as Ron White explains, the most prominent religious connection in Grant's immediate family was to his Methodist background. During their time in Galena, the Grant family attended the local Methodist church located near the bottom of the wooden steps that led to their home. Throughout her life, Julia was a devout believer and was disciplined in her church attendance. For Ulysses, devotion to God was important, and he enjoyed the opportunity to hear an interesting sermon during a church service. While he rarely expressed deep interest in theology, he loved to hear a great speaker. Listening to a passionate minister who warned against damnation was almost like going to the theater in mid-nineteenth-century America.[462]

Before Grant left Galena to join the army at the beginning of the Civil War, the family pastor, John Heyl Vincent, visited Julia to convey his hope that Ulysses "might be preserved from all harm and restored to his family."[463]

A few months later, as Grant began his ascent through the army ranks, Vincent met him on a winter morning in Dubuque, Iowa, as they both warmed themselves around a hotel stove. "Standing by the fire, in his old blue army overcoat, his hands clasped behind him, he reminded me then of the familiar picture of Napoleon." The understanding Grant had "of national questions, his knowledge of men and measures, his ... ambition and earnestness, both surprised and interested me," Vincent later wrote.[464]

Though Grant was often a man of few words, he was never reluctant to profess his faith. In addition to his visit to Chautauqua with Vincent, as president, he also attended a revival meeting led by one of the leading evangelists of the day, Dwight L. Moody.

During the nation's centennial in 1876, President Grant was asked to give a statement for Sunday school children across the country. He eloquently responded, "Hold fast to the Bible as the sheet-anchor of your liberties; write its precepts in your hearts, and PRACTISE THEM IN YOUR LIVES. To the influence of this book we are indebted for all the progress made in true civilization."[465]

PILGRIMAGE TO JERUSALEM

As a part of his two-year world tour, Grant became the first American president to visit Jerusalem. He tried to slip into the Old City undetected as a simple pilgrim, but officials found out about his arrival, and he was ushered into the ancient city with tremendous fanfare. During his stay, the general met with a delegation of American Jews who distributed relief to poverty-stricken Hebrews in Palestine. Grant promised to make their plight known to Jewish leaders in the United States.[466]

Despite their wonder at the biblical location, Ulysses and Julia arrived in the midst of a winter storm. "Our visit to Jerusalem was a very unpleasant one," Grant wrote to Adam Badeau. "The roads are bad and it rained, blew and snowed all the time."[467] The snow and rain made for a slippery walk up the famed Via Dolorosa.

As they set out to see the holy sites, Julia took the lead. Entering an ornate sanctuary, Julia was moved by a sign at the door: "Anyone who will say a prayer for the soul of Pope Pius IX will receive absolution." Julia immediately dropped to her knees in prayer. "You see," Grant said to journalist John Russell Young, "Mrs. Grant is taking all the chances"—meaning every chance to enhance her standing in heaven.[468]

Young described the exploration of the Holy City in the midst of the snow and rain in his book, *Around the World with General Grant*:

> We pass from our hotel on Mount Zion through a narrow, dingy street, paved with jagged cobblestones, rendered smooth by rain and mud. We make our way with difficulty. We stumble and slide

rather than walk. ... We can readily see as we retrace our way up the Via Dolorosa that it must have been a rough and weary road to one rent, and torn, and bleeding, and crushed under the cruel burden of the cross. Even to us—free as we are—wayfarers, in full possession of our faculties, it is a tedious task to climb the hill of Calvary. [469]

CHRISTIAN CHARITY

Grant's Christian faith also led him to be charitable to the poor. Grant's Secretary of State, Hamilton Fish, observed, "He gave to all who asked him, being often unnecessarily and unwisely profuse in his donations. I have not infrequently known him to give sums from five to ten times the amount of what the applicant could have reasonably or probably expected."[470]

To maintain his anonymity, Grant often routed his benevolence through the church where he and Julia worshiped, the Metropolitan Methodist Episcopal Church in Washington, DC. "Please give $10 to the blind man and $10 to the soldier's widow," Grant wrote in 1869. In another note to Pastor John P. Newman, Grant explained, "Please find enclosed my check for $100, for distribution among the poor."[471]

Ulysses and Julia remained friends with Rev. Newman the rest of their lives. Julia was a great admirer of his sermons, and she often called on Newman for spiritual direction and encouragement. When Grant was stricken with cancer, Julia contacted Dr. Newman, who left his vacation in the western United States to comfort the Grant family.

Ulysses was a highly moral man and continually concerned with propriety. He and Julia passed these values to their children. Grant was also an extremely private man who chose his words carefully. When the general spoke on a subject, one knew he was speaking from a place of deeply held conviction.

He believed in the concepts of right and wrong—for both individuals and nations. He followed the line of Abraham Lincoln's thinking that the Civil War was retribution for the national sin of slavery. Lincoln elucidated this concept in his second inaugural address when he quoted the Old Testament: "the judgments of the Lord are true and righteous altogether."[472]

Grant mirrored this coupling of national righteousness with the judgment of a holy God when he declared: "Nations, like individuals, are punished for their transgressions."[473]

FAMILY: "YOU KNOW MY WEAKNESSES"

During their time in Galena, Illinois, the Grant family lived on the bluff high above town. Every day at noon, Grant walked from his father's leather goods store to his home for lunch, climbing the wooden steps that led from the business district to the top of the bluff two hundred feet above. Little Jesse, the youngest of the four Grant children, eagerly waited on the porch, greeting his father in a high-pitched voice: "Mister, do you want to fight?"

Ulysses feigned seriousness as he replied, "I am a man of peace, Jess, but I will not be hectored by a person of your size!"

The two then wrestled, the father allowing his boy to use him as a punching bag with his tiny fists. Finally, Grant hugged his son, rolled over on his back, and cried out, "I give up! I give up!"[474]

Ulysses's sister-in-law criticized Grant's playfulness with Jesse. "He and the Captain would spend time rolling around on the floor-boards, kicking, wrestling and paying no mind to the dust or trouble they stirred up." As an adult, however, Jesse looked back fondly on his daily wrestling matches with his papa. With the freedom to run through the house unhindered, the Grant home became a favorite hangout for the neighborhood children.[475]

Grant's chief of staff, John Rawlins, recognized Grant's abundant love for his wife and children. He always called Fred Grant the "veteran," as the lad had been at his father's side during the assault on Vicksburg. When Vicksburg finally fell, Fred, who shared a tent with his father, was the first person the general told that the Confederates had surrendered.

JULIA AT CITY POINT

In the fall of 1864, Julia brought the children to visit their father at City Point. The children often romped with Ulysses, and he joined in their frolics as if they were all playmates. The morning after their arrival, Colonel Porter stepped into the general's tent and found him in his shirtsleeves, engaged in a wrestling match with Fred and Buck. "He had become red in the face, and seemed nearly out of breath from exertion. The lads had just tripped him up, and he was on his knees on the floor grappling with the youngsters, and joining in their merry laughter, as if he were a boy himself."

Army carpenters built Grant a T-shaped wooden cabin to replace his tent for the winter. A single room in the front served as an office, dining room, and strategy room. The cabin had two bedrooms, allowing Grant to send for Julia and the children. When she arrived with Nellie and little Jesse, the cabin was terribly cramped—but neither Ulysses nor Julia seemed to mind. They were together with their children, and that was what they loved most in life.

"I am snugly nestled away in my husband's log cabin," Julia wrote to a friend. "Headquarters can be as private as a home. I enjoy being here [and] have such long talks with my husband. ... Am I not a happy woman?"

Geoffrey Perret describes the scene at City Point: "For all her well-developed liking for comfortable surroundings, Julia would rather be with Grant in this sparse hut than be without him in a palace. Grant's staff officers often found them sitting in the room at the front, chatting quietly, finding something better than riches or luxury in the pleasure of sitting side by side and holding hands as they talked or while Grant read a book to her."[476]

The general was exceedingly fond of his family, and he allowed them to spend great amounts of time in camp. The younger ones hung about his neck while he was writing, making a terrible mess of his papers. "They were never once reproved for any innocent sport," Porter observed. "They were governed solely by an appeal to their affections. They were always respectful, and never failed to render strict obedience to their father when he told them seriously what he wanted them to do."[477]

Julia had visited Ulysses several times when he was stationed in the west, so she was used to life in camp. Ulysses and Julia were blessed with a lifelong love affair. "They would seek a quiet corner of his quarters of an evening, and sit with her hand in his, manifesting the most ardent devotion," Porter explained, "and if a staff-officer came accidently upon them, they would look as bashful as two young lovers spied upon in the scenes of their courtship."

"In addressing him she said 'Ulys,' and when they were alone, or no one was present except an intimate friend of the family, she applied a pet name which she had adopted after the capture of Vicksburg, and called him 'Victor.'"[478]

After Christmas, the children returned to school, but Julia remained with Ulysses at City Point. On January 23, the Confederates sent a fleet of six vessels floating down the James River from Richmond toward the Union headquarters. Soon after one o'clock in the morning, Ulysses and Julia were awakened with word that the rebel ships had passed obstructions set in place by the Yankees and were nearing City Point. "Ulys, will those gunboats shell the bluff?" Julia asked. "Well, I think all their time will be occupied in fighting our naval vessels and the batteries ashore," he replied.

Just then, news arrived that the captain of the Union ironclad, the *Onondaga*, had inexplicably retreated down the river away from the Confederates for no apparent reason. "General Grant's indignation knew no bounds when he heard of this retreat," Porter remembered. '… It is an inexpressible mortification to think that the captain of so formidable an ironclad, and the only of its kind we have in the river, should fall back at such a critical moment. Why, it was the great chance of his life to distinguish himself.'" Instructions were immediately telegraphed to the shore batteries to attack the rebel ships with all vigor.

Julia drew her chair a little closer to Ulysses and, in a subdued tone, asked, "Ulys, what had I better do?"

The general looked at her for a moment and then replied in a half-serious and half-teasing way, "Well, the fact is, Julia, you oughtn't to be here."

An officer offered to take Julia in an ambulance beyond the range of the gunboats, but Grant rejected the offer. "Oh, their gunboats are not down here yet, and they must be stopped at all hazards."

After two more anxious hours, the report came that only one of the enemy's boats was below the obstructions, and the rest had run aground. Ulysses and Julia decided to go back to bed. At daylight, the captain of the *Onondaga* redeemed himself by attacking the Confederate ironclad *Virginia*. At the same time, the shore batteries opened up on the rebel ship, which was struck about one hundred and thirty times, causing significant damage.[479]

LOVING EYES

Mary Robinson spent most of her life as a slave on the Dent plantation. In an interview for the *Bismarck Daily Tribune*, she shared the story of one of Julia Grant's remarkable dreams. "One day—I'll never forget it as long as I live—Mrs. Grant was sitting in a large rocking chair talking to some of her relatives about family affairs and the financial troubles of her husband. Suddenly she said, 'We will not always be in this condition. Wait until Dudie [her nickname at the time for Ulysses] becomes president. I dreamed last night that he would be elected president.' Every one laughed at this as a capital joke."[480]

But Julia pondered these things in her heart. She and her mother had seen greatness in Ulysses from nearly the time they met him. After the fall of Vicksburg, millions across America also saw this greatness in Ulysses S. Grant.

With her husband being spoken of as a future presidential candidate, Julia Grant realized that she too was becoming something of a public figure. Suddenly self-conscious of her strabismus—the condition of cross-eye that she had from birth—Julia consulted an old medical acquaintance to see if surgery could correct the problem.[481]

"I had often been urged in my girlhood by Dr. [Charles A.] Pope, the most distinguished surgeon in the country at that time, to permit him to make a very simple operation on my eyes," Julia wrote. "I had never had the courage to consent, but now that my husband had become so famous I really thought it behooved me to try to look as well as possible. So I consulted the Doctor on this, to me, most delicate subject, but alas! he told me it was too late, too late. I told the general and expressed my regret."

Grant was surprised by the notion. "What in the world put such a thought in your head, Julia?"

"Why, you are getting to be such a great man," Julia responded, "and I am such a plain little wife. I thought if my eyes were as others are I might not be so very, very plain, Ulys; who knows?"

Ulysses drew Julia to himself and said gently, "Did I not see you and fall in love with you with these same eyes? I like them just as they are, and now, remember, you are not to interfere with them. They are mine, and let me tell you, Mrs. Grant, you had better not make any experiments, as I might not like you half so well with any other eyes."[482]

A FATHER'S LOVE

In anticipation of the formal ceremony naming him lieutenant general, Grant arrived in Washington by train late in the afternoon of March 8, accompanied by his son Fred, going on fourteen, and his aides Brigadier General John A. Rawlins and Lieutenant Colonel Cyrus B. Comstock.[483] Just as he had been during the Vicksburg campaign, young Fred was by his father's side in the White House ceremony the next day when President Lincoln promoted Grant to Lieutenant General.

Later that year, the Union losses at Cold Harbor were staggering. Grant's casualties for the day totaled more than thirteen thousand, most of them during the first half hour. Lee lost far less, only twenty-five hundred troops that day.[484]

That evening, when the staff officers had assembled at head-quarters, they discussed with General Grant the events that had occured. "I regret this assault more than any one I have ever ordered," Grant told his staff. "I regarded it as a stern necessity, and believed that it would bring compensating results; but, as it has proved, no advantages have been gained sufficient to justify the heavy losses suffered."[485]

The day after the terrible battle at Cold Harbor, Grant did what many of the other soldiers were likely doing that day—he wrote home.

Nellie Grant, the general's eight-year-old daughter, was in school with her two older brothers in St. Louis. The Sanitary Commission had recently sponsored a fair, and Nellie had played the part of The Old Woman Who Lived in a Shoe. She had recently written to her father to bring him up-to-date on the events in her young life. Before he wrote the orders that would set the Army of the Potomac in motion toward their next destination, Grant sat down in his tent and wrote a letter to his much-beloved daughter.

> My Dear little Nellie:
>
> I received your pretty well written letter more than a week ago. You do not know how happy it made me feel to see how well my little girl not yet nine years old could write. I expect by the end of the year you and Buck [her 11-year-old brother] will be able to speak German, and then I will have to buy you those nice gold watches I promised. I see in the papers and also from Mama's letters that you have been representing "the old Woman that lived in a Shoe" at the Fair; I know you must have enjoyed it very much. You must send me one of your photographs taken at the Fair.
>
> Be a good little girl as you have always been, study your lessons, and you will be contented and happy.[486]

Ten years later, Nellie was wed in the White House and, much to her father's sadness, left with her aristocratic British husband, Algernon Sartoris, for Europe. Grant wept through much of the ceremony, and he missed his daughter terribly from across the Atlantic Ocean.

He did not see Nellie again until only weeks before his death in 1885.

A FINAL GOODBYE

Shortly before his death in 1885, Ulysses wrote a final letter to Julia to share what he was unable to say in person:

> Look after our dear children and direct them in the paths of rectitude. It would distress me far more to hear that one of them could depart from an honorable, upright and virtuous life than it would to know that they were prostrated on a bed of sickness from which they were never to rise alive. They have never given us any cause for alarm on this account, and I trust they never will.
>
> With these few injunctions and the knowledge I have of your love and affection and the dutiful affection of all our children, I bid you a final farewell, until we meet in another and, I trust, better world. You will find this on my person after my demise.[487]

In his final moments, his beloved family gathered around his bed. Julia still held the hand of her Ulys—her Victor. Colonel Fred Grant stroked his father's brow. The general opened his eyes and glanced about him, looking into the faces of all. The glance lingered for a moment as it met the tender gaze of his beloved Julia. Then there was the appearance of falling into a gentle sleep. He lay motionless as everyone looked on.[488] Ulysses S. Grant had passed away exactly as he desired—peacefully, in no pain, and surrounded by his loving family.

In our increasingly secular society, many have abandoned devotion to God and family, then they wonder why their attainment of financial and career success seems empty and unfulfilling. Research has shown that groups like Alcoholics Anonymous and Teen Challenge have such high success rates precisely because they maintain a focus on the necessity of a higher power. A study of the life of Ulysses S. Grant shows that his devotion to God and to his family served as an anchor in every season of his life—rich or poor, in sickness and in health, during times of fame and times of obscurity.

GRANT'S LEADERSHIP PRINCIPLES

- Make room in your life for the exploration of faith.
- Be charitable to the poor and underprivileged, both in your private life and through your corporate benevolence and community involvement.
- Maintain personal and corporate morality.
- Just as Lincoln and Grant held to the adage that "Nations, like individuals, are punished for their transgressions," understand that organizations, like individuals, are also punished for their transgressions.
- Guard your relationships with your spouse, partner, and children.
- Constantly seek a balance between a healthy professional and personal life.

Chapter Fourteen

LET US HAVE PEACE

I have never advocated war except as a means of peace. – Ulysses
S. Grant

Anyone who truly knew Ulysses S. Grant quickly realized that he
was not a bloodthirsty butcher. "He always expressed a great aversion to war for its own sake," observed close staff member Ely Parker. Grant's son Fred told an audience that, during the Vicksburg
campaign, his father's eyes "filled with tears" at seeing the wounded.[489]

"It is at all times a sad and cruel business," Grant declared. "I
hate war with all my heart, and nothing but imperative duty could
induce me to engage in its work or witness its horrors."[490]

"It was always the idea to do it with the least suffering," Grant
explained, "on the same principle as the performance of a severe
and necessary surgical operation. It was the proportion of the killed
and wounded that was the main thing to take into account. A severe
and decisive engagement prevented much subsequent and useless
slaughter."

Dr. Shrady asked if his military responsibilities had not at times
rested heavily upon him. "He significantly answered that, having
carefully studied his plan, it then became a bounden duty to the
Government to carry it out as best he could. If he then failed, he
had no after regret that this or that might have been done to alter
the result."[491]

"I never went into battle willingly or with enthusiasm," Grant
later reflected. "I was always glad when a battle was over."[492]

The general's compassion can be seen in a story told by Colonel
Horace Porter from the Overland Campaign:

> General Grant had ridden over to the light to watch the prog-
> ress of this attack. While he was passing a spot near the roadside

where there were a number of wounded, one of them, who was lying close to the roadside, seemed to attract his special notice. The man's face was beardless; he was evidently young; his countenance was strikingly handsome, and there was something in his appealing look which could not fail to engage attention, even in the full tide of battle. The blood was flowing from a wound in his breast, the froth about his mouth was tinged with red, and his wandering, staring eyes gave unmistakable evidence of approaching death.

Just then a young staff-officer dashed by at a full gallop, and as his horse's hoofs struck a puddle in the road, a mass of black mud was splashed in the wounded man's face. He gave a piteous look, as much as to say, "Couldn't you let me die in peace and not add to my sufferings." The general, whose eyes were at that moment turned upon the youth, was visibly affected. He reined in his horse, and seeing from a motion he made that he was intending to dismount to bestow some care upon the young man, I sprang from my horse, ran to the side of the soldier, wiped his face with my handkerchief, spoke to him, and examined his wound; but in a few minutes the unmistakable death-rattle was heard, and I found that he had breathed his last. I said to the general, who was watching the scene intently, "The poor fellow is dead," remounted my horse, and the party rode on.

The chief had turned round twice to look after the officer who had splashed the mud and who had passed rapidly on, as if he wished to take him to task for his carelessness. There was a painfully sad look upon the general's face, and he did not speak for some time. While always keenly sensitive to the sufferings of the wounded, this pitiful sight seemed to affect him more than usual.[493]

Having lived through the horrors of two wars, Grant later reminisced on the concept of war itself. "There never was a time when, in my opinion, some way could not be found to prevent the drawing of the sword."[494]

Servant and Leader at Appomattox

Grant carried the compassion he shared with Lincoln—and the wisdom—into the final surrender negotiations with General Lee at Appomattox. Historian Sean Murray describes the scene:

> As the Civil War was reaching its inevitable finality, Grant was worried that a humiliated South would retreat to Guerilla warfare, and the eventual reunification of North and South would take much longer than necessary. So, in a gesture of goodwill, Grant did not ask for draconian terms of surrender that may have humiliated General Lee and his officers. Instead he was gracious and offered Confederate Soldiers the right to return home to care for their families, and officers were allowed to keep their side arms and horses. When Grant asked Lee if the terms were satisfactory, Lee said, "Yes, I am bound to be satisfied with anything you offer. It is more than I expected." Lee went on to say, "This will have the best possible effect upon the men. It will be gratifying and will do much toward conciliating our people."
>
> A lesser leader might have given in to the personal need to exact vengeance and humiliate his enemy—Grant was above all that. Having endured humiliation through the failure of his civilian life, he understood the power of offering help when one needs it the most. Grant's act of generosity was also part of his strategic thinking. He was already looking beyond the war, and making decisions that were in the best interest of the future of his country."[495]

Another vitally important conversation took place between Grant and Lee at Appomattox that many people forget. The morning after the surrender at Appomattox, Grant and his staff rode out toward the enemy's lines. Grant's intention was to encourage Lee to use his influence to persuade the other Confederate army commanders to surrender so the war could be brought to a conclusion. Later that night, Grant repeated the substance of the conversation to Porter, who recorded it for posterity:

As soon as Lee heard that his distinguished opponent was approaching, he … rode out at a gallop to receive him. They met on a knoll that overlooked the lines of the two armies, and saluted respectfully by each raising his hat. The officers present gave a similar salute, and then withdrew out of ear-shot, and grouped themselves about the two chieftains in a semicircle.

Grant began by expressing a hope that the war would soon be over; and Lee replied by stating that he had for some time been anxious to stop the further effusion of blood, and he trusted that everything would now be done to restore harmony and conciliate the people of the South. He said the emancipation of the negroes would be no hindrance to the restoring of relations between the two sections of the country, as it would probably not be the desire of the majority of the Southern people to restore slavery then, even if the question were left open to them.

He could not tell what the other armies would do, or what course Mr. Davis would now take; but he believed that it would be best for the other armies to follow his example, as nothing could be gained by further resistance in the field. Finding that he entertained these sentiments, General Grant told him that no one's influence in the south was so great as his, and suggested to him that he should advise the surrender of the remaining armies, and thus exert his influence in favor of immediate peace.

Lee said he could not take such a course without first consulting President Davis. Grant then proposed to Lee that he should do so, and urge the hastening of a result which was admitted to be inevitable. Lee, however, in this instance was averse to stepping beyond his duties as a soldier, and said the authorities would doubtless soon arrive at the same conclusion without his interference.[496]

The conversation lasted a little more than half an hour. After clarifying the details of the upcoming formal surrender and the form of the paroles, the two commanders lifted their hats and bade each other farewell. Porter poetically writes of the parting of these two mighty generals:

General Grant, after shaking hands with all present who were not to accompany him, mounted his horse, and started with his staff for Burkeville. Lee set out for Richmond, and it was felt by all that peace had at last dawned upon the land. The charges were now withdrawn from the guns, the camp-fires were left to smolder in their ashes, the horses were detached from the cannon to be hitched to the plow, and the Army of the Union and the Army of Northern Virginia turned their backs upon each other for the first time in four long, bloody years.[497]

TRUE PEACE COMES WITH A PRICE

Carved into the front of the General Grant National Memorial in New York City—known by most as Grant's Tomb—are the words that were the theme for his campaign for the presidency in 1868:

LET US HAVE PEACE

Grant rose to the become general in chief of the Union army amid a Civil War fought over the same issue that we still struggle with today: race.

Some say the war was about states' rights or tariffs, but remove race-based slavery from the equation and these issues would have never flamed into a war to divide the Union. The Confederate leaders said unequivocally that the war was about racial slavery. This sentiment was clearly stated by Confederate Vice President Alexander Stephens in a March 1861 speech that has become known as "The Cornerstone Speech":

> "Our new government[']s] foundations are laid," Stephens declared, "its cornerstone rests, upon the great truth that the negro is not equal to the white man; that slavery, subordination to the superior race, is his natural and normal condition."[498]

Those who would argue that the American Civil War was not about race-based slavery neglect to mention that a state had to include the so-called right of slavery in their constitution in order to be admitted into the Confederacy.[499]

Grant, who had been ambivalent toward abolition, had an instant change of heart when the slave-holding Confederacy fired on

Fort Sumter. Years later, while speaking to Chancellor von Bismarck of Germany, Grant spoke of the hand of providence in the events surrounding the American Civil War.

"We might have had no war at all," Grant answered. "Our war had many strange features—there were many things which seemed odd enough at the time but which now seem Providential. If we had had a large regular army, as it was then constituted, it might have gone with the South. In fact, the Southern feeling in the army among high officers was so strong that when the war broke out the army dissolved. We had no army—then we had to organize one. A great commander like Sherman or Sheridan even then might have organized and put down the rebellion in six months or a year, or at the farthest two years. But that would have saved slavery, perhaps, and slavery meant the germs of a new rebellion."

"There had to be an end to slavery," Grant declared. "Then we were fighting an enemy with whom we could not make a peace. We had to destroy him. No convention, no treaty was possible—only destruction."[500]

"It was a long war," said the prince, "and a great work well done. I suppose it means a long peace."

"I believe so," Grant remarked with a slight smile. [501]

Through the course of the Civil War, Grant grew to oppose slavery on practical, military, and religious grounds. As early as the summer of 1861, he had told an army chaplain that "he believed slavery would die with this rebellion, and that it might become necessary for the government to suppress it as a stroke of military policy."[502]

Grant's brother-in-law, Michael John Cramer, confirmed that "as the war progressed [Grant] became gradually convinced that 'slavery was doomed and must go.' He had always recognized its moral evil, as also its being the cause of the war ... hence General Grant came to look upon the war as a divine punishment for the sin of slavery."[503]

In a letter to Elihu Washburne, soon after Lincoln issued the Emancipation Proclamation, Grant shared his belief that since slavery was the root cause of the war, its destruction had become the basis for settlement with the South. It was "patent to my mind early in the rebellion that the North & South could never live at peace with each other except as one nation, and that without Slavery. As anxious as I am to see peace reestablished I would not therefore be willing to see any settlement until this question is forever settled."[504]

Grant saw the drift toward the Lost Cause movement's defense of the war in the final years of his life, and in his final message to the country and the world—the closing of Grant's *Personal Memoirs*—he reminded the country of the true cause of the war:

> The cause of the great War of the Rebellion against the United States will have to be attributed to slavery. For some years before the war began it was a trite saying among some politicians that "A state half slave and half free cannot exist." All must become slave or all free, or the state will go down. I took no part myself in any such view of the case at the time, but since the war is over, reviewing the whole question, I have come to the conclusion that the saying is quite true.[505]
>
> This war was a fearful lesson, and should teach us the necessity of avoiding wars in the future.[506]
>
> It is possible that the question of a conflict between races may come up in the future, as did that between freedom and slavery before. The condition of the colored man within our borders may become a source of anxiety, to say the least. But he was brought to our shores by compulsion, and he now should be considered as having as good a right to remain here as any other class of our citizens.[507]
>
> I feel that we are on the eve of a new era, when there is to be great harmony between the Federal and the Confederate. I cannot stay to be a living witness to the correctness of this prophecy; but I feel it within me that it is to be so. The universally kind feeling expressed for me at a time when it was supposed that each day would prove my last, seemed to me the beginning of the answer to "Let us have peace."[508]

Ironically, a mob recently tore down a statue of Ulysses S. Grant in San Francisco because they were angry about racial relations in modern-day America. They either did not know or did not care that next to Lincoln, Grant was one of the foremost defenders of African Americans in the history of this country. As stated earlier, the Civil Rights Act of 1875, establishing equality between the races, was perhaps his greatest accomplishment as president. Tragically, it was struck down by the Supreme Court in 1883, but not before it created the prototype for Civil Rights legislation in the twentieth century.

The greatest African-American mind of the nineteenth century, Frederick Douglass, eulogized Grant as "a man too broad for prejudice, too humane to despise the humblest, too great to be small at any point. In him the Negro found a protector, the Indian a friend, a vanquished foe a brother, an imperiled nation a savior."[509]

In some ways, the modern world seems to have lost its way. While we certainly live in turbulent times, America has endured even darker periods, such as the Revolution, World War Two—and perhaps the darkest time of all, the Civil War. During the conflagration of the Civil War, Ulysses S. Grant emerged from relative obscurity to guide this nation first to victory, then to the beginnings of reconciliation.

Within six months of the outbreak of the Civil War, Grant was appointed brigadier general. Six months later, he was named major general by President Lincoln. In two years, he was named lieutenant general—the rank last held by George Washington—and took command of an army of a million men. Four years later, U. S. Grant was elected president of the United States.

As general, he defeated the rebellion. As chief of the army, he was a stabilizing presence in the midst of the Andrew Johnson impeachment. As a candidate for president, he coined the slogan that represented the heart cry from millions of Americans, "Let us have peace."

That is an example of leadership for the ages.

"Out of the hubbub of the war Lincoln and Grant emerge, the towering majestic figures," wrote Walt Whitman. Observing how these two men rose from obscurity to the highest office in the land, Whitman believed their lives demonstrated how people lifted from the lower classes of American society could overcome all obstacles in a climb to greatness. "I think," Whitman said, "this is the greatest lesson of our national existence so far."

At nearly every step along the way, Grant was underestimated, criticized, betrayed, and disappointed, yet he persevered. He was a man of few words but monumental actions. He loved being with his family, but he spent years away from them in service to his country. He had few close friends, but he was loved and admired by millions in America and around the world. He was intensely private, but he was thronged by massive crowds wherever he went in America and overseas. He was born in a small clapboard house on the Ohio frontier, but his New York City funeral attracted 1.5 million people—still the largest in American history.

Such a leader is worthy of our enduring respect. His leadership should be studied and emulated. He is worthy of the reexamination of his contribution and reputation currently underway by historians.

He was a truly great leader, and the modern world can learn much from his example.

We owe a great debt to Ulysses S. Grant—and today, we can all echo the plea for harmony in his immortal words, "Let us have peace."

GRANT'S LEADERSHIP PRINCIPLES

- Engaging in a "just war" (or conflict) is sometimes a necessary means of seeking a long-term peace.
- Enter into any conflict with the goal of inflicting the least amount of suffering.
- Be gracious in victory. Do not gloat over the downfall or setback of an opponent.

- Recognize the power of offering help when someone needs it the most.
- Enduring unpleasant and difficult conflict is sometimes necessary for the continued life and prosperity of the organization.

ACKNOWLEDGMENTS

As *Forward!* is a companion to my biography of Ulysses S. Grant, *Victor!*, I've utilized many of the same sources from my research. I'm most grateful for the assistance and encouragement from Ben Kemp, Operations Manager at the U. S. Grant Cottage State Historical Site on Mount McGregor in Wilton, NY. Thanks also to John Marszalek, Executive Director of the Ulysses S. Grant Presidential Library at Mississippi State University and his staff, David S. Nolen, Ryan P. Semmes, Eddie Rangel, and Kate Salter Gregory.

Thanks to Greg Roberts, Curator of the U.S. Grant Birthplace, Point Pleasant, Ohio, and the Village Administrator in New Richmond, Ohio. Thanks also to Jim Godburn, Education Specialist at Sailor's Creek Battlefield Historical State Park in Rice, Virginia.

Thanks to the project manager from LPC Books/Iron Stream Media for my last three books, Ann Tatlock, and to my editor, Denise Kelso Loock. Thanks to the support team at LPC Books/Iron Stream Media: John Herring, Bradley Isbell, Shonda Savage Whitworth, Kim McCulla, Tina Atchenson, Ramona Pope Richards, Cindy Sproles, and Eddie Jones. Thanks to my agent, Del Duduit, for his support and encouragement.

Thanks to the staff and leadership at Inspiration Ministries. Special thanks for the support of my colleagues on the Digital team, in particular Michael Black, Greg Bentley, Bernard Baker, John Farrell, and Willie Mangum.

Thanks to Colonel Aaron Zook, US Army (retired) for his generous foreword to this book and for his friendship and support.

I give special thanks to my friends and colleagues in the leadership field for their encouragement and support: Dr. Bruce Winston, Director, PhD in Organizational Leadership Program, Regent University; Dr. Gregory Stone, Professor, School of Business, Regent University; Dr. Almarie Donaldson, Associate Professor of Leadership, Indiana Wesleyan University; Wendy Griffith, co-host of *The 700 Club*; Andy Freeman, television producer of *The Huckabee Show* and *The 700 Club*; Lieutenant Colonel Baxter Ennis, US Army (Retired), author; Edie Melson, author and director of the Blue Ridge Mountains Christian Writers Conference; Dr. Daniel Gilbert, Assistant Professor, Regent University School of Divinity, President of EmPowered Living Int'l Ministries & Bible Schools; Lieutenant Commander David R. Lavender, US Navy (Retired), and Julie Lavender, author; Peter M. Kairuz, President and CEO, CBN Asia; Dr. Mitch Land, Dean of Media and Worship Arts, The King's University; Rev. Joel Palser, PhD, retired chaplain & Vice President Ministry Relations, The Christian Broadcasting Network; Jenny L. Cote, award-winning historical author; Rob Dickson, Doctor of Strategic Leadership, Vice President of Partner Relations, Inspiration Ministries; April Ballestero, leadership coach, author, founder of One Light Ahead; Muriel Gregory, Planting Roots Military Outreach and author.

My thanks and gratitude to the amazing historical guides and expert staff at the battlefields, museums, national parks, and various historical sites I've visited in doing research for these books. You can find a list of these sites at vonbuseck.com/single-post/usgrant-sites-visited.

Thanks to my parents, Clem and Carol Buseck, for their ongoing love and support. Thanks to my siblings who have given their encouragement and support over the years—Barbie MacFarland, Dawn Buseck, Sean von Buseck, and Erin Staaf. I also thank my children, Aaron and Julie, David, and Margo for their unending love, assistance, and encouragement. With much love and gratitude.

NOTES

INTRODUCTION

[1] Ulysses S. Grant Homepage Editors, "Grant's Genius," Ulysses S. Grant Homepage, granthomepage.com/grantgenius.hm.

[2] Chernow, *Grant,* 957–958.

[3] Waugh, Joan. *U. S. Grant: American Hero, American Myth* (Chapel Hill, NC: UNC Press, 2009), 262.

[4] Farris, Scott, *Freedom on Trial: The First Post-Civil War Battle Over Civil Rights Voter Suppression* (Lanham, MD: Rowman & Littlefield, November 15, 2020), 84.

[5] Waugh, *American Hero,* 185–186.

[6] White, Ronald C., *American Ulysses* (New York: Penguin Random House, 2016), xxiv.

[7] Behn, Richard J., "The Generals and Admirals: Ulysses S. Grant (1822–1885)," Mr. Lincoln's White House, mrlincolnswhitehouse.org/residents-visitors/the-generals-and-admirals/generals-admirals-ulysses-s-grant-1822-1885/.

[8] Phillips, Donald T., *Lincoln on Leadership* (New York: Hachette Book Group, 1992), 42.

[9] Chernow, *Grant,* 354.

[10] Chernow, *Grant,* 366.

[11] Porter, Horace. *Campaigning with Grant* (New York: Time Life Books, 1981), reprinted from The Century Company, 1897, 46–47.

[12] Green, Horace, *General Grant's Last Stand* (New York: Charles Scribner's Sons, 1936)

[13] Grant, Ulysses S., *Personal Memoirs of Ulysses S. Grant* (New York: Barnes & Noble Books, 2005). Originally published by Charles L. Webster and Company, New York, 1885, 104.

[14] Porter, *Campaigning,* 98.

[15] Milton, John, *Areopagitica.* First Amendment Watch at New York University. https://firstamendmentwatch.org/history-speaks-essay-john-milton-areopagitica-1644/.

[16] White, Ronald C., "Leadership, Life, and Legacy of Ulysses S. Grant: An interview between General David Petraeus and Dr. Ronald White," November 9, 2016, https://youtube/m7HQPxSxKas.

[17] White, Ronald C., "Why Ulysses S. Grant Was One of America's Greatest Leaders," *The Daily Signal,* October 05, 2016. https://nationalinterest.org/blog/the-buzz/why-ulysses-s-grant-was-one-americas-greatest-leaders-17952.

CHAPTER ONE

[18] Waldo, Whitson G., *Classic Leadership Principles* (Portland, OR: Inkwater Press, 2004), 109.

[19] Rank, Scott Michael, "The Peninsula Campaign in the Civil War (1862)," Historyonthenet.com. © 2000–2020, Salem Media.

November 16, 2020. https://www.historyonthenet.com/peninsula-campaign-in-civil-war-1862

[20] National Public Radio, Talk of the Nation, "Lincoln Was A President 'Tried By War'" https://www.npr.org/templates/story/story.php?storyId=95906257.

[21] History.com Editors, "General George McClellan snubs President Lincoln" https://www.history.com/this-day-in-history/mcclellan-snubs-lincoln.

[22] McPherson, James M., *Battle Cry of Freedom* (Oxford: Oxford University Press, 1988), 364.

[23] National Park Service Editors, "Casualties of Battle" https://www.nps.gov/anti/learn/historyculture/casualties.htm.

[24] Foote, Shelby, "Episode 3: Forever Free" *The Civil War: A Film by Ken Burns* PBS Video, 1990.

[25] Marvel, William, "Ambrose E. Burnside (1824-1881)," Encyclopedia Virginia, https://www.encyclopediavirginia.org/Burnside_Ambrose_E_1824-1881.

[26] Knighton, Andrew, "American Civil War: The Battle of Chancellorsville—Fighting Joe Hooker and Robert E. Lee," War History Online, September 11, 2017, https://www.warhistoryonline.com/american-civil-war/the-battle-of-chancellorsville.html.

[27] History.com Editors, "George G. Meade" History.com, November 9, 2009, https://www.history.com/topics/american-civil-war/george-g-meade.

[28] Phillips, Donald T., *Lincoln on Leadership*, 3.

[29] Brands, H. W., *The Man Who Saved the Union: Ulysses Grant in War and Peace*. New York: Doubleday–Random House, 2012), 188.

[30] Blanchard, Ken and Renee Broadwell, *Servant Leadership in Action* (Oakland, CA: Berrett-Koeler Publishers, 2018), 15.

[31] Brands, *Man Who Saved*, 162.

[32] Porter, *Campaigning*, 331–332.

[33] Blanchard and Broadwell, *Servant Leadership*, 15.

[34] Perrett, Geoffrey, *Ulysses S. Grant: Soldier & President* (New York: Modern Library–Random House, 1999/1997), 111.

[35] Blanchard and Broadwell, *Servant Leadership*, 15–16.

[36] Burns, Ken, "Episode 8: War Is All Hell" *The Civil War: A Film by Ken Burns*, PBS Video, 1990.

[37] Greeley, Horace, "Horace Greeley's Estimate of Lincoln," Our American Holidays: Lincoln's Birthday, Edited by Robert Haven Schauffler, New York: Moffat, Yard and Company, 1916. https://www.gutenberg.org/files/21267/21267-h/21267-h.htm.

[38] Chernow, *Grant*, 475.

[39] Blanchard and Broadwell, *Servant Leadership*, 16.

[40] Perrett, *Soldier and President*, 94–96.

[41] Blanchard and Broadwell, *Servant Leadership*, 16.

[42] Simpson, Brooks D., *Ulysses S. Grant: Triumph over Adversity, 1882–1865* (New York: Houghton Mifflin Company, 2000), 183.

[43] Simpson, *Ulysses S. Grant*, 183.

[44] Simpson, *Ulysses S. Grant*, 184.

[45] Blanchard and Broadwell, *Servant Leadership*, 16.

[46] Porter, *Campaigning*, 250.

[47] Blanchard and Broadwell, *Servant Leadership*, 17.

[48] Burns, Ken, "Episode 6: Valley of the Shadow of Death—1864," *The Civil War: A Film by Ken Burns*, PBS Video, 1990.

[49] Porter, *Campaigning*, 172–173.

[50] Melton, Brian C., *Robert E. Lee: A Biography* (Santa Barbara, CA: ABC-CLIO, 2012), 110.

[51] Blanchard and Broadwell, *Servant Leadership*, 17.

[52] Catton, Bruce, *Grant Moves South* (Boston: Little, Brown and Company, 1960), 190.

[53] Lincoln, Abraham, *The Collected Works of Abraham Lincoln: Volume 7*, https://quod.lib.umich.edu/l/lincoln/lincoln7/1:719?rgn=div1;view=fulltext.

[54] Brands, *Man Who Saved*, 297.

[55] Burns, Ken "Episode 7: Most Hallowed Ground," *The Civil War: A Film By Ken Burns*, PBS Video, 1990.

[56] Blanchard and Broadwell, *Servant Leadership*, 17.

[57] Samet, Elizabeth D. "7 Reasons Ulysses S. Grant Was One of America's Most Brilliant Military Leaders," History.com, May 13, 2020. https://www.history.com/news/ulysses-s-grant-civil-war-general-strengths/.

[58] Blanchard and Broadwell, *Servant Leadership*, 17.

[59] Porter, *Campaigning*, 249–250.

CHAPTER TWO

[60] Kennedy, John F. https://www.goodreads.com/quotes/36676-there-are-costs-and-risks-to-a-program-of-action.

[61] Perrett, *Soldier and President*, 313–314.

[62] Simpson, Brooks D., *Ulysses S. Grant: Triumph over Adversity, 1882–1865,* 215 (quoted in mrlincolnswhitehouse.org/residents-visitors/the-generals-and-admirals/generals-admirals-ulysses-s-grant-1822-1885/).

[63] Derose, Chris, "Those Not Skinning Can Hold a Leg," *The President's War*, Chapter 39. https://erenow.net/ww/the-presidents-war-six-american-presidents-and-the-civil-war/40.php.

[64] Brands, *Man Who Saved*, 18.

[65] Porter, *Campaigning*, 92.

[66] Brands, *Man Who Saved*, 151.

[67] Duncan, Rodger Dean, "Ken Blanchard: Why Servant Leadership Requires Humility," *Forbes*, May 8, 2019, https://www.forbes.com/sites/rodgerdeanduncan/2019/05/08/ken-blanchard-why-servant-leadership-requires-humility/#461ff35425f2.

[68] Blanchard and Broadwell, *Servant Leadership,* 7.

[69] White, "Leadership, Life."

[70] Porter, *Campaigning*, 80–81.

[71] Catton, *Grant Takes Command* (Edison, NJ: Castle Books – Book Sales Inc., 2000), 235.

[72] Simon, *The Papers,* Volume 10, 422.

[73] Collins, Jim, *Good to Great* (New York: HarperCollins Publishers, 2001), 12–13.

[74] Collins, *Good to Great,* 27.

[75] Collins, *Good to Great,* 13.

[76] Collins, *Good to Great,* 13.

[77] Flood, Charles Bracelen, *Grant and Sherman: The Friendship That Won the Civil War* (New York: Farrar, Straus and Giroux, 2005), https://erenow.net/ww/grant-and-sherman-the-friendship-that-won-the-civil-war/1.php.

[78] Wicker, Tom, "A Case of 'the Slows,'" *The New York Times*, October 30, 1988. https://www.nytimes.com/1988/10/30/books/a-case-of-the-slows.html.

[79] Waldo, *Classic Leadership,* 103.

[80] Grant, Ulysses S., *Personal Memoirs*, 384–385.

[81] Porter, *Campaigning*, 29.

[82] Collins, *Good to Great,* 13.

[83] Foote, Shelby, *Ken Burns's The Civil War Deluxe Ebook*, Edited by Geoffrey C. Ward, Ric Burns, Ken Burns New York: Knopf, 2011, https://books.google.com/books?id=Zrx0UkoF4BkC&pg=PT252&lpg=PT252&dq=#v=onepage&q&f=false.

[84] Collins, *Good to Great,* 90.

[85] Collins, *Good to Great,* 97.

[86] Waldo, *Classic Leadership,* 79.

[87] Simpson, *Ulysses S. Grant*, 461.

[88] Simpson, *Ulysses S. Grant*, 461–462.

[89] Collins, *Good to Great,* 13.

[90] Brands, *Man Who Saved*, 130.

[91] Waldo, *Classic Leadership*, 112.

[92] Collins, *Good to Great,* 13.

[93] Burns, Ken. "Episode 2: A Very Bloody Affair – 1862," *The Civil War: A Ken Burns Film*, PBS Video, 1990.

[94] Green, 279.

[95] Spangenberger, Phil, "The Yankee Sixteen Shooter," *True West Magazine*, Truewestmagazine.com/the-yankee-sixteen-shooter/.

[96] Collins, *Good to Great,* 30.

CHAPTER THREE

[97] Simpson, *Triumph over Adversity*, 10.

[98] Simpson, *Triumph over Adversity*, 13.

[99] Smith, Jean Edward, *Grant* (New York: Simon and Schuster, 2001), 25.

[100] Murray, Sean P., "Ulysses S. Grant: 12 Leadership Lessons," RealTime Performance, February 20, 2018, https://www.realtimeperformance.com/ulysses-s-grant-12-leadership-lessons/.

[101] Proverbs 22:29, Modern English Version (Lake Mary, FL: Charisma House, 2014), https://www.biblegateway.com/passage/?search=Proverbs+22%3A29&version=MEV.

[102] Scott, Steven K. *The Richest Man Who Ever Lived* (New York: Currency/Doubleday, 2006), 12.

[103] Scott, *Richest Man*, 14.

[104] History.com Editors, "Union Disaster at Cold Harbor," History.com, November 13, 2009. https://www.history.com/this-day-in-history/union-disaster-at-cold-harbor.

[105] Simpson, *Triumph over Adversity*, 341.

[106] Simpson, *Triumph over Adversity*, 341.

107 Scott, *Richest Man*, 14.

108 Scott, *Richest Man*, 15.

109 White, *American Ulysses,* 587.

110 Smith, *Grant,* 605.

111 Smith, *Grant*, 608.

112 Scott, *Richest Man*, 15.

113 Chernow, *Grant,* 250.

114 Chernow, *Grant*, 251.

115 Chernow, *Grant*, 252.

116 Brands, *ManWho Saved*, 229.

117 Chernow, *Grant*, 252.

118 Scott, *Richest Man*, 16.

119 Grant, Julia, *The Personal Memoirs of Julia Dent Grant*, Edited by John Y. Simon (NewYork: G. Putnam's Sons, 1975), 328.

120 Green, *General*, 55.

121 Chernow, *Grant*, 201.

122 Grant, Ulysses S., *Personal Memoirs*, 197.

123 Bonekemper, Edward H. *Grant and Lee: Victorious American and Vanquished Virginian* (Washington: Regnery History, 2012), 58.

124 Perrett, *Soldier and President*, 196.

125 Waldo, *Classic Leadership*, 85.

126 Simpson, *Ulysses S. Grant*, 134.

127 Grant, Ulysses, *Personal Memoirs*, 194.

128 Waldo, *Classic Leadership*, 86.

129 Waldo, *Classic Leadership*, 86.

130 Hymel, Kevin M. "A General's Heroes." Army.mil, April 27, 2010. https://www.army.mil/article/38075/a_generals_heroes.

131 Perrett, *Soldier and President*, 198.

132 Brands, *ManWho Saved*, 187.

133 Waldo, *Classic Leadership*, 86.

134 Grant, Ulysses S., *Personal Memoirs*, 205.

135 Brands, *ManWho Saved*, 188.

Chapter Four

136 History.com Editors. "Ulysses S. Grant," History.com, October 29, 2009. https://www.history.com/topics/us-presidents/ulysses-s-grant-1.

137 Chernow, *Grant*, 151.

138 Chernow, *Grant*, 151.

139 Chernow, *Grant*, 670–671.

140 Catton, *Command*, 137.

141 Chernow, *Grant*, 671.

142 Young, John Russell, *Around the World with General Grant* (Baltimore: The Johns Hopkins University Press, 2002/1879), 388.

143 Perrett, *Soldier and President*, 24.

144 Smith, *Grant*, 314.

145 Catton, *Command*, 138.

146 Dabney, Emmanuel, "City Point During the Civil War" www.encyclopediavirginia.org/city_point_during_the_civil_war#start_entry.

[147] Army.mil. "Brigadier General Rufus Ingalls 16th Quartermaster School Commandant February 1882-July 1883" https://quartermaster.army.mil/bios/previous-qm-generals/quartermaster_general_bio-ingalls.html.

[148] Kouzes, James M. and Barry Z. Posner, *The Leadership Challenge* (San Francisco: John Wiley & Sons–Jossey-Bass, 2002), 13.

[149] Kouzes and Posner, *Leadership Challenge*, 15.

[150] Porter, *Campaigning*, 35–37.

[151] Kouzes and Posner, *Leadership Challenge*, 14–15.

[152] Burns, Ken, "Episode 6: The Valley of the Shadow of Death—1864," *The Civil War: A Film by Ken Burns*, PBS Video, 1990.

[153] Smith, *Grant*, 337–338.

[154] Bonekemper, *Grant and Lee*, 298.

[155] Perrett, *Soldier and President*, 314.

[156] Porter, *Campaigning*, 78–79.

[157] Porter, *Campaigning*, 291.

[158] Kouzes and Posner, *Leadership Challenge*, 16–17.

[159] Bonekemper, *Grant and Lee*, 288.

[160] Green, *General*, 161.

[161] Bonekemper, *Grant and Lee*, 330.

[162] Bonekemper, *Grant and Lee*, 330–331.

[163] Bonekemper, *Grant and Lee*, 330.

[164] Catton, *Command*, 359.

[165] Bonekemper, *Grant and Lee*, 342.

[166] Kouzes and Posner, *Leadership Challenge*, 18.

[167] Grant, Ulysses S., *Personal Memoirs*, 503–504.

[168] Catton, *Command*, 364.

[169] Perrett, *Soldier and President*, S352.

[170] Kouzes and Posner, *Leadership Challenge*, 19–20.

[171] Simpson, *Triumph over Adversity*, 283.

[172] The 700 Club, "Leading With Love" https://www1.cbn.com/700club/joel-manby-love-works.

[173] The 700 Club, "Leading With Love" https://www1.cbn.com/700club/joel-manby-love-works.

[174] The 700 Club, "Leading With Love" https://www1.cbn.com/700club/joel-manby-love-works.

[175] Simon, *The Papers*, Volume 31, 404.

[176] Mr. Lincoln and Friends, "The Officers: Ulysses Grant," MrLincolnandfriends.org, http://www.mrlincolnandfriends.org/the-officers/ulysses-grant/.

[177] Mr. Lincoln and Friends, "The Officers: Ulysses Grant."

[178] Mr. Lincoln and Friends, "The Officers: Ulysses Grant."

[179] Klein, Christopher, "How Lincoln and Grant's Partnership Won the Civil War," History.com, May 5, 2020. https://www.history.com/news/abraham-lincoln-ulysses-s-grant-partnership-civil-war.

[180] Longstreet, General James, "Confederate General James Longstreet discusses his friendship with Grant," *The New York Times*, July 24, 1885, Grant Homepage Editors, granthomepage.com/intlongstreet.htm.

[181] Longstreet, Grant Homepage.

[182] Cozzens, Peter, "The War Was a Grievous Error: General Longstreet Speaks His Mind," History.net, https://www.historynet.com/war-grievous-error.htm.

CHAPTER FIVE

[183] Grant, Ulysses S., *Personal Memoirs*, 133–134.

[184] Waldo, *Classic Leadership*, 20.

[185] Merriam-Webster, "Courage," https://www.merriam-webster.com/dictionary/courage.

[186] Stanley, Thomas J., *The Millionaire Mind*, (Kansas City, MO: Andrews McMeel Publishing, 2000), 142.

[187] Porter, *Campaigning*, 65.

[188] Porter, *Campaigning*, 63.

[189] Perrett, *Soldier and President*, 311.

[190] Porter, *Campaigning*, 59.

[191] History.com Editors, "Ulysses S. Grant."

[192] Hugo, Victor, Wikiquote, https://en.wikiquote.org/wiki/Victor_Hugo.

[193] Reeves, John, "Review of Ron Chernow's 'Grant,'" History News Network, https://historynewsnetwork.org/article/167256.

[194] Welles, Gideon, "Admiral Farragut and New Orleans: with an account of the origin and command of the first three naval expeditions of the war," *The Galaxy, v. 12*, 669–683, 817 832 (November and December 1871), https://babel.hathitrust.org/cgi/pt?id=uc1.$b201039;view=1up;seq=685.

[195] Bonekemper, *Grant and Lee*, 213.

[196] Bien, Madeleine, "Vicksburg Is the Key," National Parks Foundation, https://www.nationalparks.org/connect/blog/vicksburg-key.

[197] Smith, *Grant*, 120.

[198] Smith, *Grant*, 120–121.

[199] Smith, *Grant*, 208.

[200] Smith, *Grant*, 208.

[201] AbrahamLincolnOnline.org quoted from Basler, Roy P. *The Collected Works of Abraham Lincoln: Volume 7*, http://www.abrahamlincolnonline.org/lincoln/speeches/grant.htm.

[202] AbrahamLincolnOnline.org quoted from Basler, Roy P. *The Collected Works of Abraham Lincoln: Volume 7*, http://www.abrahamlincolnonline.org/lincoln/speeches/grant.htm.

[203] Brands, *Man Who Saved*, 308.

[204] Brands, *Man Who Saved*, 308.

[205] Grant, Ulysses S., *Personal Memoirs*, 479.

[206] Green, *General*, 145–146.

[207] Inghram, Lt. Col Richard B., "Grant and Sherman: Development of a Strategic Relationship," U.S. Army War College, 4/5/1991, https://apps.dtic.mil/sti/pdfs/ADA236277.pdf.

[208] Porter, *Campaigning*, 248–250.

[209] Chernow, *Grant*, 632.

[210] Chernow, *Grant*, 708.

[211] Chernow, *Grant*, 709.

[212] Chernow, *Grant*, 795.

[213] Chernow, *Grant*, 795.

[214] Strook, William, "Sherman's March to the Sea," Warfare History Network. https://warfarehistorynetwork.com/2018/12/31/shermans-march-to-the-sea/.

[215] Perrett, *Soldier and President*, 353.

[216] Simpson, *Triumph over Adversity*, 383–384.

[217] History.com Editors, "General Sherman Presents President Lincoln with a Christmas Gift," history.com/this-day-in-history/Sherman-presents-lincoln-with-a-christmas-gift.

[218] Green, *General*, 151.

[219] Troolin, Amy, "The Costs of the Civil War: Human, Economic & Cultural," Study.com. https://study.com/academy/lesson/the-costs-of-the-civil-war.html.

[220] Smith, *Grant*, 409.

CHAPTER SIX

[221] Chernow, *Grant*, 102.

[222] Fulfer, Johnny, "The Panic of 1857," The Economic Historian, https://economic-historian.com/2020/07/panic-of-1857.

[223] Seaman, Ezra C., "The Panic and Financial Crisis of 1857," *Hunt's Merchants' Magazine and Commercial Review*, December 1857, 659, https://fraser.stlouisfed.org/title/merchants-magazine-commercial-review-5733/december-1857-577181.

[224] Chernow, Ronald, "Ulysses S. Grant with General (Ret.) David H. Petraeus," 92nd Street Y, November 13, 2017, YouTube video, https://youtube/_jeNRrNf7Us.

[225] Grant, Julia, *Memoirs*, 82.

[226] Chernow, *Grant*, 109.

[227] Chernow, *Grant*, 114.

[228] Chernow, *Grant*, 115.

[229] Chernow, *Grant*, 109.

[230] Waldo, *Classic Leadership*, 19.

[231] White, "Leadership, Life."

[232] American Battlefield Trust Editors, "Ulysses S. Grant: The Myth of 'Unconditional Surrender' Begins at Fort Donelson" https://www.battlefields.org/learn/articles/ulysses-s-grant-myth-unconditional-surrender-begins-fort-donelson.

[233] Hindley, Meredith, "Allied Leaders at Casablanca: The Story Behind a Famous WWII Photo Shoot," *Time*, January 16, 2018. https://time.com/5101354/churchill-fdr-casablanca-photo/.

[234] White, "Leadership, Life."

[235] American Battlefield Trust, "The Myth of 'Unconditional Surrender.'"

[236] Waldo, *Classic Leadership*, 21.

[237] Brands, *Man Who Saved*, 164–165.

[238] Brands, *Man Who Saved*, 165.

[239] American Battlefield Trust, "The Myth of 'Unconditional Surrender.'"

[240] History.com Editors, "Battles of Cold Harbor," History.com, December 2, 2009, https://www.history.com/topics/american-civil-war/battles-of-cold-harbor.

[241] Maxwell, John C., "Leadership Gold," Soundview Executive Book Summaries, https://vuthedudotorg.files.wordpress.com/2015/04/leadership-gold.pdf.

[242] Perrett, *Soldier and President*, 334.

[243] Green, *General*, 148.

[244] Chernow, *Grant*, xxi.

[245] Maxwell, John, "Leadership Gold Notes & Review" Vialogue, January 29, 2012, https://vialogue.wordpress.com/2012/01/29/leadership-gold-notes-review/.

[246] Catton, *Command*, 276.

[247] Porter, *Campaigning*, 190.

[248] Smith, *Grant*, 373.

[249] Bonekemper, *Grant and Lee*, 315.

[250] Perrett, *Soldier and President*, 335–336.

[251] Catton, *Command*, 284.

[252] Chernow, *Grant*, 411–412.

[253] Bonekemper, *Grant and Lee*, 314.

CHAPTER SEVEN

[254] Knighton, Andrew, "Ulysses S. Grant —Military Genius of the Civil War," War History Online, July 14, 2017, https://www.warhistoryonline.com/american-civil-war/8-features-ulysses-s-grants-military-leadership.html.

[255] Simpson, *Triumph over Adversity*, 284.

[256] Waldo, *Classic Leadership*, 45.

[257] Waldo, *Classic Leadership*, 112.

[258] Simpson, *Triumph over Adversity*, 392–393.

[259] Porter, *Campaigning*, 41-42.

[260] Murray, "12 Leadership Lessons."

[261] Murray, "12 Leadership Lessons."

[262] Ketcham, Henry, "Lincoln and Grant: Chapter XXXIV," *The Life of Abraham Lincoln*. http://www.authorama.com/life-of-abraham-lincoln-36.html.

[263] Simpson, *Triumph over Adversity*, 273.

[264] Covey, Stephen R., *The 7 Habits of Highly Effective People* (New York: Simon & Schuster, 1989, 2014), 105–106.

[265] Phillips, *Lincoln on Leadership*, 129.

[266] Simpson, *Triumph over Adversity*, 257.

[267] Simpson, *Triumph over Adversity*, 257.

[268] Simpson, *Triumph over Adversity*, 257.

[269] Simpson, *Triumph over Adversity*, 257.

[270] History.com Editors, "Robert E. Lee Surrenders," History.com, November 24, 2009. https://www.history.com/this-day-in-history/robert-e-lee-surrenders.

[271] Brands, *Man Who Saved*, 363–364.

[272] Lincoln, Abraham, "Lincoln Home National Historic Site, Illinois," National Park Service, https://www.nps.gov/features/liho/1864/02.htm.

[273] Chamberlain, Joshua Lawrence, *The Passing of the Armies* (Gettysburg, PA: Stan Clark Military Books, 1994/1915), 246–247.

274   Catton, *Command*, 464.

275   Brands, *Man Who Saved*, 366.

276   Porter, *Campaigning*, 472.

277   Porter, *Campaigning*, 473–475.

278   Porter, *Campaigning*, 486.

279   Porter, *Campaigning*, 477.

CHAPTER EIGHT

280   Waldo, *Classic Leadership*, 24.

281   Shenk, Rob, "The Long, Gruesome Fight to Capture Vicksburg," American Battlefield Trust. https://www.battlefields.org/learn/articles/long-gruesome-fight-capture-vicksburg.

282   History Collection Editors, "This Day In History: Sherman Orders Assault At The Battle Of Chickasaw Bluffs (1862)," History Collection, https://historycollection.com/day-history-sheridan-orders-assault-battle-chickasaw-bluff-fought-1862/.

283   Grant, Ulysses S., *Personal Memoirs*, 256–257.

284   Bonekemper, *Grant and Lee*, 214.

285   Bonekemper, *Grant and Lee*, 214–215.

286   Green, *General*, 71.

287   Bonekemper, *Grant and Lee*, 215.

288   Green, *General*, 71.

289   Chernow, *Grant*, 259–260.

290   Smith, *Grant*, 238.

291   Grant, Ulysses S., *Personal Memoirs*, 269.

292   Bonekemper, *Grant and Lee*, 223.

293   Perrett, *Soldier and President*, 254.

294   History.com Editors, "Siege of Vicksburg," History.com, November 9, 2009. https://www.history.com/topics/american-civil-war/vicksburg-campaign.

295   Green, *General*, 79.

296   Grant, Ulysses, *Personal Memoirs*, 295–296.

297   Brands, *Man Who Saved*, 239.

298   Green, *General*, 79.

299   Brands, *Man Who Saved*, 239.

300   Grant, Ulysses, *Personal Memoirs*, 317.

301   Perrett, *Soldier and President*, 263–264.

302   Perrett, *Soldier and President*, 264.

303   Waldo, *Classic Leadership*, 25.

304   Cunningham, Jeff, "Grant's Quiet Fortitude by General David Petraeus," May 24, 2017. https://thunderbird.asu.edu/knowledge-network/grants-quiet-fortitude.

305   Grant, Ulysses S., "Appendix: Report of Lieutenant-General U. S. Grant, of the United States Armies 1864-65," The Memoirs of General Ulysses S. Grant, http://www.historyofwar.org/sources/acw/grant/report01.html.

306   Brands, *Man Who Saved*, 300–301.

307   Wert, Jeffry D., *The Sword of Lincoln: The Army of the Potomac* (New York: Simon & Schuster, 2005), 344–345.

308   Phillips, *Lincoln on Leadership*, 133.

[309] Thomas, Benjamin, *Abraham Lincoln: A Biography* (Carbondale, Il: Southern Illinois University Press, 2008), 441.

[310] Smith, *Grant*, 381–382.

CHAPTER NINE

[311] Rafuse, Ethan S., "'My Earnest Endeavor': Grant Takes Command, 1864," March 13, The Kansas City Public Library. https://youtube/MPgZnlbqpxY.

[312] Grant, Ulysses S., *Personal Memoirs*, 18.

[313] Grant, Ulysses S., *Personal Memoirs*, 18.

[314] National Park Service Editors, "Graduation Day: Ulysses S. Grant and the West Point Class of 1843," National Park Service, Ulysses S. Grant National Historic Site, https://www.nps.gov/articles/000/graduation-day-ulysses-s-grant-and-the-west-point-class-of-1843.htm.

[315] National Park Service, "Graduation Day."

[316] Habecker, Eugene, *The Softer Side of Leadership* (Sisters, Oregon: Deep River Books, 2018), 23.

[317] Habecker, *Softer Side*, 128–130.

[318] Habecker, *Softer Side*, 131–132.

[319] Maxwell, John C., *Thinking for a Change* (New York: Warner Books, 2003), 104.

[320] Chernow, *Grant*, 105.

[321] Chernow, *Grant*, 105.

[322] Simpson, *Triumph over Adversity*, 458.

[323] Deforest, Tim, "Grierson's Raid During the Vicksburg Campaign," History.net, September 2000. https://www.historynet.com/griersons-raid-during-the-vicksburg-campaign.htm.

[324] History.com Editors, "Union Colonel Abel Streight's raid into Alabama and Georgia begins," History.com, November 13, 2009. https://www.history.com/this-day-in-history/streights-raid-begins.

[325] Grant, Ulysses S., *Personal Memoirs*, 267.

[326] Grant, Ulysses S., *Personal Memoirs*, 267.

[327] Green, *General,* 74.

[328] History.com Editors, "Siege of Vicksburg."

[329] Flood, *Grant and Sherman,* 184.

[330] Perrett, *Soldier and President*, 265.

[331] Waugh, *American Hero,* 66.

[332] Waldo, *Classic Leadership*, 30.

[333] Chernow, *Grant*, 928.

[334] Flood, Charles Bracelen, *Grant's Final Victory* (Cambridge, MA: Da Capo Press, 2011), 98.

[335] Brands, *The Man,* 610.

[336] Flood, *Grant's Final,* 130–131.

[337] Twain, Mark, *Autobiography of Mark Twain, Volume 1*, Edited by Harriet Elinor Smith (Berkeley, CA: University of California Press, 2010), 84.

[338] Perry, Mark, *Grant and Twain* (New York: Random House, 2004), 162.

[339] Simon, *The Papers*, Volume 31, 293–294.

CHAPTER TEN

340 Gilbert, Peter A., "Union General Rosecrans was 'confused and stunned like a duck hit on the head,'" Civil War Book of Days, https://civilwarbookofdays.org/2013/09/13/union-general-rosecrans-was-confused-and-stunned-like-a-duck-hit-on-the-head/.
341 Porter, *Campaigning*, 5.
342 Smith, *Grant*, 267.
343 White, *American Ulysses*, 299–300.
344 Porter, *Campaigning*, 10.
345 White, *American Ulysses*, 300.
346 Knighton, "Military Genius."
347 White, *American Ulysses*, 309–310.
348 White, *American Ulysses*, 310.
349 Bonekemper, Edward H. *Ulysses S. Grant: A Victor, Not a Butcher* (Washington: Regnery Publishing, 2010), 137.
350 Knighton, "Military Genius."
351 Knighton, "Military Genius."
352 Grant, Ulysses S., *Personal Memoirs*, 633.
353 Brands, *Man Who Saved*, 311.
354 Simpson, *Triumph over Adversity*, 378.
355 Brands, *Man Who Saved*, 311.
356 Chernow, *Grant*, 417–418.
357 Biography.com Editors, "Sam Walton Biography," Biography.com, March 26, 2015. https://www.biography.com/business-figure/sam-walton.
358 Borritt, Gabor S., *Why the Confederacy Lost* (Oxford: Oxford University Press, 1993), 74.
359 Robertson, James, "Desertion," Radio IQ, July 30, 2019. https://www.wvtf.org/post/desertion#stream/0.
360 Grant, Ulysses S., *Personal Memoirs*, 560.
361 Bonekemper, *Grant and Lee*, 353.
362 Burns, Ken, "War Is All Hell–1865," *The Civil War*.
363 Chernow, *Grant*, 488.
364 Sherman, William T., *The Personal Memoirs of William T. Sherman* (New York: Literary Classics of the United States, 1990), 408.
365 Simpson, *Triumph over Adversity*, 415.
366 Simpson, *Triumph over Adversity*, 419.
367 Simpson, *Triumph over Adversity*, 423.

Chapter Eleven

368 Chernow, *Grant*, 22.
369 New York Times Editors, "The Career of a Soldier," *The New York Times*, July 24, 1885, https://archive.nytimes.com/www.nytimes.com/learning/general/onthisday/bday/0427.html.
370 Perrett, *Soldier and President*, 13.
371 Chernow, *Grant*, 954.
372 Chernow, *Grant*, xx.
373 Chernow, *Grant*, 106.
374 Chernow, *Grant*, 124.
375 Brands, *Man Who Saved*, 123.

376 Chernow, *Grant,* 874-875.

377 Simpson, *Triumph over Adversity*, 162–163.

378 Young, *Around the World,* 157.

379 Morrow, Kevin, "Lincoln's Triumphant Visit to Richmond," *The New York Times*, April 7, 2015. https://opinionator.blogs.nytimes.com/2015/04/07/lincolns-triumphant-visit-to-richmond/.

380 Hamilton, J. G. De Roulhac, and Mary Thompson Hamilton, "The Life of Robert E. Lee for Boys and Girls: Chapter XIV, After the War," Lee Family Digital Archive. http://leefamilyarchive.org/reference/books/hamilton/14.html.

381 Chernow, *Grant,* xvii.

382 Perry, *Grant and Twain*, xx–xxi.

383 Green, *General,* 271.

384 Goldhurst, Richard, *Many Are the Hearts: The Agony and the Triumph of Ulysses S. Grant* (New York: Readers Digest Press, 1975), 14–15.

385 Perry, *Grant and Twain*, xx–xxi.

386 Goldhurst, *Many Are the Hearts,* 14–15.

387 Firstladies.com, First Lady Biography: Julia Grant, www.firstladies.org/biographies/firstladies.aspx?biography=19.

388 Perry, *Grant and Twain*, xx–xxi.

389 Lynghaug, Fran, *The Official Horse Breeds Standards Guide*, Voyageur Press; First Edition, October 15, 2009, 70.

390 Huntington, Randolph, *History in Brief of "Leopard" and "Linden," General Grant's Arabian Stallions* (Philadelphia: J. B. Lippincott Company, 1885), https://www.wiwfarm.com/LEOPARD_AND_LINDEN.htm.

391 Flood, *Grant's Final Victory*, 11–13.

392 Goldhurst, *Many Are the Hearts,* 3.

393 Flood, *Grant's Final Victory,* 11–13.

394 Smith, *Grant,* 620.

395 Chernow, *Grant,* 921.

396 Flood, *Grant's Final Victory,* 11–13.

397 Chernow, *Grant,* 921–922.

398 Perry, *Grant and Twain*, xxix–xxx.

399 Flood, *Grant's Final Victory,* 43–44.

400 Simon, *The Papers,* Volume 31, 387–388.

401 Chernow, *Grant,* 953.

402 Powers, Ron, *Mark Twain: A Life* (New York: A Free Press/Simon & Schuster, 2005), 504.

Chapter Twelve

403 Madaras, Larry, "Rethinking the Life and Presidency of Ulysses S. Grant," *America Magazine*, February 21, 2018. https://www.americamagazine.org/arts-culture/2018/02/21/rethinking-life-and-presidency-ulysses-s-grant.

404 Chernow, *Grant,* xxiii.

405 Ingraham, Christopher, "One in eight American adults is an alcoholic, study says," *The Washington Post*, August 11, 2017, https://www.washingtonpost.com/news/wonk/wp/2017/08/11/study-one-in-eight-american-adults-are-alcoholics/.

[406] Hazelden Betty Ford Foundation, "Stages of Alcoholism," March 13, 2019. https://www.hazeldenbettyford.org/articles/stages-of-alcoholism.

[407] WebMD, "Understanding Alcohol."

[408] Hazelden Betty Ford Foundation, "Stages of Alcoholism."

[409] Chernow, *Grant*, 58.

[410] Chernow, *Grant*, 58.

[411] Chernow, *Grant*, 899.

[412] Chernow, *Grant*, 67.

[413] Ulysses S. Grant Homepage Editors, "Interview with Colonel James E. Pitman," https://www.granthomepage.com/intpitman.htm.

[414] Alcoholics Anonymous, "There is a Solution," *Alcoholics Anonymous: The Big Book*, https://www.aa.org/assets/en_US/en_bigbook_chapt2.pdf.

[415] Garland, Hamlin, *Ulysses S. Grant: His Life and Character* (NewYork: Doubleday & McClure Co., 1898) 111.

[416] Chernow, *Grant*, 69.

[417] Perrett, *Soldier and President*, 87.

[418] Garland, *Grant: His Life and Character*, 111.

[419] Chernow, *Grant*, 70.

[420] Garland, *Grant: His Life and Character*, 117.

[421] Chernow, *Grant*, 73.

[422] Smith, *Grant*, 638.

[423] Smith, *Grant*, 83.

[424] Alcoholics Anonymous, "The Doctor's Opinion," *Alcoholics Anonymous: The Big Book*, Online version, https://www.aa.org/assets/en_US/en_bigbook_foreworddoctorsopinion.pdf.

[425] Blakeslee, Sandra, "Scientists Find Key Biological Causes of Alcoholism," *The New York Times*. https://www.nytimes.com/1984/08/14/science/scientists-find-key-biological-causes-of-alcoholism.html.

[426] Simpson, *Triumph over Adversity*, 73.

[427] Chernow, *Grant*, 80.

[428] Chernow, *Grant*, 81.

[429] Chernow, *Grant*, 81.

[430] White, *American Ulysses*, 118.

[431] White, *American Ulysses*, 119-120.

[432] Chernow, *Grant*, 84.

[433] Chernow, *Grant*, 84.

[434] Chernow, *Grant*, 84.

[435] Chernow, *Grant*, 85.

[436] Chernow, *Grant*, 85.

[437] Brands, *ManWho Saved*, 73.

[438] Smith, *Grant*, 88.

[439] Chernow, *Grant*, 282.

[440] Chernow, *Grant*, 85.

[441] Chernow, *Grant*, 97.

[442] Chernow, *Grant*, 97.

[443] Smith, *Grant*, 92.

[444] Alcoholics Anonymous, "The Doctor's Opinion."

[445] Chernow, *Grant*, 135.

446 Simpson, *Triumph over Adversity*, 82.

447 Simpson, *Triumph over Adversity*, 82.

448 Smith, *Grant*, 103.

449 White, *American Ulysses*, 182–183.

450 Chernow, *Grant*, 252.

451 Chernow, *Grant*, 272–273.

452 Chernow, *Grant*, 272–273.

453 Chernow, *Grant*, 193.

454 Chernow, *Grant*, 211.

455 Quote Investigator, "I Will Send a Barrel of This Wonderful Whiskey to Every General in the Army," https://quoteinvestigator.com/2013/02/18/barrel-of-whiskey/.

456 Catton, *Command*, 115

457 Chernow, *Grant*, 350.

458 Simpson, *Triumph over Adversity*, 385.

459 Chernow, *Grant*, 649.

CHAPTER THIRTEEN

460 Grant, Ulysses S., *Personal Memoirs*, 5.

461 White, "Leadership, Life."

462 Perrett, *Soldier and President*, 117.

463 Chernow, *Grant*, 129.

464 Chernow, *Grant*, 122.

465 Chernow, *Grant*, 811.

466 Chernow, *Grant*, 872.

467 Brands, *Man Who Saved*, 583–584.

468 Chernow, *Grant*, 872.

469 Young, *Around the World*, 122–123.

470 Chernow, *Grant*, 648-649.

471 Chernow, *Grant*, 649.

472 Psalm 19:9, King James Version, public domain. https://www.biblegateway.com/passage/?search=Psalm+19%3A9&version=KJV.

473 History on the Net Editors, Grant, Ulysses. "Commanding General Ulysses S. Grant: (1822-1885)," History on the Net, Salem Media. https://www.historyonthenet.com/commanding-general-ulysses-s-grant-1822-1885.

474 Perrett, *Soldier and President*, 116.

475 Chernow, *Grant*, 116.

476 Perret, *Soldier and President*, 348–349.

477 Porter, *Campaigning*, 284.

478 Porter, *Campaigning*, 284–285.

479 Porter, *Campaigning*, 379–380.

480 Fay, John, "Reminiscences of Grant," *Bismarck Daily Tribune*, Bismarck, North Dakota, Sunday, October 2, 1887. https://libguides.css.edu/ld.php?content_id=10102489.

481 Flood, *Grant's Final Days*, 28.

482 Grant, Julia, *Memoirs*, 126–127.

483 Blumberg, Arnold, "Grant Takes D.C.," Warfarehistorynetwork.com, https://warfarehistorynetwork.com/2018/12/21/grant-takes-d-c/.

484   History.com. "Battles of Cold Harbor."

485   Porter, *Campaigning*, 179.

486   Catton, *Command*, 270.

487   Simon, *The Papers*, 387–388.

488   Flood, *Grant's Final Victory*, 229.

CHAPTER FOURTEEN

489   Simpson, *Triumph over Adversity*, 463.

490   Grant, Ulysses S., "Excerpts from Ulysses S. Grant–Personal Memoirs," 3. https://econclubchi.org/media/2114/readings-on-ulysses-s-grant.pdf.

491   Shrady, George F., MD, "General Grant's Last Days," *The Century Magazine*, 106–107.

492   Simpson, *Triumph over Adversity*, 464.

493   Porter, *Campaigning*, 123–124.

494   Dymond, Jonathan, "On the Principles of Morality," 280. https://www.google.com/books/edition/Essays_on_the_Principles_of_Morality/2RYUpSQAOOIC?hl=en&gbpv=1&dq=inauthor:%22Jonathan+Dymond%22&printsec=frontcover.

495   Murray, "12 Leadership Lessons."

496   Porter, *Campaigning*, 490–491.

497   Porter, *Campaigning*, 490–492.

498   Stephens, Alexander H., "Cornerstone Speech: Savannah, Georgia, March 21, 1861," American Battlefield Trust. https://www.battlefields.org/learn/primary-sources/cornerstone-speech.

499   Bomboy, Scott, "On This Day, the Confederate Constitution Is Approved," Constitution Daily, March 11, 2020. https://constitutioncenter.org/blog/looking-back-at-the-confederate-constitution.

500   Young, *Around the World,* 158.

501   Young, *Around the World,* 158.

502   Chernow, *Grant,* 243.

503   Chernow, *Grant,* 243.

504   Chernow, *Grant,* 243.

505   Grant, Ulysses S., *Personal Memoirs*, 626.

506   Grant, Ulysses S., *Personal Memoirs*, 627.

507   Grant, Ulysses S., *Personal Memoirs*, 630.

508   Grant, Ulysses S., *Personal Memoirs*, 632.

509   Gregory, James M., "Frederick Douglas The Orator," Willey Company, Springfield, MA, 1893, 170. http://libraryweb.org/~digitized/books/Frederick_Douglass_The_Orator.pdf.

511   Chernow, *Grant*, 955.

BIBLIOGRAPHY

AbrahamLincolnOnline.org. Quoted from Basler, Roy P. *The Collected Works of Abraham Lincoln: Volume 7.* http://www.abraham-lincolnonline.org/lincoln/speeches/grant.htm.

Alcoholics Anonymous. "The Doctor's Opinion." *Alcoholics Anonymous: The Big Book.* Online version. https://www.aa.org/assets/en_US/en_bigbook_foreworddoctorsopinion.pdf.

———. "There is a Solution." *Alcoholics Anonymous: The Big Book.* https://www.aa.org/assets/en_US/en_bigbook_chapt2.pdf.

American Battlefield Trust Editors. "Ulysses S. Grant: The Myth of 'Unconditional Surrender' Begins at Fort Donelson." https://www.battlefields.org/learn/articles/ulysses-s-grant-myth-unconditional-surrender-begins-fort-donelson.

Army.mil. "Brigadier General Rufus Ingalls 16th Quartermaster School Commandant February 1882-July 1883." https://quartermaster.army.mil/bios/previous-qm-generals/quartermaster_general_bio-ingalls.html.

Behn, Richard J. "The Generals and Admirals: Ulysses S. Grant (1822–1885)." Mr. Lincoln's White House. mrlincolnswhitehouse.org/residents-visitors/the-generals-and-admirals/generals-admirals-ulysses-s-grant-1822-1885/.

Bien, Madeleine. "Vicksburg Is the Key." National Parks Foundation. https://www.nationalparks.org/connect/blog/vicksburg-key.

Biography.com Editors. "Sam Walton Biography." Biography.com, March 26, 2015. https://www.biography.com/business-figure/sam-walton.

Blakeslee, Sandra. "Scientists Find Key Biological Causes of Alcoholism." *The New York Times.* https://www.nytimes.com/1984/08/14/science/scientists-find-key-biological-causes-of-alcoholism.html.

Blanchard, Ken and Renee Broadwell. *Servant Leadership in Action.* Oakland, CA: Berrett-Koeler Publishers, 2018.

Blumberg, Arnold. "Grant Takes D.C." Warfarehistorynetwork. com. https://warfarehistorynetwork.com/2018/12/21/grant-takes-d-c/.

Bomboy, Scott. "On This Day, the Confederate Constitution Is Approved." *Constitution Daily*, March 11, 2020. https://constitutioncenter.org/blog/looking-back-at-the-confederate-constitution.

Bonekemper, Edward H. *Ulysses S. Grant: A Victor, Not a Butcher*. Washington: Regnery Publishing, 2010.

———. *Grant and Lee: Victorious American and Vanquished Virginian*. Washington: Regnery History, 2012.

Borritt, Gabor S. *Why the Confederacy Lost*. Oxford: Oxford University Press, 1993.

Brands, H. W. *The Man Who Saved the Union: Ulysses Grant in War and Peace*. New York: Doubleday–Random House, 2012.

Burns, Ken. "Episode 2: A Very Bloody Affair – 1862." *The Civil War: A Ken Burns Film*, PBS Video, 1990.

———. "Episode 6: Valley of the Shadow of Death—1864." *The Civil War: A Film by Ken Burns*, PBS Video, 1990.

———. "Episode 7: Most Hallowed Ground." *The Civil War: A Film By Ken Burns*, PBS Video, 1990.

———. "Episode 8: War Is All Hell." *The Civil War: A Film by Ken Burns*, PBS Video, 1990.

Catton, Bruce. *Grant Moves South*. Boston: Little, Brown and Company, 1960.

———. *Grant Takes Command*. Edison, NJ: Castle Books – Book Sales Inc.

Chamberlain, Joshua Lawrence. *The Passing of the Armies*. Gettysburg, PA: Stan Clark Military Books, 1994/1915.

Chernow, Ronald, *Grant*, New York: Penguin Press, 2017.

———. "Ulysses S. Grant with General (Ret.) David H. Petraeus." 92nd Street Y, November 13, 2017. YouTube video, https://youtube/_jeNRrNf7Us.

Collins, Jim. *Good to Great*. New York: HarperCollins Publishers, 2001.

Covey, Stephen R. *The 7 Habits of Highly Effective People.* New York: Simon & Schuster, 1989.

Cozzens, Peter. "The War Was a Grievous Error: General Longstreet Speaks His Mind." History.net. https://www.historynet.com/war-grievous-error.htm.

Cunningham, Jeff. "Grant's Quiet Fortitude by General David Petraeus." May 24, 2017. https://thunderbird.asu.edu/knowledge-network/grants-quiet-fortitude.

Dabney, Emmanuel. "City Point During the Civil War." www.encyclopediavirginia.org/city_point_during_the_civil_war#start_entry.

Deforest, Tim. "Grierson's Raid During the Vicksburg Campaign." History.net, September 2000. https://www.historynet.com/griersons-raid-during-the-vicksburg-campaign.htm.

Derose, Chris. "Those Not Skinning Can Hold a Leg." *The President's War*, Chapter 39. https://erenow.net/ww/the-presidents-war-six-american-presidents-and-the-civil-war/40.php.

Duncan, Rodger Dean. "Ken Blanchard: Why Servant Leadership Requires Humility." *Forbes*, May 8, 2019. https://www.forbes.com/sites/rodgerdeanduncan/2019/05/08/ken-blanchard-why-servant-leadership-requires-humility/#461ff35425f2.

Dymond, Jonathan. "On the Principles of Morality." https://www.google.com/books/edition/Essays_on_the_Principles_of_Morality/2RYUpSQAOOIC?hl=en&gbpv=1&dq=inauthor:%22Jonathan+Dymond%22&printsec=frontcover.

Farris, Scott. *Freedom on Trial: The First Post-Civil War Battle Over Civil Rights Voter Suppression.* Lanham, MD: Rowman & Littlefield, November 15, 2020.

Fay, John. *Reminiscences of Grant. Bismarck Daily Tribune*, Bismarck, North Dakota, Sunday, October 2, 1887. https://libguides.css.edu/ld.php?content_id=10102489.

Firstladies.org. First Lady Biography: Julia Grant. www.firstladies.org/biographies/firstladies.aspx?biography=19.

Flood, Charles Bracelen. *Grant and Sherman: The Friendship That Won the Civil War.* New York: Farrar, Straus and Giroux, 2005.

https://erenow.net/ww/grant-and-sherman-the-friendship-that-won-the-civil-war/1.php.

———. *Grant's Final Victory*. Cambridge, MA: Da Capo Press, 2011.

Foote, Shelby. "Episode Three: Forever Free." The Civil War: A Film by Ken Burns. PBS Video, 1990.

———. *Ken Burns's The Civil War Deluxe Ebook*. Edited by Geoffrey C. Ward, Ric Burns, and Ken Burns. New York: Knopf, 2011. https://books.google.com/books?id=Zrx0UkoF4BkC&pg=PT252&lpg=PT252&dq=#v=onepage&q&f=false.

Fulfer, Johnny. "The Panic of 1857." The Economic Historian. https://economic-historian.com/2020/07/panic-of-1857/.

Garland, Hamlin. *Ulysses S. Grant: His Life and Character*. New York: Doubleday & McClure Co., 1898.

Gilbert, Peter A. "Union General Rosecrans was 'confused and stunned like a duck hit on the head.'" Civil War Book of Days. https://civilwarbookofdays.org/2013/09/13/union-general-rosecrans-was-confused-and-stunned-like-a-duck-hit-on-the-head/.

Goldhurst, Richard. *Many Are the Hearts: The Agony and the Triumph of Ulysses S. Grant*. New York: Readers Digest Press, 1975.

Grant, Julia. *The Personal Memoirs of Julia Dent Grant*. Edited by John Y. Simon. New York: G. Putnam's Sons, 1975.

Grant, Ulysses S. "Appendix: Report of Lieutenant-General U. S. Grant, of the United States Armies 1864-65." *The Memoirs of Ulysses S. Grant*. http://www.historyofwar.org/sources/acw/grant/report01.html

———. "Commanding General Ulysses S. Grant: (1822-1885)." History on the Net.

© 2000-2021, Salem Media. https://www.historyonthenet.com/commanding-general-ulysses-s-grant-1822-1885.

———. "Excerpts from Ulysses S. Grant–Personal Memoirs," 3. https://econclubchi.org/media/2114/readings-on-ulysses-s-grant.pdf.

———. *Personal Memoirs of Ulysses S. Grant*. New York: Barnes & Noble Books, 2005. Originally published by Charles L. Webster and Company, New York, 1885, 104.

Greeley, Horace. "Horace Greeley's Estimate of Lincoln." *Our American Holidays: Lincoln's Birthday*. Edited by Robert Haven Schauffler, New York: Moffat, Yard and Company, 1916. https://www.gutenberg.org/files/21267/21267-h/21267-h.htm.

Green, Horace. *General Grant's Last Stand*. New York: Charles Scribner's Sons, 1936.

Gregory, James M. *Frederick Douglas: The Orator*. Springfield, MA: Willey Company, 1893. http://libraryweb.org/~digitized/books/Frederick_Douglass_The_Orator.pdf.

Habecker, Eugene. *The Softer Side of Leadership*. Sisters, Oregon: Deep River Books, 2018.

Hamilton, J. G. De Roulhac, and Mary Thompson Hamilton. *The Life of Robert E. Lee for Boys and Girls*, Chapter XIV, "After the War." Lee Family Digital Archive. http://leefamilyarchive.org/reference/books/hamilton/14.html.

Hazelden Betty Ford Foundation. "Stages of Alcoholism." March 13, 2019. https://www.hazeldenbettyford.org/articles/stages-of-alcoholism.

Hindley, Meredith. "Allied Leaders at Casablanca: The Story Behind a Famous WWII Photo Shoot." *Time*, January 16, 2018. https://time.com/5101354/churchill-fdr-casablanca-photo/.

History Collection Editors. "This Day In History: Sherman Orders Assault At The Battle Of Chickasaw Bluffs (1862)." History Collection. https://historycollection.com/day-history-sheridan-orders-assault-battle-chicksaw-bluff-fought-1862/.

History on the Net Editors. Grant, Ulysses, "Commanding General Ulysses S. Grant: (1822-1885)." History on the Net, Salem Media. https://www.historyonthenet.com/commanding-general-ulysses-s-grant-1822-1885.

History.com Editors. "Battles of Cold Harbor." History.com, December 2, 2009. https://www.history.com/topics/american-civil-war/battles-of-cold-harbor.

———. "General George McClellan snubs President Lincoln." https://www.history.com/this-day-in-history/mcclellan-snubs-lincoln.

———. "General Sherman Presents President Lincoln with a Christmas Gift." history.com/this-day-in-history/Sherman-presents-lincoln-with-a-christmas-gift.

———. "George G. Meade." History.com. November 9, 2009. https://www.history.com/topics/american-civil-war/george-g-meade.

———. "Robert E. Lee Surrenders." History.com. November 24, 2009. https://www.history.com/this-day-in-history/robert-e-lee-surrenders.

———. "Siege of Vicksburg." History.com. November 9, 2009. https://www.history.com/topics/american-civil-war/vicksburg-campaign.

———. "Ulysses S. Grant," History.com. October 29, 2009. https://www.history.com/topics/us-presidents/ulysses-s-grant-1.

———. "Union Colonel Abel Streight's raid into Alabama and Georgia begins." History.com. November 13, 2009. https://www.history.com/this-day-in-history/streights-raid-begins.

———. "Union Disaster at Cold Harbor." History.com. November 13, 2009. https://www.history.com/this-day-in-history/union-disaster-at-cold-harbor.

Hugo, Victor. Wikiquote. Wikimedia. https://en.wikiquote.org/wiki/Victor_Hugo.

Huntington, Randolph. *'Leopard' and 'Linden,' General Grant's Arabian Stallions*. Philadelphia: J. B. Lippincott Company, 1885. https://www.wiwfarm.com/LEOPARD_AND_LINDEN.htm.

Hymel, Kevin M. "A General's Heroes." Army.mil. April 27, 2010. https://www.army.mil/article/38075/a_generals_heroes.

Ingraham, Christopher. "One in eight American adults is an alcoholic, study says." *The Washington Post*. August 11, 2017. https://www.washingtonpost.com/news/wonk/wp/2017/08/11/study-one-in-eight-american-adults-are-alcoholics/

Inghram, Lt. Col. Richard B. "Grant and Sherman: Development of a Strategic Relationship." U.S. Army War College, 4/5/1991. https://apps.dtic.mil/sti/pdfs/ADA236277.pdf.

Kennedy, John F. https://www.goodreads.com/quotes/36676-there-are-costs-and-risks-to-a-program-of-action.

Ketcham, Henry. "Lincoln and Grant: Chapter XXXIV." *The Life of Abraham Lincoln*. http://www.authorama.com/life-of-abraham-lincoln-36.html.

King James Version of the Bible. Psalm 19:9. https://www.biblegateway.com/passage/?search=Psalm+19%3A9&version=KJV.

Klein, Christopher. "How Lincoln and Grant's Partnership Won the Civil War." History.com, May 5, 2020. https://www.history.com/news/abraham-lincoln-ulysses-s-grant-partnership-civil-war.

Knighton, Andrew. "American Civil War: The Battle of Chancellorsville—Fighting Joe Hooker and Robert E. Lee." War History Online. September 11, 2017. https://www.warhistoryonline.com/american-civil-war/the-battle-of-chancellorsville.html.

———. "Ulysses S. Grant—Military Genius of the Civil War." War History Online. July 14, 2017. https://www.warhistoryonline.com/american-civil-war/8-features-ulysses-s-grants-military-leadership.html.

Kouzes, James M. and Barry Z. Posner. *The Leadership Challenge*. San Francisco: John Wiley & Sons–Jossey-Bass, 2002.

Lincoln, Abraham. *The Collected Works of Abraham Lincoln: Volume 7*. https://quod.lib.umich.edu/l/lincoln/lincoln7/1:719?rgn=div1;view=fulltext.

———. "Lincoln Home National Historic Site, Illinois." National Park Service. https://www.nps.gov/features/liho/1864/02.htm.

Longstreet, General James. "Confederate General James Longstreet discusses his friendship with Grant." *The New York Times*, July 24, 1885. Grant Homepage Editors, granthomepage.com/intlongstreet.htm.

Lynghaug, Fran. *The Official Horse Breeds Standards Guide.* First Edition. Stillwater, MN: Voyageur Press. October 15, 2009.

Madaras, Larry. "Rethinking the Life and Presidency of Ulysses S. Grant." *America Magazine*, February 21, 2018. https://www.americamagazine.org/arts-culture/2018/02/21/rethinking-life-and-presidency-ulysses-s-grant.

Marvel, William. "Ambrose E. Burnside (1824-1881)." Encyclopedia Virginia. https://www.encyclopediavirginia.org/Burnside_Ambrose_E_1824-1881.

Maxwell, John C. "Leadership Gold." Soundview Executive Book Summaries. https://vuthedudotorg.files.wordpress.com/2015/04/leadership-gold.pdf

———. "Leadership Gold Notes & Review." *Vialogue.* January 29, 2012. https://vialogue.wordpress.com/2012/01/29/leadership-gold-notes-review/

———. *Thinking for a Change.* New York: Warner Books, 2003.

McPherson, James M. *Battle Cry of Freedom.* Oxford: Oxford University Press, 1988.

Melton, Brian C. *Robert E. Lee: A Biography.* Santa Barbara, CA: ABC-CLIO, 2012.

Merriam-Webster. "Courage." https://www.merriam-webster.com/dictionary/courage.

Milton, John. *Areopagitica.* First Amendment Watch at New York University. https://firstamendmentwatch.org/history-speaks-essay-john-milton-areopagitica-1644/.

Modern English Version. Proverbs 22:29. https://www.biblegateway.com/passage/?search=Proverbs+22%3A29&version=MEV.

Morrow, Kevin. "Lincoln's Triumphant Visit to Richmond." *The New York Times*, April 7, 2015. https://opinionator.blogs.nytimes.com/2015/04/07/lincolns-triumphant-visit-to-richmond/.

Mr. Lincoln & Friends Editors. "The Officers: Ulysses Grant." MrLincolnandfriends.org. http://www.mrlincolnandfriends.org/the-officers/ulysses-grant/.

Murray, Sean P. "Ulysses S. Grant: 12 Leadership Lessons." RealTime Performance, February 20, 2018. https://www.realtime-performance.com/ulysses-s-grant-12-leadership-lessons/.

National Park Service Editors. "Casualties of Battle." https://www.nps.gov/anti/learn/historyculture/casualties.htm.

———. "Graduation Day: Ulysses S. Grant and the West Point Class of 1843." National Park Service, Ulysses S. Grant National Historic Site. https://www.nps.gov/articles/000/graduation-day-ulysses-s-grant-and-the-west-point-class-of-1843.htm.

National Public Radio. Talk of the Nation. "Lincoln Was a President 'Tried by War.'" https://www.npr.org/templates/story/story.php?storyId=95906257.

New York Times Editors. "The Career of a Soldier." *The New York Times*, July 24, 1885. https://archive.nytimes.com/www.nytimes.com/learning/general/onthisday/bday/0427.html.

Perrett, Geoffrey. *Ulysses S. Grant: Soldier & President.* New York: Modern Library–Random House, 1999/1997.

Perry, Mark. *Grant and Twain.* New York: Random House, 2004.

Phillips, Donald T. *Lincoln on Leadership.* New York: Hachette Book Group, 1992.

Porter, Horace. *Campaigning with Grant.* New York: Time-Life Books, 1981. Reprinted from The Century Company, 1897.

Powers, Ron. *Mark Twain: A Life.* New York: A Free Press/Simon & Schuster, 2005.

Quote Investigator. "I Will Send a Barrel of This Wonderful Whiskey to Every General in the Army." https://quoteinvestigator.com/2013/02/18/barrel-of-whiskey/.

Rafuse, Ethan S. "'My Earnest Endeavor': Grant Takes Command, 1864." March 13, The Kansas City Public Library. https://youtube/MPgZnlbqpxY.

Rank, Scott Michael. "The Peninsula Campaign in the Civil War (1862)." Historyonthenet.com. © 2000–2020, Salem Media.

Reeves, John. "Review of Ron Chernow's 'Grant.'" History News Network. https://historynewsnetwork.org/article/167256.

Robertson, James. "Desertion." Radio IQ, July 30, 2019. https://www.wvtf.org/post/desertion#stream/0.

Samet, Elizabeth D. "7 Reasons Ulysses S. Grant Was One of America's Most Brilliant Military Leaders." History.com, May 13, 2020.

Shenk, Rob. "The Long, Gruesome Fight to Capture Vicksburg." American Battlefield Trust. https://www.battlefields.org/learn/articles/long-gruesome-fight-capture-vicksburg.

Scott, Steven K. *The Richest Man Who Ever Lived*. New York: Currency/Doubleday, 2006.

Seaman, Ezra C. "The Panic and Financial Crisis of 1857." *Hunt's Merchants' Magazine and Commercial Review*, December 1857. https://fraser.stlouisfed.org/title/merchants-magazine-commercial-review-5733/december-1857-577181.

The 700 Club. "Leading with Love." https://www1.cbn.com/700club/joel-manby-love-works.

Simpson, Brooks D. *Ulysses S. Grant: Triumph over Adversity, 1822–1865*. New York: Houghton Mifflin Company, 2000.

———. *Ulysses S. Grant: Triumph over Adversity, 1882–1865*. Quoted in mrlincolnswhitehouse.org/residents-visitors/the-generals-and-admirals/generals-admirals-ulysses-s-grant-1822-1885/).

Sherman, William T. *The Personal Memoirs of William T. Sherman*. New York: Literary Classics of the United States, 1990.

Shrady, George F., MD. "General Grant's Last Days." *The Century Magazine*.

Smith, Jean Edward. *Grant*. New York: Simon and Schuster, 2001.

Spangenberger, Phil. *The Yankee Sixteen Shooter, True West Magazine*. Truewestmagazine.com/the-yankee-sixteen-shooter/.

Stanley, Thomas J. *The Millionaire Mind*. Kansas City, MO: Andrews McMeel Publishing, 2000.

Stephens, Alexander H. "Cornerstone Speech: Savannah, Georgia, March 21, 1861." American Battlefield Trust. https://www.battlefields.org/learn/primary-sources/cornerstone-speech.

Strook, William. "Sherman's March to the Sea." Warfare History Network. https://warfarehistorynetwork.com/2018/12/31/shermans-march-to-the-sea/

Thomas, Benjamin. *Abraham Lincoln: A Biography*. Carbondale, Il: Southern Illinois University Press, 2008.

Troolin, Amy. "The Costs of the Civil War: Human, Economic & Cultural." Study.com. https://study.com/academy/lesson/the-costs-of-the-civil-war.html.

Twain, Mark. *Autobiography of Mark Twain, Volume 1*. Edited by Harriet Elinor Smith. Berkeley, CA: University of California Press, 2010.

Ulysses S. Grant Homepage Editors. "Grant's Genius." Ulysses S. Grant Homepage, granthomepage.com/grantgenius.hm.

———. "Interview with Colonel James E. Pitman." https://www.granthomepage.com/intpitman.htm.

Waldo, Whitson G. *Classic Leadership Principles*. Portland, OR: Inkwater Press, 2004.

Waugh, Joan. *U. S. Grant: American Hero, American Myth*. Chapel Hill, NC: UNC Press, 2009.

WebMD. "Understanding Alcohol Use Disorder—the Basics." https://www.webmd.com/mental-health/addiction/understanding-alcohol-abuse-basics#1.

Welles, Gideon. "Admiral Farragut and New Orleans: with an account of the origin and command of the first three naval expeditions of the war." *The Galaxy, v. 12*, 669–683, 817–832 (November and December 1871). https://babel.hathitrust.org/cgi/pt?id=uc1.$b201039;view=1up;seq=685.

Wert, Jeffry D. *The Sword of Lincoln: The Army of the Potomac* (New York: Simon & Schuster, 2005), 344–345.

White, Ronald C. *American Ulysses*. New York: Penguin Random House, 2016.

———. "Leadership, Life, and Legacy of Ulysses S. Grant: An interview between General David Petraeus and Dr. Ronald White." November 9, 2016. https://youtube/m7HQPxSxKas.

Wicker, Tom. "A Case of 'the Slows.'" *The New York Times*, October 30, 1988. https://www.nytimes.com/1988/10/30/books/a-case-of-the-slows.html.

Young, John Russell. *Around the World with General Grant*. Baltimore: The Johns Hopkins University Press, 2002/1879.

Photo Credits

1. "Jesse and Hanna Grant," photo. Reprinted from Wikimedia Commons. Public domain in the United States. https://commons.wikimedia.org/wiki/File:Jesse_and_Hannah_Grant.jpg.
2. Grant Birthplace, Point Pleasant, OH, author photo. Photo by Craig von Buseck. Author collection.
3. "Brevet Second Lieutenant Ulysses S. Grant in 1843," photo. Reprinted from Wikimedia Commons. Public domain in the United States. https://commons.wikimedia.org/wiki/File:Brevet_Second_Lieutenant_Ulysses_S._Grant_in_1843.jpg.
4. "Julia Dent Grant with Frederic & Ulysses Jr., 1854," photo. Reprinted from Wikimedia Commons. Public domain in the United States. https://commons.wikimedia.org/wiki/File:-Julia_Dent_Grant_with_Frederic_%26_Ulysses_Jr,_1854.jpg.
5. "File: Julia Grant with family - Brady-Handy.jpg," photo. Reprinted from Wikimedia Commons. Public domain in the United States. https://commons.wikimedia.org/wiki/File:Julia_Grant_with_family_-_Brady-Handy.jpg.
6. "Grant & Perkins leather store.jpg," photo. Reprinted from Wikimedia Commons. Public domain in the United States. https://commons.wikimedia.org/wiki/File:Grant_%26_Perkins_leather_store.jpg.
7. "File: General_Grant_and_horse,_Cincinnati,_photo.jpg," photo. Reprinted from Wikimedia Commons. Public domain in the United States. https://commons.wikimedia.org/wiki/File:General_Grant_and_horse,_Cincinnati,_photo.jpg.
8. "John_Aaron_Rawlins_-_Brady-Handy.jpg," photo. Reprinted from Wikimedia Commons. Public domain in the United States. https://commons.wikimedia.org/wiki/File:John_Aaron_Rawlins_-_Brady-Handy.jpg.

9. "William-Tecumseh-Sherman.jpg," photo. Reprinted from Wikimedia Commons. Public domain in the United States. https://commons.wikimedia.org/wiki/File:William-Tecumseh-Sherman.jpg.

10. "Colorized_portrait_of_Abraham_Lincoln.jpeg," photo. Reprinted from Wikimedia Commons. Public domain in the United States. Author: Samuele Wikipediano 1348. No changes have been made to this photo. https://commons.wikimedia.org/wiki/File:Colorized_portrait_of_Abraham_Lincoln.jpeg.

11. "Horace_Porter_-_Brady-Handy.jpg," photo. Reprinted from Wikimedia Commons. Public domain in the United States. https://commons.wikimedia.org/wiki/File:Horace_Porter_-_Brady-Handy.jpg.

12. "James Longstreet photograph.jpg," photo. Reprinted from Wikimedia Commons. Public domain in the United States. https://en.wikipedia.org/wiki/File:James_Longstreet_photograph.jpg.

13. "Grant_crop_of_Cold_Harbor_photo.png," photo. Reprinted from Wikimedia Commons. Public domain in the United States. https://commons.wikimedia.org/wiki/File:Grant_crop_of_Cold_Harbor_photo.png.

14. "Mark_Twain_by_AF_Bradley.jpg," photo. Reprinted from Wikipedia.org. Public domain in the United States. https://commons.wikimedia.org/wiki/File:Mark_Twain_by_AF_Bradley.jpg.

15. Grant Whitehaven Home, Saint Louis, MO, author photo. Photo by Craig von Buseck. Author collection.

16. "Ulysses_S_Grant_by_Brady_c1870-restored.jpg," photo. Reprinted from Wikimedia Commons. Public domain in the United States. https://commons.wikimedia.org/wiki/File:Ulysses_S_Grant_by_Brady_c1870-restored.jpg.

17. "Ulysses_Grant_and_Family_at_Long_Branch,_NJ_by_Pach_Brothers,_NY,_1870.jpg," photo. Reprinted from Wikimedia Commons. Public domain in the United States. https://commons.wikimedia.org/wiki/File:Ulysses_Grant_

and_Family_at_Long_Branch,_NJ_by_Pach_Brothers,_
NY,_1870.jpg.

18. "Ulysses S. Grant Cottage, Long Branch, NJ - drawing from Harper's Weekly.jpg.," photo. Reprinted from Wikipedia.org. Public domain in the United States. https://en.wikipedia.org/wiki/Ulysses_S._Grant_Cottage#/media/File:Ulysses_S._Grant_Cottage,_Long_Branch,_NJ_-_drawing_from_Harper's_Weekly.jpg.

19. "Gen._Fred_Grant_LOC_2162739645.jpg," photo. Reprinted from Wikimedia Commons. Public domain in the United States. https://commons.wikimedia.org/wiki/File:Gen._Fred_Grant_LOC_2162739645.jpg.

20. "Ulysses_S._Grant_Jr._cph.3a38515.jpg," photo. Reprinted from Wikimedia Commons. Public domain in the United States. https://commons.wikimedia.org/wiki/File:Ulysses_S._Grant_Jr._cph.3a38515.jpg.

21. "Mrs._Algernon_Sartoris_(Nellie_Grant)_LCCN2017893285_(cropped).jpg," photo. Reprinted from Wikimedia Commons. Public domain in the United States. https://commons.wikimedia.org/wiki/File:Mrs._Algernon_Sartoris_(Nellie_Grant)_LCCN2017893285_(cropped).jpg.

22. "Jesse_R._Grant,_youngest_son_of_President_Ulysses_S._Grant.jpg," photo. Reprinted from Wikimedia Commons. Public domain in the United States. https://commons.wikimedia.org/wiki/File:Jesse_R._Grant,_youngest_son_of_President_Ulysses_S._Grant.jpg

23. "Li_Hongzhang_and_Ulysses_S_Grant.jpg," photo. Reprinted from Wikimedia Commons. Public domain in the United States. https://commons.wikimedia.org/wiki/File:Li_Hongzhang_and_Ulysses_S_Grant.jpg.

24. "George Frederick Shrady," photo. Reprinted from Internet Archive – Archive.org. Public domain in the United States (copyright in the name of Dr. Shrady's wife, Hester Ellen Cantine Shrady, expired in 1986, 70 years after her death in 1916). File: https://ia800200.us.archive.org/

BookReader/BookReaderImages.php?zip=/0/items/generalgrantslas00shra/generalgrantslas00shra_jp2.zip&file=-generalgrantslas00shra_jp2/generalgrantslas00shra_0018.jp2&id=generalgrantslas00shra&scale=1&rotate=0.   From: https://archive.org/details/generalgrantslas00shra/page/n19/mode/2up.

25. "Karl_Gerhardt_1879.jpg," photo. Reprinted from Wikimedia Commons. Public domain in the United States. https://commons.wikimedia.org/wiki/File:Karl_Gerhardt_1879.jpg.

26. "US_Grant_in_1885.jpg," photo. Reprinted from Wikimedia Commons. Public domain in the United States. https://commons.wikimedia.org/wiki/File:US_Grant_in_1885.jpg.

27. "Ulysses_S._Grant_death_mask_Gerhardt.jpg," photo. Reprinted from Wikimedia Commons. Public domain in the United States.   https://en.wikipedia.org/wiki/File:Ulysses_S._Grant_death_mask_Gerhardt.jpg.

INDEX